The
Art and Science
of Flowers

# The
# Art and Science
# of Flowers

Nicolette Scourse

*7143*

*London*
MICHAEL JOSEPH

First published in Great Britain by
Michael Joseph Ltd., 52 Bedford
Square, London WC1   1973

ISBN 0 7181 1073 0

Photoset and printed in Great Britain
by BAS Printers Limited, Wallop,
Hampshire, Colour plates: reproduc-
tion by City Engraving, Hull and
printed by Hollen Street Press, Slough,
Bucks., Paper supplied by P. F. Bingham,
Croydon, Surrey and bound by Dorstel
Press, Harlow.

# Acknowledgments

Maurice Cosgreave Colour Plate 7, Plates 15, 21, 32, 36, 37; Jenni Norman-Walker Colour Plate 1, Plates 2, 3, 11, 13, 14, 16, 17, 18, 19, 24, 26, 27, 31, 43, 46, 50; Nicolette Scourse Colour Plate 2, Plates 1, 4, 23, 41; Peter Scourse Colour Plates 3, 4, 5, 10, Plates 6, 8, 9, 10, 12, 20, 22, 28, 29, 30, 33, 34, 35, 38, 40, 42, 44, 45, 48, 49, 51; Richard Simpson Colour Plate 6, Plate 25; John Tucker Colour Plate 8, Plates 5, 7; Robert Walters Colour Plate 9.

# Contents

# Illustrations

## *Drawings*

# Preface

The need for short snatches of quiet and relaxation in a world governed by speed, tension and change cannot be disputed. The idea of peace of mind through handling natural materials—of losing mundane worries for a moment in a timeless lovely flower—is not modern; the Japanese have practised Ikebana, the art of arranging living plant material, for more than ten centuries.

Classical Ikebana is a time consuming and philosophical study, but its impeccable placing of few materials has rubbed off on western floral art, and has inspired uncluttered, quickly created designs ideal for modern rooms. Simplicity with few materials has necessarily formed the basis of my own designs as I have no garden, and in the scope of manipulation, treatment and preservation of flowers for arrangments I have been carefully limited by the dictum that, for most of us, time is the least available commodity. Even so, the lucky ones with time to spend will still find plenty of food for thought, vision and investigation.

I have scrupulously avoided step by step directions for arrangements; rather, there is an introduction to the elements of design—harmony, balance, unity, and to the theory of colour, so that a personal feel for design and self expression are brought out rather than squashed through blind mimicry. Most of all, the book seeks to stimulate the art of seeing and appreciating beauty in commonplace things—an art that is innate in all of us.

Heightened awareness and observation soon extend beyond aesthetic appreciation of natural forms to the intricate structures of natural materials, to the reasons for things being as they are. Why are flower shapes different? What were the first flowers like and why did they change? Are grasses and catkins really flowers? Why are wild flowers and stones typical of some localities? Why do stones have different colours and textures? How old are stones? What makes cut plants wilt indoors? Can their life be prolonged? What has been the history of the plant world so far, and what does the future hold? How does man dictate the form of new plants? The plant world is part of the living world of which we are a part; in observation and understanding of the nature of things as they seem and things as they are, the two channels of art and science meet. One is a natural progression of the other.

The natural world is certainly not exclusive to the country dweller or the garden owner. The book has been written with fellow flat dwellers in mind. Creating designs with plant life is an art without barriers (and taking it to its ultimate conclusion, avant-garde arrangers include no plant life at all).

Arranging flowers is an absorbing form of self-expression that does not demand any innate ability to draw, balance or move; it merely demands looking and feeling—a cheap price for the discovery of the perfection of unsuspected beauty and intricate scientific design.

I wish to acknowledge my debt to my mother, Margaret Somerville West, who passed to me the notes collected over many years by herself and my grandmother. As well as providing an invaluable background for the book, these were its initial inspiration. My mother also supplied numerous photographs and drawings of arrangements of which twelve appear in this book.

My thanks are due to Peter Scourse for taking photographs and criticising the manuscript in detail, Richard Scourse for advice on geology, James Parlane for advice on indoor plants and the use of his Nursery for photography, Rehana Savul for the loan of her prize winning arrangements, John and Louise Goss for devising an arrangement in an antique setting, and Irene Christie for advice on Ikebana.

Nicolette Scourse 1971.

INTRODUCTION

# The Art and the Science

*Flowers And You*

'Leaving the harder part to the servant, the mistress might well do the other:
. . . ' but people and ideas have progressed a long way since Mrs. Beeton.
Flower arranging is now for everyone to enjoy, a creative outlet from the chores
of everyday, and above all a breath of sanity when the rain pours on the washing
and the children are fidgety. In common with painting, sport, dancing, music,
yoga and the myriad of physical and mental disciplines, flower arrangement can
demand complete involvement of the senses, the hands and the mind, thus
relaxing tension. The ability to see beauty in everyday plants and objects and
to create something tangible out of an inspiration breeds pleasure and a sense
of achievement as well as 'gracing a table'.

Raw materials have changed, too; flowers are no longer a necessity for floral
art, which in its very broadest sense envelops almost the entire plant world and
much of the mineral and animal worlds too. Inspiration can stem as much from
a twig of spring leaves and fairy-tale toadstools (*Colour Plate 1*) as a bunch of
rich red roses or a heap of peach-lipped sea shells.

Once arranged, natural materials can lighten the dowdiest, darkest room, can
make an elegant peaceful space in a chaotic utilitarian study, can highlight a
colour scheme, make a poor room rich, and above all give continuing pleasure
and inspiration. Plant life plays a more psychological part in our lives than we
imagine. In the face of past experience, the psychological need for personal
contact with natural things cannot be denied. The nature-gobbling industrial
revolution was followed by a spate of floral decoration on pottery and in paintings; the Victorian age saw flower mania—potted aspidistras on pedestals,
lavish conservatories, floral petit point cushions, fire-screens, footstools, silken
pictures, pressed flowers, bead posies and dainty handbags—flowers with everything. It is tempting to draw an analogy with the present day inclusion into

interior decor of naturalistic building and furnishing materials, living plants, and gaudy artificial flowers—plastic and traditional, tissue and trendy. Live plant material can, however, add delicacy, grace, creativity, and emotion which is never still as buds turn to flowers and flowers grow old. The mellowed colours and texture of preserved plant materials, be they flowers or driftwood, cannot be imitated by mass production.

Escape to the beauties of nature also happened in the East. Japan, during its turbulent and violent period of history—the fifteenth and sixteenth centuries— saw the wealthy and the men of taste seeking withdrawal from worldly tribulations in their exquisite tea houses built for flower and moon-viewing and set in specially designed landscape gardens. One of the main features of their carefully rustic and simple design was an alcove for flower arrangements. Earlier, during the thirteenth and fourteenth centuries, the Moors had built the Alhambra Palace in Spain with niches within arches to hold flowers.

The place of flowers, floral decoration and gardens throughout history is a fascinating topic—their symbolism in religion, their use in art and their reflection of everyday life and attitudes. Such a study really merits a book to itself; all that it has been possible to include here is a single short Chapter—Flowers Through the Centuries.

Although Mrs. Beeton's days of elegance and industrial engulfment are now part of history, it is still a popular misconception that arranging fresh flowers is a delicate, ladylike occupation for the woman who has time on her hands, a colossal flower garden or florist's bill, and shelves of attractive containers.

This book has been written bearing in mind people who are not in the enviable position of having gardens, time or quantities of money to spend. Perhaps it should again be mentioned here that it has not been written by someone with these commodities, trying to visualise what it is like to be without them. Much of the book was written and illustrated while camping without vases or collections of 'useful objects' in a one-room caravan in the northernmost tip of Scotland at the coldest time of year—at first sight not very promising prospects for floral creativity! The only requirement for floral art is that there should be a love of beauty, flowers, and the countryside, or an appreciation of pleasing surroundings in which to live.

No matter if one is rich or poor, the incredible variety and wonder of the natural world is all around, waiting to be discovered.

*The Art and Science of Seeing.* How can one make attractive arrangements without vases and a choice of foliage and flowers, possibly without any flowers at all?

Firstly it is largely a matter of talent spotting—of getting into the way of recognising the essential design qualities of materials—of being inspired. This is the basis of an original design, and it soon develops once one starts looking. One must allow the nature of the material to dictate the nature of the arrangement. To assist the process, plant and other natural materials have been grouped and tabulated in the first chapter, The Art of Seeing, according to their line, form, texture and so on.

The Art of Seeing also includes thoughts on what combinations make designs pleasing, and attempts to stimulate the reader into deciding what it is that makes a pleasing and possibly artistic creation out of 'making do', which may influence future selection and arrangements. Before coming to grips with a branch of blossom and the agonising choice of partners and container, it is suggested that the reader spare a moment for this not so theoretical preamble. In the illustrated arrangements reasons for personal choices, combinations and placing are explained as a pointer to a personal way of seeing.

Beyond the inspiration of a gossamer petal, tortuous driftwood forms, and the filmy lace of fern, there is the fascination of design for survival, both visible and miniature—the other world where destiny lies in air currents, mammoth dew drop discs, and puncturing insects tongues, where a bee's flight and fancy is deciding future plant generations, and an inadvertent sheep's hoof smashes years of miraculous growth and tenacious life. These shapers of survival are timeless in man's experience, for they belong to a world in which plant history, about a thousand million years of it, fills but a chapter.

The science behind the art materials is given at the end of chapter sections, and as far as possible scientific jargon has been avoided. Where scientific terms are inevitable explanations appear close at hand. Except where there is no common name and a flower is popularly known by its generic name, Latin names have been omitted as they are complicated for the non-specialist and when casually used often cause the very ambiguity the Latin terms seek to avoid. Alternative names to those used can be traced through the index. The basis of classification of plants and the scientific naming conventions are explained for those who have an interest in the subject.

*Flowers in Practice.* Most people buy or pick flowers and foliage haphazardly to suit their pocket or fancy. Rather than selecting a variety on the basis of a preconceived floral design, one gets back to the kitchen with an apparently incongruous and incompatible sample of what's pickable. The next step is to make the best of what you have got—a massive recovery operation, in effect!

Being able to make an arrangement from unpromising and limited material involves using the material one has to best advantage, to choose an inspiring line or form as a basis and to select things that complement and balance each other, and make the arrangement look 'just right' as a design in a container and in its location. Practical points and suggested combinations for few items and for the classical British mass style are given separately for easy reference, according to one's own supply and demand.

In Chapter 2, Practical Suggestions for Few Flowers, and Chapter 3, Masses of Flowers, raw materials particularly suited for different parts of a design have been grouped according to their source and type, and set out in tables. Thus quick reference can be made, whether one's source is a florist specialising in the exotic, a tiny garden, a vegetable basket, or if one is starting with only a handful of leaves from the wayside and a few pot plants. It should be noted that wild versus unusual cultivated flowers have been classified from the British viewpoint: foreign weeds are often British exotics. With the time factor in mind, the technique of wiring flowers has been omitted—the designs illustrated make use of the material as it is, without forcing branches into curves, or bending stems. Locations of arrangements and suiting design to occasion are discussed in Chapter 7.

### A THREE SMALL TWIGS, ONE BUNCH OF BERRIES

Can these few materials make an arrangement? The answer is definitely yes, provided one has a driftwood store from which to choose a partner to the live plants.

Here a beautiful shiny piece of driftwood has been used—silver grey, smooth and mellowed by countless years of wind and rain. It is part of the knotted roots of the old tree relic in *Colour Plate 2*.

The perpendiculars of the wood are extended with a leafless twig of rowan (mountain ash). Linking this strong vertical line with the lower part of the arrangement, alder leaves echo the horizontal bunches of hanging berries. Alder twigs intertwine amongst the driftwood contortions—extending the horizontal base line to the left, and large leaves radiate from a focus of bright rowan berries on the right. Alder catkins peep out from below the berries.

At the back of the driftwood, hidden slim containers (lipstick lids) hold stems, which are steadied by wire wrapped round driftwood projections. A grey and white granular stone made a plain and appropriately shaped base.

*On Hoarding.* To be able to select well suited combinations for good designs, one needs at least some variety of raw material even if one is 'making do'. Materials other than fresh blooms open up other sources of large quantities of cheap material, extend the scope, interest and vitality of design possibilities and, above all, open one's eyes. Hoarding, then, is the answer.

Beyond the horizons of live material, there are the endless possibilities of dried oddments, such as driftwoods, seed heads, leaves, and pebbles, shells, and curiosities gleaned from roadside, sea-shore, field and hedgerow. These make an invaluable store from which a wide selection of materials for mixing and matching with any live plants can be chosen, or simply used in arrangements of storage items (*Fig A*). Build up a good supply of driftwood shapes, and problems of quantity are over—a few leaves and berries are all that is necessary as embellishment or interest.

Hints on collection, preservation and storage without bother, demanding little or no time, are given in Chapter 6, Collecting and Preserving Plant Beauty. Building up a collection of semi-permanent materials is an important part of arranging and is necessary just as a painter needs paints, canvas and brushes, and the poet requires words. Who would say that the raw materials for painting and poetry constitute either art? But with ordinary bare branches, twigs, cones or seed pods, grasses and stones, an attractive and artistic creation can be made and for very little cost—truly something out of nothing.

Hoarding seems to become part and parcel of existence once one has found the first beautiful driftwood, or cupped a handful of variegated pebbles; it extends to accessories and curios too—carved gourd containers, china figures, stuffed birds, delicate old fans, tiles, bottles, candlesticks and candles, baskets, oriental tea boxes, trinkets, and baubles of past and present. How much more do-it-yourself and satisfying to create a beautiful original composition from forest, road-side and junk shop, than to follow-step-by-step instructions of a floral kit in order to achieve an expensive and standardised arrangement, the same as everybody else's.

As well as being useful, building up a collection of 'useful items' is enjoyable—one becomes aware of unexpected variety on the regular walk with the dog. No two pieces of driftwood are identical, and on the sea-shore each tide brings in its own kind of trophy. Attached to a piece of driftwood is its often amusing story of acquisition; then there is the expression of the customs officer's face when one brings a prickly pear skeleton back from a beachcombing holiday abroad! Making the stock box brings lots of enjoyment to all concerned. (A heartbreak note here: the joy of it all extends also to dogs, cats and destructive small children!)

*Milestones of Time and Distance*

*The Year*. Flowers and fruits mirror the pattern and character of the seasons—they are the quintessence of the yearly cycle. The classical schools of Ikebana all recognise, and are strictly bound to, types of flowers and trees setting the background and atmosphere of the seasons. This is not surprising when one realises that the typical Japanese room is completely bare, and the walls consist of sliding doors, the outer ones of glass. Thus the garden is almost inside the house, even in winter. Inside the room there is close contact with nature—traditionally there is the recess in which the flower arrangement stands; with the view outside the glass walls it forms the only focus of the room, so it follows that the two must be in keeping with each other.

In a uniform city world of concrete and asphalt there is little to mark the passage of time, and the quiet yearly renaissance and demise. That is, there is no manifestation of the joyful resurgence of spring until narcissi and daffodils tower in a column above bark and moss, primroses and violets peep from baskets and laburnum, wisteria and bluebells cascade in curves from high placed vases. Blackthorn (sloe), hyacinths, anemones, buttercups and thrift bring spring vigour and colour into the house—a reminder that lean winter days are over at last. To be dependent on common wild flowers for arrangements is a positive advantage if one seeks to capture the seasons (*Plate 1*).

Robert Browning captured spring with words:

> '. . . the lowest boughs and the brushwood sheaf
> Round the elm-tree bole are in tiny leaf,
> While the chaffinch sings on the orchard bough.'

Summer is beautiful and brash; the flowers almost shout with their brightness.

> 'The summer's flower is to the summer sweet'
> Though to itself it only live and die.'
> Shakespeare

The new felt warmth of the sun and the hint of first summer fruits is captured in myriads of roses, delphiniums and lupins, whether arranged in shopping baskets or silver bowls. The warm sweet smell of summer hedgerows, 'All the live murmur of a summer's day' in the words of Arnold, is brought into the house with a bunch of honeysuckle, and meadow sweet; a tub of cow parsley and marguerites epitomises the unsophisticated abandon of the summer countryside.

Sad, yet glorious, is autumn, simultaneously bright and subtle.

> 'Season of mists and mellow fruitfulness!
> Close bosom-friend of the maturing sun;
> Conspiring with him to load and bless
> With fruit the vines that round the thatch-eaves run.'

Few can compete with Keats, but anyone can make an autumn portrait—a mass of copper-tinted dahlias, chrysanthemums and beech leaves. Glistening bright berries are enthusiastic reminders of lost summer blooms, and turning leaves and swelling fruits herald the return of grey wind and cold. Trees and hedgerows become grey skeletons of autumn plenty.

> 'Late lies the wintry sun a-bed,
> A frosty, fiery sleepy-head;
> Blinks but an hour or two; and then,
> A blood-red orange, sets again.'
> Robert Louis Stevenson

Winter withering and austerity is epitomised in matt fibrous seed heads, brown glycerined leaves and snowy leaf skeletons. The unleashable tenacity and hope of life shouts from glossy ivy leaves, holly and fir branches: spring is manifested in the promise of rebirth of green richness, or as Keats put it so aptly, 'The simple flowers of our Spring are what I want to see again.'

**1** SPRING CAPTURED
Bluebells and spring are inseparable: dainty flowers, and a casual bunch arrangement combine to capture the freshness of a reawakened world.

*Scenic Change and Environment.* Wherever one goes in the world, there are always flowers and trees supplying colour, movement and beauty: to describe a place no verbal language is necessary; a handful of plants, stones and bark says it all. The essence of different regions of the world, even areas of one country, lies in the characteristic flowers and trees. The relatively small area of Britain has many faces: the colour and feeling of autumn Hampshire is captured in misty white mantles of traveller's joy, yellowing deciduous trees, bronze and crimson berries. Flint stone white and grey, straggling blue-pink roses in a pure blue setting symbolise a Sussex summer day; northern and southern moorland are crystallised in autumnal bracken brown, rusty orange lichen, grey misty green, and wind blown blue emerging from grey hard stone. In a country the size of the United States the extremes of scenery are dynamic. In the Central Plains of North America, tall bending grasses and vivid flowers of the spring Prairie depict a scene worlds away from the swampy South, with Spanish moss festooned in canopies over green trees. Different again is the autumn brilliance of New England, foiled by the evergreen magnificence of the coniferous giants of western mountains. Design ideas for landscape portraits are suggested in Chapters 2 and 3.

Up to two thousand years ago the British Isles were covered by a natural forest (*Colour Plate 2*)—south-east vegetation being deciduous, northern Scotland coniferous. Since that time, man's activities have altered the environment, grazing animals causing the forest to give way to grassland. There remain parts of the country which still contain indigenous species, and where there is little interference by man—rough mountain and hill pastures which are practically unused at high altitudes, bogs and fens, salt-marshes and sand-dunes, native woodlands and heath. These provide truly natural colour schemes and plant combinations.

Some factors which decide the type of vegetation in any area are climatic; rainfall, temperature range, amount of frost, light duration and intensity, and wind. These things on their own affect plants, and also they all alter humidity which, as will be seen in Chapter 6, is very important to plants. Vegetation and scenery illustrate the variation in these environmental factors, which in turn mirror the topography of the land. Along the Pacific Coast of America rainfall is high due to moisture-laden winds from the ocean cooling as they rise over the mountains. Inland the land is lower and rainfall small, until the land rises from the plateaux to the heights of the Rockies and the rainfall increases. Predictably the vegetation reflects the rainfall pattern: the northern mountain ranges near the Pacific are covered with imposing forests of conifers including the giant redwoods, and further south dense scrub with stunted trees and grassland. Straggling trees at high levels, sagebrush and cactus, and some desert areas manifest the scarcity of rain in the inland plateaux and basins, while in the high watered Rockies woodlands once more prevail. These differences of climate and vegetation, although occurring at such relatively close proximity, are great enough to show on rainfall and vegetation maps of the world. The minute area of Britain shows an overall sameness on these maps. However, within the homogeneous damp and temperate climate there is still regional variation. The South-east and Midlands are drier and warmer in summer than other parts of Britain, while in Northern Scotland, temperatures are lower and there is often cloud and mist. Deciduous and coniferous forests attest the difference.

These, then, are factors behind the different types of vegetation and scenery typical of particular regions of any country. In fact the environmental conditions outweigh geography; vegetation bears the stamp of the climate. Two comparable habitats with similar conditions are likely to have vegetation of the same general appearance if not the same species. For example in most temperate regions of the world there are deciduous forests, green in summer and bare in winter. Separation by barriers of thousands of miles, seas and deserts does not detract from the similarity of summer green forests in temperate areas of Europe, Eastern Asia and North America. Local species are comparable in physical form from one forest to another. Oak woods of Western and Central Europe share types of oak, ash, elm and birches, and many others, with the forests of eastern North America. Within this area the Appalachians and surrounding regions show marked differences in the types and relative numbers of the many different trees which make up the luxuriant forests of the Eastern States; beeches, birches, basswoods, elms, oaks, tulip-trees, hickories, maples, walnuts, hornbeams, sweet chestnuts, and pines and spruces. Also, within an area there are tiny differences: local geography, such as exposed hillsides and sheltered pockets, have a marked effect on the distribution of plants. Common wild flowers of one place are the rarities of another.

The soil particle size, which ultimately depends on weathering factors and the type of rock from which it was formed (see page 171), affects the amount of water held by the soil which is of vital importance for some species of plants. Acidity or alkalinity of the soil depends somewhat on the type of the underlying rock, the nature of which also determines the drainage of the soil and thus waterlogging and loss of soil and nutriments. Salt in the soil, as in salt-marshes and sand-dunes, is obviously not desirable to many plants.

The geography and geology of an area, apart from determining the physical features of scenery such as hill and valley shape, river beds and coastline, also influence the clothing of the countryside—the vegetation and the animal life. Geographical features and the underlying rocks shape the environment in which plants have to survive.

It is not surprising therefore that certain plants with similar preferences grow together in a plant community which becomes typical of an area. For instance, species typical of a beech-wood of southern England are ash, wild cherry, holly, elder, box, hazel, spurge laurel, dogwood, traveller's joy and ivy. The plants at ground level are dictated by the amount of light filtering through the canopy of beech and its partners. Dog's mercury, violets, helleborines, cuckoo-pint, Solomon's seal, herb robert and grasses are typical. Often beech trees create so much shade there is no ground flora.

The plants in the community affect each other in other ways besides the amount of light they cut off; trees affect plants growing round their roots by their falling leaves—dead pine needles exclude other vegetation. Often one has the situation of one plant colonising an area and altering the soil by its decaying remains and by its shelter, allowing a second type to become established, and so on, ending in many cases with the first species being ousted from the environment.

This happens in the case of marram grass (*Plates 38 and 46*) which is abundant on sand dunes, but almost unknown on inland soils. This species has long and strong creeping underground stems which produce many fibrous roots—these serve as anchorage for the dunes and stop them from shifting further inland (marram grass is often planted specifically for the purpose of building dunes). Sand is blown inshore and drifts onto the dune, and, as one layer is anchored, the grass grows up through the new sand which it soon fixes. Such a cumulative process soon establishes dunes fifty feet high, and other plants infiltrate the area and slowly the marram disappears. Marram grass and other plants of the sea shore, such as couch grass, sea rocket, and sea kale are very tolerant hardy plants, resisting fresh water scarcity, salt and drying winds. The clever adaptations of marram leaves to deal with their adverse surroundings are shown in *Fig N.*

*Environment and Man.* Some inkling of the complex interaction of the living and non-living in a land environment has been outlined; apparently unconnected living things indirectly affect each other extensively, and man tips the see-saw of balance and relationships most of all. The continuous web of relationships extends into air and sea. In ecology, the study of the environment and its organisms, nothing is simple—disturb one insect-plant relationship and one sets in motion a far-reaching chain of events, the end of which may be unpredictable.

In this age of man taking over control of his environment, the study and understanding of ecology is of the utmost importance. Insecticides increase the harvest but their effects extend beyond the crops at which they are aimed— the soil, visiting beneficial insects, birds and the final product for human consumption may be deleteriously affected if the chain of interactions and its mechanics are not understood.

Pollution can happen so slowly and deviously as to be invisible and unnoticed. Cases of reservoir pollution have been accounted for by accumulated fertilizers being washed out of farmland by heavy rain. Poisonous liquids seeping out of rubbish tips can ultimately find their way to rivers, fish and drinking water. Innocent disposal of a disused chemical container has been the instrument of poisoning for river fish. The round-about route through the living and non-living connections in the environment makes tracking and control difficult.

One of the big dangers of chemical pollution is accumulation—small amounts are harmless and cause little alarm or suspicion; however there is the complicating factor of food chains to be considered before shutting one's eyes. In the sea, microscopic plants and animals (plankton) are the food of small fish, which are preyed on by large fish, which are in turn eaten by the largest fish and sea birds. If every link in the chain contains a minute amount of a foreign chemical which cannot be expelled from the body, the creature at the top of the food chain, the fish and the sea birds receive a correspondingly large dose. Exactly the same situation occurs on land. Man is at the end of many food chains, and like many of the animals, his body is not equipped to deal with some harmful man-made chemicals; once there they are there to stay.

The sea is often treated as an oversize bottomless dustbin. Mile upon mile of the coastline is made unfit for the healthy existence of seaweeds and the animals feeding on them by the tipping of colliery waste and untreated sewage from an astounding number of cities. It is a sobering thought that in the space age some methods of large scale dumping of waste continue unchanged since Victorian times, and, in the Tudor tradition, sewage and other effluent are discharged directly to 'rivers' flowing through town and country and to the sea direct. Boat loads of dead fish have testified the far-reaching effects of industrial waste in rivers.

No-one yet knows the cumulative effects of this type of sea pollution, nor the limit of the amount of waste the sea can handle without stifling and killing its variety of life on which our own food chain depends. The healthy survival of the very lowest of the chain, the plankton, is vitally important, for these miniscule dots of living matter, apart from manufacturing food for creatures higher up the chain, help purify the atmosphere.

Treatment of industrial and domestic waste and sewage is expensive, but in some places demand for pure water is already outstripping availability, or is forecast to in the near future. The whole of life depends on water; Keats felt the vitality of water:

> 'The moving waters at their priestlike task
> Of pure ablution round earth's human shores.'

Undoing years of pollution will be the only answer, and a more expensive one in the long run, if yesterday's and today's warnings are not heeded today.

It is now necessary to accept the possibility of man being suffocated by his environment 'control', for the plants, directly or indirectly, support all life on this planet and above all are the vital oxygen producers. On their survival the survival of man and other animals depends. Conservation is not the old school denying progress in order to preserve the prettiness of the countryside for weekend entertainment; it is ultimately a matter of survival and tolerable conditions for living.

There is the psychological effect of plants too. The common wild flowers of hedgerow and woodland may be only a tiny link in the ecological chain, but even so, vandalism is not too strong a word for stripping a plant of too many of its flowers or seed heads, or picking a rare species. So, with the ordinary man and woman in the street lies the responsibility to allow our great grandchildren, and their children, the privilege of seeing the art and science of flowers.

In the context of appreciation and conservation of the plant world—our world—the author dedicates this book to the 'Tree Planting Year' 1973.

CHAPTER ONE

# The Art of Seeing

An elegant design can be concocted by cleverly teaming one or several flowers with fresh greenery, dried material, natural 'props', and an appropriate container, all placed in a well chosen setting. What are the things that make up a beautiful design?

An important factor is *unity*—several different things are brought together under the roof of one idea, such as a curve or a certain hue. *Interest* involves variety of shapes and forms, colour combinations, and different relationships of parts of the design to each other and the overall whole. *Balance* of an asymmetrical idea demands that one item or attraction of the design should not outweigh and steal all attention away from the other parts, while at the same time allowing one form to dominate the picture, giving it a theme. For example a design made of predominantly solid perpendiculars could be set off well by the addition of delicate curves, or a feathery flimsy item, each retaining its identity and contrasting with the other while at the same time contributing to a solid perpendicular whole. A dominant theme is present but there is still an awareness of the other material in the design in order that there should be *harmony*, or definite relationships between the parts. A satisfying design should not contain too much material, or too much space—a sense of *proportion* is essential.

All of these things, and others not mentioned, are involved in beauty, so that it is a difficult task to single out one and consider it in isolation from its partners. Design can convey movement, static peace, and a multitude of subjective feelings; so too can single items which can be the initial inspiration for a design.

This is not intended to be an exhaustive artistic analysis of natural objects. It is merely a collection of natural materials which have given inspiration—in retrospect it has been attempted to put the nature of the inspiration into words. If it triggers off any new awareness it will have served its purpose; a cross section of mundane, wild, cultivated and exotic items have been included to suit all tastes, facilities, and pockets.

## 2 MEANDERING CURVE

A curved orchid spray can hold its own as a single beautiful shape, or inspire an original design.

In creating a design around an inspiration it is imperative that the initial theme shape should not be swamped—balance is essential. The choice of partner materials for the design must be governed by the sweeping curve, the sculptured spurs and lobes of individual orchid flowers, waxy yellow texturing and scarlet highlights. Unity and contrast play off against each other.

## B NEW LIFE UNFURLS

Stylised scrolls of unfurling fern fronds make an unusual starting point for a design. Snaking and curved like a lyre-bird's tail, fern leaves look almost unreal when picked from their natural shady niche.

The unfurling, erupting effect of opening scrolls is enhanced by the close packed point of radiation of the stems from a large uninterrupted area of water. Leaf bases have been superimposed to avoid a clutter of radiating stems. Two basic curves have been embellished and a few single scrolls placed low down to break the severity of the lines. Large purplish tradescantia leaves make a contrast of shape and colour and the lack of pattern adds a solid feeling to the base of the arrangement. The natural forms are echoed in the carved Indian table used as a stand for the arrangement.

| INSPIRATION FROM | NATURAL MATERIALS (*material can be preserved) |
|---|---|
| *Lines and Shapes* (two dimensional) | |
| *Curves.* Meandering, smooth curve, from graceful to swirling, but can always suggest movement. | Driftwood derived from seaweed* (*Fig G and Plate 38*), foliage of a few species of euphorbia, black bryony with berries or leaves, grapevine,* some ivy,* clematis, passion vine, many creeping wild flowers such as vetch, wisteria stem,* tendrils. |
| Contorted, convoluted curve, awkward and angular, a solid and interesting foil for elegant simplicity. | Driftwood* (*Plate 11 and Fig O*)—gorse stems, ivy stems dried and smooth, or fresh without leaves, knotted branches, trimmed twigs of beech,* heather,* apple, almond, azalea. |
| Wide and tapering with a definite outline, simple, solid, and graceful; simplicity often accented by parallel veining. | Leaves of aspidistra, plantain, lily-of-the-valley,* arum lily, canna, foxglove, hosta*—all with curved outlines and leaves hang in a curve. Flower of arum and cuckoo-pint (*Fig E*). |
| Narrow curve, slender and elegant. | Leaves of daffodil, bluebell, iris,* spider plant (*Plates 31 and 44*), grasses, reedmace (also known as bulrush) (*Fig L*), liriope. |

| | |
|---|---|
| Stylised geometric curve, a hint of unreality and orderliness. | Shepherd's crook appearance—sprouting fern fronds (*Fig B*) such as bracken, male-fern, and others. |
| Impression of a curve, not a continuous line; delicate and light, but a less elegant feeling about them than continuous lines. | Flowers of some grasses (*Figs R and T*), bluebell (*Plate 1*), Solomon's seal, bleeding heart. Foliage of tamarisk, willow, cypress, silk-oak,* some ferns,* some bamboos. |
| *Straight Lines.* Straight sided shapes— perpendiculars, dramatic, sometimes abrupt, sometimes gracious. | Daffodil buds, wheat,* flower spikes of foxglove and lupin* (*Colour Plate 4*), speedwell (*Plate 32*), central leaves of iris* (*Plate 36*). |
| Topped perpendiculars— elongated heads and round sprays topping thick stems accentuates their line. | Reedmace (bulrush) heads,* stem of cuckoo-pint berries (*Plate 18*), teasel,* red hot poker,* papyrus,* agapanthus, wood garlic, cow parsley* and relatives, seed heads of dandelion,* plantain* (*Plate 49*), poppy (*Colour Plate 10*). |
| Perpendiculars emphasized with horizontals, giving a stylised pagoda-like appearance. | Horsetail (*Fig C and Plate 6*), bamboo stem, dried stem and fruits* (seed cases) of shepherd's purse and dead-nettle, fir and spruce twigs stripped of lateral branches,* stem of dock with flowers, seeds* or bare.* |

→

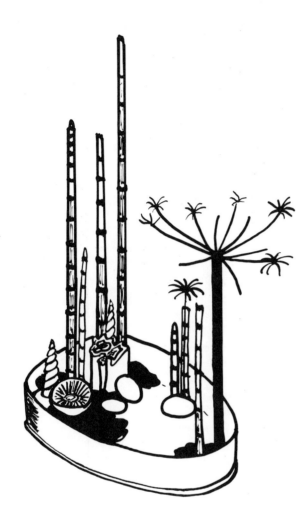

## C PERPENDICULAR LANDSCAPE

In a sense this is an abstract pattern of an imaginary world, where palm tree skeletons and giant gaunt columns, almost man-made in their striped repetition, tower over pastel coloured minarets, smooth and striated domes, set on a dark island in a still lake. The fact that the stylised regular striations, spirals and spokes are provided by horsetails, shells, an upturned toadstool, and a dried umbellate head (see also *Plate* 26) is irrelevant; the fusion into a single idea loses their individual identity.

As for the container and the mechanics of the arrangement, they are improvised in the extreme—as will be seen in Chapter 4.

| | |
|---|---|
| Spikey lines. | Gladioli buds, leaves of iris,* yucca, and bamboo, gorse, twigs and sprays of pine, barley* (*Colour Plate 10*), dried seed heads of iris, columbine. |
| *Forms* (three dimensional) | |
| Simplicity of form, a contrast to the complex. | Beach pepples—quartz, sandstone, slate (*Plate 46*). arum lily, acorn, cactus stem. |
| Sculptured and complex, interesting, demanding investigation of intricacies. | Rose* (*Plate 13*), chrysanthemum,* iris (*Plates 8 and 27*), draped and folded material; eroded sandstone, weathered driftwood (*Fig A, Colour Plate 2, Plate 11 and Fig O*). |
| *Surface Texture* | |
| Smooth and striated. | Leaves of hosta, plantain, viburnum. Some sea shells (*Plate 46*). |
| Smooth and matt, the feel of unglazed pottery.

Depth and intensity of velvet. | Some toadstools and mushrooms,* sloe berries* (*Colour Plate 10*), banana skin, sandstone, driftwood, eucalyptus leaves,* sheath ('petal') of arum lily, leaves of chrysanthmums. Grapes with bloom, petals of some purple pansies, petals of some roses in bud. |

→

Groups of plants growing together often give inspiration; for instance, the majestic simple curves of reedmace leaves growing near a radiating bundle of sedge perpendiculars, or the contrasted stripes of sunlit larch trunks topped by

**3 SUNLIGHT SCULPTURE**
The petalled intricacy of flowering cherry is caught for a moment by the sun. A complex form such as this is a striking contrast to simple shapes and forms and makes an eye-catching focus in a design.

| | |
|---|---|
| Smooth and shiny, in sympathy with glass, enamel lacquer, and polished metal. | Leaves of spindle shrub* (euonymus), ivy (*Plate 44 and Fig O*), bluebell, laurel,* young rhododendron, begonia (*Plate 44*), holly,* rowan (*Plate 10*), cotoneaster berries, rose hips (*Plate 50*), aubergine, peppers* and chillis,* tomato (*Colour Plate 3*), polished apples (*Colour Plate 7*), yellow and red toadstools. Fool's gold (iron pyrites) mica, quartz and other minerals. Bark of silver birch.* |
| Rough and granular. | Lichens on rocks* (*Plate 48*), granite, sand, melon skin (honeydew), gourds* and coconuts,* orange skin* (particularly if old), many tree barks* (*Plate 10*). |
| Rough and striated, often giving a repetitive pattern. | Flaky slate and rock formed by layers of different coloured sediments, some fungi, cedar tree, some shells. |
| Rough and bushy. | Some lichens,* particularly tree types (*Plate 48*). |
| Soft and downy. | Cotton-grass, leaves of lamb's ears, and dusty miller (*Plate 8*); fluffy fruits of traveller's joy. |

downward flowing delicate branches and cascades of filmy green. Natural and contrived combinations can be the seed of design ideas.

| *Pattern* of shapes, form, colour, texture | |
| --- | --- |
| Regular, rhythmic, and repetitive. | Lilac, hydrangea,* phlox, grape hyacinth, lupin* (*Colour Plate 4*), berries of cuckoo-pint, a bunch of grapes,* ferns* (*Plates 31 and 44*), palm fronds,* fir branch,* corn cob,* chrysanthemun globe* (*Plate 48*), fir cone* (*Plates 5, 49, and 51*), daisy,* horse-chestnut flower spike, and many other flower clusters (*Plate 36*). |
| Mathematical symmetry, two-sided or circular. | Fern frond;* undamaged organisation of leaves on a twig, e.g. lime, beech;* faces of some flowers such as wallflower; starfish, shell of sea urchin (*Plate 46*). |
| Random irregularity, a foil for repetition. | Wood (*Plates 11 and 35*), chunky stones, lichen, leaves partly eaten by insects, sprawling seaweeds,* knot of tree roots (*Figs A and O*). |
| Lack of pattern, a plain impression of space, a foil to pattern. | Aubergine, green apple (single colour), still water, (plain container—artificial material which should be borne in mind). |

So far, physical and tangible characteristics of rocks, plant and animal life have been considered. These natural things also evoke diverse subjective feelings. Some of these 'moods' have been recorded below, but are, of course, very personalised. When one stops to think, the list is as endless as personal feelings. The inspiration from which the illustrated arrangements developed is included in most of the captions.

**D** OFF-BEAT CONTRASTS
A beautiful leaning Z-shape is made by a few spring flowers, and the courage to mix opposites. The apple blossom provides the diagonal which is broken by delicate green hellebores. The unity of the diagonal line is retained by the similarity in form of the apple flowers and hellebores. The clean solid form of the tulip leaf contrasts with the pattern of the blossom, and balances the composition. The spreading base of the vase is emphasized with broad leaves.

| *Contrast of Opposites (Fig D)* | |
|---|---|
| Dark and light. | Variegated leaves—ivy, begonia (*Plate 44*), holly (*Fig T*), coleus (*Plate 35*). |
| Dramatic and interesting, an important feature in the Japanese style. | Bi- or multi-coloured varieties of flowers such as pansy, cineraria, tulip, dahlia. A combination of two separate materials: light pink or white rose with dark red rose; foliage of dusty miller with viburnum; green and black grapes, dark larva rock, basalt (*Plate 40*), or coal and white quartz. |
| Contrast of surfaces—dull with shiny (*Figs A, D, U, Colour Plates 3 and 10, Plate 39*), rough with smooth (*Fig A, Plate 10 and Fig O*). | Combinations of materials listed under suface texture, see p. 35. |
| Combination of contrasting shapes and forms (*Figs D, G, O, U, Plates 32, 39, 44, 48*, all contain some opposites). | Materials listed above under appropriate heading. |
| Combination of pattern and lack of it. | Lack of pattern often provided by container (*Fig D, Plates 21 and 44*). |

Having appreciated the form of, say, a well shaped branch with leaves forming an intricate pattern, the next step is to build on this inspiration without overshadowing it. By intuition and thoughtful selection of more material one

| 'Mood' (*material can be preserved) | |
|---|---|
| Whimsy and delicate, fine and feathery, essentially feminine, and light. | Some grasses* (*Figs R and T*), asparagus tops,* geraldton wax plant, gypsophila (baby's breath),* papyrus tops; flowers and foliage of mimosa, love-in-a-mist; skeletonised leaves and seed heads; foliage of parsley family (Umbelliferae, p. 121), many ferns,* larkspur, larch (*Fig S*), tamarisk, branching horsetail. |
| Solid shapes, sturdy and masculine, visually heavy, often majestic. | Hosta and yucca* leaves, foliage of iris* and mother-in-law's tongue (*Plates 36 and 44*), wood, stones, gourds, most fruits and vegetables, chrysanthemum flower (*Plate 48*). |
| Cascading, and gracefully bowed, delicate, but with visual weight. | Catkins* (*Plate 51*), laburnum foliage and flowers (fruits are very poisonous), larch foliage (*Fig S*), boughs of fir trees,* fuschia, quaking grass,* Himalayan honeysuckle flowers and berries, wisteria. |

can build up a whole, contrasting geometry with randomness, dark with light, smooth with granular, solid with feathery, straight with curved, or by echoing similar features in different materials one can make unity and harmony (*Plates*

**4 LEAFY WET LOOK**

Far from being common place or 'good for background' material a collection of leaves can make a beautiful composition on their own, particularly if they have an interesting texture or pattern.

Gleaming leaves such as these are a brilliant foil for furry leaves such as dusty miller, or a pure contrast to the metallic sheen of patterned begonia leaves.

Coupled with a few large flowers such as the giant lilies from the same plant, these giant leaves link beautifully with a polished glass container or bring out the dull bloom of fired clay.

*32, 33, 38, 39, 44, 47, Figs C, D, L, Colour Plate 3*). Such contrasts and similarities can be pictured in the same container, or in two sharing a similarity making an unusual unified group (*Fig O*).

Once having seen natural things in terms of design and their essential features, one automatically starts to see the aesthetic qualities in apparently ordinary things. Man-made articles can be equally inspiring—the soft smooth shine of pewter trays and beautifully contoured container shapes, whether they be priceless silver or mass-produced make-up bottles. An art of seeing soon develops,

**5 PATTERNS IN A WYOMING WOODLAND**
Leaves, a fir cone and a flower spike are three very different forms, but here they share the same pattern of regular repetition. These mix better with unpatterned forms, random or plain, than with each other.

as with a painter or a photographer—beauty and interest lie all around; many pass it by, but the mind of the artist sees it, understands it, and captures it. Photographers can compose a picture from a heap of rope, corroding metal, or a dusty street; similarly a beautiful composition with plant life can spring from any road-side. Grass, from green animal feed and excessively fast-growing lawn plant, the same day in day out, transforms into flowing curves in an ever-changing composition. An oddly shaped chunk of firewood by a stone becomes a fascinating and complex entwined shape, its rough lined texture contrasting to its smooth and simple contoured partner.

*The Art of Seeing Further*

*Floral Trap*. Beyond form, line, texture and pattern lies an even greater beauty, an even more sophisticated design.

Within the pure contour of cuckoo-pint (Jack-in-the-pulpit) lies an unexpected, but organised, trapping mechanism, the product of slow change by trial and error through countless April days. Cuckoo-pint, also known as wild arum, lords-and-ladies, wake-robin, cuckoo-pintle, is a very unusual flower, or to be accurate, community of flowers (*Fig E*). Instead of attracting the momentary attention of passing insects by the orthodox appeal of brightly coloured

**E SOLITARY AND COMMUNAL LIVING**

The figure shows a true flower, the daffodil, and an erroneous 'flower', cuckoo-pint or Jack-in-the-pulpit, which is really a community of many male (a) and female (a') flowers. The two have in common an enveloping leaf-like structure, the spathe (1), which in the cuckoo-pint is often wrongly called the petal.

The daffodil is a single flower on a single stem. In the cuckoo-pint there is a flower spike made of lots of tiny stalkless flowers arranged around an elongated central stem, forming a cylindrical mass. The common weed plantain and also catkins, have a similar arrangement of small flowers up a central stem. Cuckoo-pint differs from these other flower spikes in its very much enlarged fleshy central stem (sp), and in its large spathe (1), both of which are enlarged specially for attracting insects to the flower.

A      *daffodil* flower cut in half to show the structure of a typical flower.
B      *cuckoo-pint*, whole and cut in half.
1      *spathe*—an enlarged bract (modified leaf), enveloping and protecting a flower bud as in A, is leaf-like; enveloping a group of flowers as in B, attracting insects, is petal-like.
2      *sepals*—at flower base, usually green and leaf-like and protective as in rose and magnolia (*Plates 13* and *16*) and the sage (*Colour Plate 5*), but often act and therefore look like petals, as in A.
3      *petals*—brightly coloured and showy, used for advertisement.

4      *ovary*—'seed box', contains unfertilised seeds. ⎫
5      *style*—elongated stalk connecting ovary and stigma. ⎬ *pistil*—female part
6      *stigma*—receptive surface for pollen. ⎭
7      *filament*—flimsy stalk holding up anther. ⎫ *stamen*—male part
8      *anther*—produces pollen, 'pollen box'. ⎭
2–8    flower parts.
9      *receptacle*—top of flower stalk bearing flower parts.
sp.    *spadix*—fleshy central axis around base of which is a cylinder of tiny flowers.
h      *downward pointing hairs*—part of fly-trap mechanism.

a      male flowers having only stamens ⎫ sepals and petals reduced as their function is
a'     female flowers having only pistil ⎭ taken over by spathe.

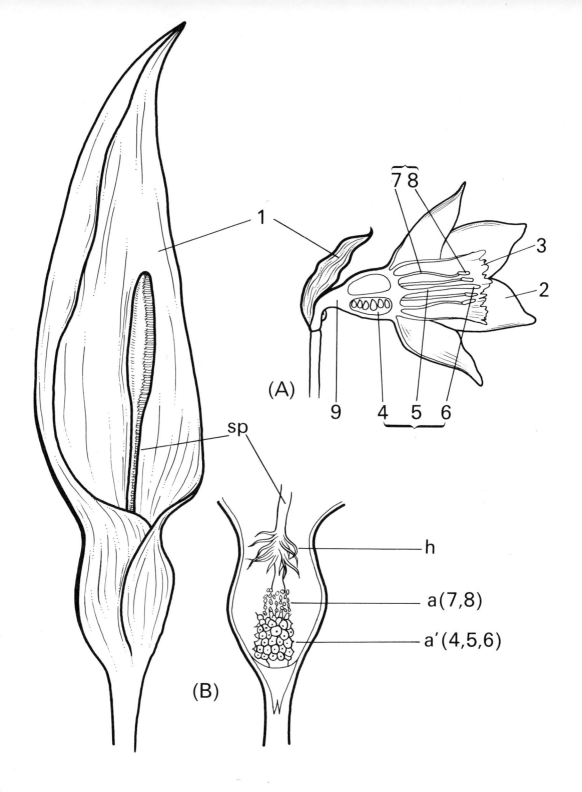

(A)

(B)

showy petals and perfume, this group of flowers lures and then traps small flies.

Flies are attracted by decaying flesh or vegetable matter, foul smelling and brown or purple coloured. Flowers that use flies to spread their pollen therefore attract the insects by producing the smell of decay, or imitate its appearance. The showy and protective cowl-like sheath of cuckoo-pint is green and purple, its prominent central column is purplish, and it has an unpleasant odour: the flies are attracted.

At the base of the central column is a group of female flowers (a') and a group of male flowers (a). Once it has crawled down to the base of the column the fly is trapped among the flowers; the inside walls of the sheath are slippery barring its exit, the sheath's neck is constricted, and below it there are stiff hairs projecting downwards. The flies are thus imprisoned inside the bulbous base: in crawling about inside their trap they dust pollen over the ripe female flowers; the male flowers are as yet unripe.

Later the male flowers ripen and the barricading hairs wither. As the fly makes its escape, it crawls over loose pollen released from the ripe male flowers. The pollen adheres to its hairy body and it is brushed off on ripe female flowers in the next community the fly visits.

The advantages of the trapping mechanism are fairly obvious: by having its pollinating insect at hand and on the job, the cuckoo-pint guarantees an insect visitor at the critical moment when the stigma (see caption of *Fig E*) is receptive and just as the pollen ripens. Less apparent is an even greater expedience. A single flower could adopt the same trapping method, assuming a similar appearance with petal sheath and female and male parts grouped around the base. In such a single flower arrangement one trapped fly would pollinate only the one flower. Where there is a community of flowers within the base as in cuckoo-pint one fly pollinates the whole host. Not only is the pollination mechanism economical—many fertilized seeds in many flowers for the price of attracting one fly— but also many flowers and seeds for the price of one root, and one plant's quota of leaves. A community of flowers on one stem thus means economy of plant material and growth, in the same way that centralisation in industry means economy of administration and costs; another analogy is the comparison of mass production with individual workmanship. Other less extreme and more easily recognisable communities are hawthorn, clover, Queen Anne's lace, and other members of family Umbelliferae, and family Compositae (*Colour Plate 6*).

*Communal Living*. Protection of the flower and its advertisement are usually the tasks of sepals (typically green and leaf-like, but often resembling petals) and petals of each individual flower. In a community of flowers these functions are most economically taken over by a few enlarged sepal or petal-like structures which protect and advertise for the whole group, rather than each flower retaining its own small and less conspicuous sepals and petals. In some communities each flower is thus reduced to the essential minimum: the sexual structure. In cuckoo-pint the parts of advertisement and protection are taken over by one spathe—a massive magnified bract. The latter is usually a tiny scale or leaf-like structure growing out of the stem just below the flower, as in the bluebell and more prominently the daffodil.

The spathe of cuckoo-pint does the same job as a petal, and so has come to look like a petal. This often happens in nature: different structures which have the same use tend to become superficially similar, leading to common misnomers. Examples of other flowers in which bracts act as petals and look superficially like them are poinsettia (*Plate 19*), bougainvillea, and dogwood.

**6** SHADOW OF THE PAST
Destined to remain in a wet environment, modern horsetails are a humble shadow of their ancient predecessors from swamp forests of the Carboniferous Age.

The dark horizontal striations up the stems are tiny scaly leaves which are joined in a collar encircling the stem. A circle of side branches grow out from this collar, making the horsetail look superficially like a Chinese pagoda.

The striated perpendicular line of horsetails has been used in an arrangement in *Fig C*.

*Survivors of 300 Million Years.* 'Unnatural', geometric and stylized perpendiculars; broad, serene curves; delicate filigrees of green: all improbable relics of the sultry swamps of the Carboniferous Period. These are the horsetails and ferns, the much humbled descendants of once glorious lines of giants seventy feet high, girded by thick bark-like covering and elevating long flowing leaves.

The ancient horsetails, together with the colossal predecessors of club mosses and ferns, were prolific in the swampy environment of Carboniferous times (Table 1). The swamps were near sea level and extended across Western Europe, Britain and Eastern North America. From studies on the fossil trees that remain there is evidence that the soil was peaty and waterlogged. During this age there was a large rainfall and it was warm, even hot and humid. When the giant trees died their decomposition was slow as the swamp conditions prevented fast decay, and this together with the pressures of overlying later rock deposits led to the formation of coal from the old rotting wood. Coal that is mined and burnt today is the remains of the ancestral horsetails and their relatives; recognisable fragments can sometimes be seen in coal seams.

The trees of these prolific swamp forests were solely horsetails, ferns and their kind—evergreens and deciduous trees had not yet appeared. In their structure and their way of reproducing the Carboniferous trees were very much simpler and less efficient than the modern trees of which they were the forerunners. The roots, stems and leaves of the ancients were unsophisticated: for example, modifications to reduce water loss were feeble, thus these plants could not exist except in very moist conditions. There were no flowers in which fertilisation occurred to produce seeds, reproduction was by means of spores borne in cones at the top of the stem in horsetails and club mosses or inside dark umbrella-like structures hanging on the underside of leaves in the ferns. Once freed spores gave rise to an intermediate stage which in turn produced male and female cells. In order to reach the female cell, the male cell was dependent on water through which it had to swim, possibly for some distance: a tiny unprotected unit of living 'jelly' at the mercy of coincidence and accident. The ancient trees were well suited to their swamp environment but could never leave the watery safety of the swamps and spread over drier ground.

As long as the wet climate of the Carboniferous persisted the forests were safe; however, widespread earth movements occurred towards the close of the Carboniferous Period, and new mountain chains were formed in Asia, Europe and North America, accompanied by volcanic activity. Climatic conditions changed and fluctuated: deserts and salty inland seas developed, there were

## TABLE 1

In this Table, the geological eras in the earth's history have been arranged in chronological order, and a figure in millions of years ago gives the approximate time scale. In addition, in an attempt to bring the enormity of geological time into focus, a 'relative calendar date' is given, which supposes the origin of the earth to have occurred at the beginning of January, and the present day to be exactly midnight on the following 31st December.

| GEOLOGICAL ERA | MILLION YEARS AGO | RELATIVE CALENDAR DATE | ENVIRONMENT | LIFE |
|---|---|---|---|---|
| Origin of the earth (Pre-Cambrian) | about 4,500 | beginning of January | A mass, heating and cooling, eventually forming a barren landscape of rivers, seas, mountains, deserts, and volcanoes. | None. |
| | | mid-July | Warm seas. Rocks of inner gorge of Grand Canyon (*Plate 7*) formed. | Life begins in the warm seas—simple soft-bodied forms, such as seaweeds, and animals, such as sponges. |
| Cambrian | 500 | early November | Shallow warm seas, advancing and receding; volcanic activity in Europe— no important mountain building. | Seaweeds the only plants, providing food for the animals— sponges, jellyfish, sea worms, starfish etc. |
| Ordovician | 450 | | Sea continues to advance and recede; mud and sand deposited on ocean floor forming dry land in places; volcanic activity; mountain ranges formed. | Only plants still seaweeds; higher forms of life appear—first animals with backbones (fish); squids dominate the seas. |

→

| GEOLOGICAL ERA | MILLION YEARS AGO | RELATIVE CALENDAR DATE | ENVIRONMENT | LIFE |
|---|---|---|---|---|
| Silurian | 400 | 12th December | Seas still rise and fall periodically; volcanic activity wanes, but new mountain ranges begin to form; climate warm, but very dry in places. | Leafless plants appear on land; greater variety of sea plants. |
| Devonian | 350 | | Land area increases; extensive mountain building and volcanic activity; warm and semi-arid in places with heavy seasonal rain. | Plants with roots, stems, leaves; later ferns, horsetails, have appeared, some forty feet high; wingless insects and other lowly land animals. |
| Carboniferous— the coal age | 300 | | Shallow seas; brackish swamps; many regions warm and humid (tropical). | Giant evergreen forests, later forming peat and coal; insects with wings, and reptiles. |
| Permian | 230 | | Inland lakes starting to evaporate, high mountains formed; tropical conditions disappear. | Evergreens decrease as seasonal drought and frost develop— deciduous plants have the advantage; land animals increase as vegetation established; great insect variety. |
| Triassic | 200 | | Dry deserts and mountains; salt lakes; climate becomes wetter later. Rocks at the top of the outer walls of the Grand Canyon being formed. | Dryness discourages plant life until wet conditions return to foster conifers and ferns; warm-blooded creatures (mammals). |
| Jurassic | 150 | | Seas advance; wet conditions return; swamps, lakes and rivers. | Conifers and ferns abundant; flower-like cones are formed—the first step towards flowers. |

PALAEOZOIC (Silurian–Permian)

MESOZOIC (Triassic–Jurassic)

| GEOLOGICAL ERA | MILLION YEARS AGO | RELATIVE CALENDAR DATE | ENVIRONMENT | LIFE |
|---|---|---|---|---|
| Cretaceous | 120 | mid-December | Swamps; mountain-building; mild climate with seasonal variation. | Deciduous trees abundant, e.g. magnolia, poplar; insects and flowers develop side by side; the age of dinosaurs. |
| Eocene | 70 | | Seas advance, mountain ranges grow; large-scale volcanic activity forms Atlantic and Indian oceans; tropical conditions prevail. | Flowering plants and deciduous trees flourish; tropical plants in Southern England, all present-day groups of insects are now living. |
| Oligocene | 40 | | Land mass increases; earth movements; temperate climate, but cold in parts. | Forests decline and grasses take their place, assisting evolution of grazing mammals; tail-less primitive apes appear. |
| Miocene | 27 | after Christmas | Sea recedes due to earth movements which form Alps and Himalayas; much volcanic activity; climate varies in different regions. | Deciduous woods; apes become common. |
| Pliocene | 12 | | Continents take up present shapes; less mountain building; climate like the present. | Apes develop, some walk upright. |
| Pleistocene (glacial) | 1 | just before midnight, 31st December | Ice sheets form and then melt, forming lakes; landscape begins to look as we know it; extreme climatic variation. | Many European plants exterminated by cold; primitive man (with stone implements) emerges. |
| Recent | | | Ice retreats; deserts develop; Britain no longer linked to Europe; climate becomes warmer. | Spread of forests in Europe; man cultivates plants and alters the environment. |

MESOZOIC

CAINOZOIC

## 7 GEOLOGICAL TIME-SHEET

Climate and life have changed continuously throughout the earth's history (see Table 1). These changes, taking place over millions of years, were reflected in the characteristics of the rocks formed at the time. As one era gave way to another, new rocks covered the old, and the time-sheet of the past was covered by the present, possibly to be exposed by the effects of earth movements and erosion in some later era.

The photograph shows one dramatically exposed time-sheet; layers of old and new rock which form the wall of the Grand Canyon. The formation of this wonder of the world was due to uplift of the area and the resultant erosion accomplished by the rejuvenated river. Less spectacular erosion of outer crusts of plateaux and mountains is going on continuously, gradually shifting the upper layers to expose the geological past. In the case of the Grand Canyon, earth movement caused uplift of the land and the Colorado River cut its course through many strata of the uplifted area relatively quickly, geologically speaking. Meanwhile the newly exposed rock walls of the Canyon were subjected to the destruction of the elements and the gorge was widened. Even now the river is still eroding the gorge away and it removes thousands of tons of debris in one day.

The vertical incision of the Colorado River path is about a mile deep through the horizontal layers of rock which form the Colorado Plateau, revealing dramatically each layer in turn with relatively new rock in the top layer, and very old volcanic rock forming the inner gorge of the Canyon. Each layer is a product of its time, some being formed by compression of particles and debris, some being blown and laid down like sand dunes, and some being the

periods of glacial cold, and the large areas of humid low lying swamps disappeared. With the swamp conditions went the characteristic plants, giant insects and other animals. The changes in the environment and consequent mass extinction that occurred during these years were the most dramatic in the known history of the world.

In some areas there were still swamp conditions and in spite of millions of years of changing environment and changing life, moist pockets have persisted in which horsetails, club-mosses, ferns and the still imposing tree ferns have continued to carry on as a shadow of their primitive existence.

### Colour—(Art and Science)

Qualities other than colour have so far been considered—the ideas of form and pattern have been discussed at length as they have a less obvious appeal than colour and in the Japanese styles are more important. A beautiful colour hits you in the eye. It is tempting to be carried away with colour: each is so lovely it seems criminal not to include it. In a simple modernistic design, colour is as important as form and can make or mar a perfectly planned form. Colour combines with form, so that intensities, amounts and hues must be delicately balanced and 'fit in' to make one overall effect.

In arranging colour, it is useful to think of the colour wheel—colour can be put in a circular arrangement according to the physical nature of light. Within the wheel (see diagram) are a series of triangles—the primary colours, green, red, and violet-blue forming one; secondary colours, yellow, magenta, and turquoise forming another; with the tertiary colours in between: green-yellow, orange, magenta-red, violet, blue, and turquoise-green. Pure colours are yellow, orange, red, green, violet, and blue. Within the wheel, complementary colours are directly opposite one another; for example, green and magenta, turquoise and red, blue and orange. This can be tested with the eye by staring hard at a block of colour against a white background in a bright light. When the colour is taken away one sees its opposite colour in its place against the white back-

result of deposition at the bottom of a sea which has long since vanished. The lower strata were formed during the Cambrian (see Table 1) and contain fossils of the earliest complicated creatures. The recent flat-lying layers of rock derived from different sediments can be seen in the photograph. These belong mainly to the Palaeozoic era.

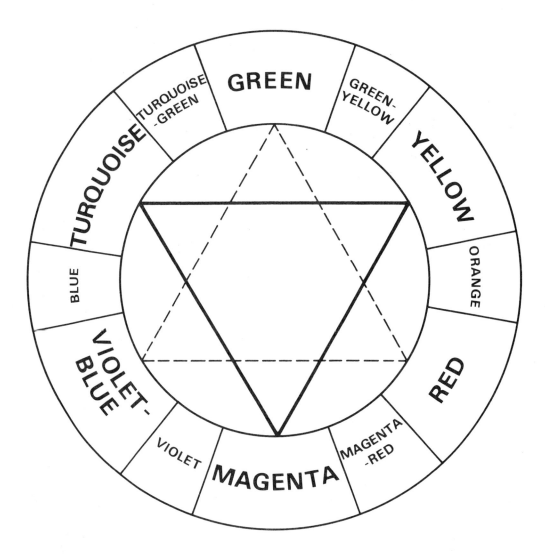

**F** THE COLOURS AND PHYSICAL NATURE OF LIGHT
Colours arranged according to the physical nature of light give a circular sequence of one leading into another. The nature of light is such that by mixing light of all of these colours, one obtains white light.

Colours opposite each other on the colour wheel are complementary—green is complementary to magenta, which can be tested with the eye by staring very hard at a strongly illuminated block of colour, say green, against a white background. If while still looking at it, the colour is removed, one sees its complementary colour, in this case magenta—an interesting optical phenomenon to try.

The solid lined triangle links primary colours, the dotted lines link secondary colours. For use of the wheel in colour schemes, see *Colour Plates*.

ground. Going round the wheel, each colour is related to its next door neighbour; violet-blue, blue, turquoise, turquoise-green, and green form a continuous gradation in colour.

A good colour scheme can be made by combining related colours; for example, a combination of green-yellow, yellow, orange, and adding the complementary colour to yellow which is violet-blue, or a related colour such as blue or violet. The kind of colour, the hue, is not the only consideration. Within each colour there is variation of dark and light and also brightness and dullness. All of these things combine in a single effect on the observer. Black and white react well with colours and relieve the colour scheme.

Once you build up an awareness of colour, you can achieve dramatic contrasts with it, or radiate colours from a main focal point giving a movement effect. There is no end to the possibilities; variation of colour within a single flower, such as the larkspur or tulip, can often suggest good 'natural' colour schemes centred round themselves.

*How Do Flowers Get Their Colours?* Long a mystery, the basis of flower colourings has been uncovered by research in recent years. There are not thousands of chemical dyes in flowers to account for their infinite variety of colour, as one might imagine. There are in fact surprisingly few substances involved. There are three main types of pigments, shown in the following table.

| Pigment type and solubility in plant sap | Colours | Flowers, leaves, fruits in which found |
|---|---|---|
| Plastid pigments (1) Not soluble, so contained in small bodies (plastids) | Orange yellow cream white | Deep yellow tulip, narcissus, tomato fruit. |
| Flavones (2) Soluble | Yellow ivory-white | Rarely colours flowers, except deep yellow dahlia and snapdragon, pale lemon wallflower. |
| Anthocyanins (3) Soluble | Red, violet, blue. | Responsible for some autumn leaf colours, young shoots and buds tinted in spring. Acts with (2) in many flowers. |

Depending on the relative amounts and colour of pigment types present, different end colours are produced. The scarlet dahlia owes its colour to crimson type 3 and yellow type 2; the rich brown wallflower is the unlikely product of the interaction of bluish type 3 and yellow type 2. Besides the quantities of pigments present, acidity of the sap is important; the more acid, the redder the colour, in the same way that the pigment litmus varies according to its chemical surroundings.

Genes, the units of inheritance, control pigments. The nature of the control is not the obvious one gene: one colour pigment. The control is much finer—one pigment is made under the direction of one gene, and modified by another, enabling very fine adjustment to be made of the quantity of pigment produced. Thus a few genes can by their action and interaction control accurately the amounts of the three types of pigments and make a very wide range of colours. The colossal variety of dahlia colours and patterns are organised by six pairs of genes. More is said about genes and their effect on the appearance of flowers in Chapter 5.

CHAPTER TWO

# Practical Suggestions for Few Flowers

*Few Materials and Imagination*

A northern climate does not make life at all easy for those who love living with flowers. For almost a third of the year flowers are scarce, and growth, if any, is slow. It only rubs salt in the wound to think of those in warm-temperate climes throwing away freesias ('weeds'), regularly cutting such eye-catching exotics as anthurium and strelitsia, hacking handfuls off pot plants ('Oh, it will grow again in a fortnight'), and putting masses of camellias and dinner plate size magnolias in the bathroom because every other room already has too many!

One can only make the best of what one has available, and since for most people this is precious little for a large grey part of the year, this chapter deals solely with arrangements tailor made for these starting limitations. It is the longest chapter as improvising with little starting material presents most problems and involves most people. Apart from professional and amateur specialists few people keep up a garden or greenhouse adequate for the provision of material for well balanced bouquets of flowers or berries throughout the year, or can afford to buy large quantities of flowers necessary to keep even one vase full continually. Even the relatively humble conventional designs one sees illustrated in magazines and books involve several bunches of well formed flowers.

The answer, then, is design with few materials, Japanese inspired design. Classically a disciplined and intricate art governed by rules, the Japanese simplicity of design and impeccable use of very few materials in Ikebana (the Art of Arranging Plant Material) have rubbed off on the West. East and West meet in the appreciation of the beautiful qualities of a single branch or flower, and in the urge to create something which will convey this. With sensitivity, imagination, and improvisation, the few green leaves and bare twigs which are our winter heritage go a very long way.

Improvisation with what is available is one key to success with original

**8** SIMPLE AND STRIKING

To have few starting materials can be a positive advantage. A striking feature of one branch or shoot can be transformed into a stunning design when coupled with appropriate partner and container.

Here, a pair of sculptured purple iris stand serene in a slim glass cylinder with only one addition of foliage. However the selection and placing of the materials is vital to the effect. The stepped position of the flowers and the low-placed shoot continue the elongated line of the vase. Greyish-blue tinted dusty miller makes a quiet transition between purple and yellowish hues as well as providing a velvety contrast to the shining glass.

designs, but there is another angle. Most housewives cannot afford the time, nor the money, to embark on a full scale collection of different styled containers, stands, wire and cutters, and varieties of holders necessary for a classic approach to western or Japanese arrangements. Wiring and trimming flowers and greenery, even simply to achieve a classic Hogarth curve (elongated leaning S-shape), for example, demands time and organisation, as do many of the traditional short and long-term preservation treatments prior to arranging. Apparently casual arrangements that one admires have often taken much thought, time, and background experience in technique and artistry.

In the following pages, there is no wiring of material at all; it is used in its natural state except for trimming off odd leaves and twigs here and there which interfered with the main line or direction of the stem. This also applies to the arrangements with few materials illustrated in Chapters 4, 6, and 7. A small pinholder, wire netting, and one block of Oasis were the only financial outgoings for a lot of pleasure in making and living with the designs.

*Rules—To Have or Not To Have?* Having been inspired by a beautifully shaped branch, how does one attain the ethereal effects of unity, balance, harmony and the other aspects of beauty in flower arrangement talked of in the previous chapter?

Within the limits of almost any starting materials one can create the basis of a Line Design. This style is discussed more fully in Chapter 5, but in summary a Line Design is essentially simple, relies on a few well placed lines and forms, and it reflects very much the elegance and austerity of Japanese Ikebana, to which it owes its origin. Ikebana, the genuine article undiluted to western taste, is illustrated in *Figs K* and *M* (kindly lent by a teacher of the Sogetsu School).

Line Design in the West has assumed various rules:
The height of the arrangement should be one and a half times the width of the container.
The highest point of the arrangement should be over the centre of the container. Odd numbers of components are usually used, for instance a favourite combination is a tall branch, a smaller branch three-quarters the height of the first, and an even smaller branch about three-quarters the height of the second. Even numbers are particularly undesirable in Japanese arrangements.
All of the stems in the arrangement should appear to spring or radiate from one point, the focal point, which should also be the visual centre of the display.

Often the linear material, such as branches, is used to frame a focus of a single or several blooms.

How much one adheres to these rules depends on one's personal point of view. Rules are very good guides but at the same time an excess of rules can create artificiality and overshadow initiative. Blind step-by-step imitation is a sure killer of inspiration and personal creation. Throughout this book there is an explanation of the selection and relationships of the material in illustrated arrangements, so that by appreciating the inspiration behind the decoration and what went on back-stage, the reader cultivates the habit of seeing possible combinations and designs, while retaining his or her individuality and inspiration.

*Without a Focus—Playing it by Eye.* Rules were made to be broken, and it is not by accident that one of the first arrangements in this book lacks any point from which stems radiate, and contradicts most rules of arrangement, ancient and modern. In a sense it is an abstract pattern of an imaginary landscape of perpendiculars.

Less remote, a real landscape picture makes an interesting decoration. Striking features of the north-eastern tip of Scotland are the flat and undulating vistas of dunes and moors, covered with heather, sedge and grasses, also the horizontal wafers of local stone caked with golden lichen. The feeling of wind-swept perpendiculars and horizontals was used in an unusual arrangement of three perpendicular groups—placed according to the source: marram blades and heads from the dunes and sea shore, flag leaves from low lying banks, yellowing sedges with orange, black and brown fruits and flowers, and white bob-tail heads of cotton-grass from moorlands. Linking the groups were smooth and lichen textured slate and flat beach pebbles. For interest and pattern there were heather and cliff-top succulents, green-yellow and red tinged rosettes creeping out from among the stones.

Vegetation to a large extent characterizes an area, and it is a challenge in observation and artistry to capture a typical landscape as a decorative plant arrangement. A scenic inspiration worth capturing is the repetitive flickering light-dark pattern of slanting sunlight through parallel tree trunks.

A completely different style of arrangement is the apparently casual placing of natural and ornamental objects for a pleasing overall effect, without the appearance of 'having been arranged'. The division line between designs involving placing of objets d'art and interior decor is slim, since the impact is largely

## 9 LANDSCAPE COMPOSITION

By Scottish mountain streams, alder, birch, and rowan (mountain ash) grow wild; in fact, they are some of the few species that happily withstand waterlogging of the soil.

This autumn arrangement in a roll of bark was suggested by the curve of the rowan with its spreading leaves of green, edged with coppery pink. The diagonal line of the rowan is continued by the birch twig and accented by the placing of berries spilling downwards from the focus. The third element of the design, making a triangular outline and offsetting the diagonal, is an alder branch, its solid round leaves contrasting with those of the rowan.

The bark made a shallow base which was in keeping with the tree materials used in the design. The branches were held in wire netting in an inner jar, hidden inside the bark.

With the arrangement completed, can it be improved by removal of any material (*Plate 10*)?

dependent on the setting and a lack of nearby clutter. Examples of this type of design are to be seen all around, particularly in advertising media where, for example, perfectly placed flowers, lengths of silk and elegant cosmetic bottles (not to be forgotten as container ideas) speak for each other.

An antique Persian tray, oval and of solid copper—the old patina, glossy with oil-on-water colours of blue, mauve, pink, rose and gold sympathizes beautifully with the varying tones within living petals, far more than any highly polished modern metal-plate. Mimicking the enviable oriental habit of strewing flowers on tea trays, this tray makes a unique centre piece with a few fragrant and carefully placed flower heads with cotton wool and foil clad stems, meticulously covered. (Often, if one is lucky, oriental brass trays, rarely copper, can be found in auction sales and junk shops, and as a flat container or backdrop they are invaluable.)

A variation on this theme, requiring only an austere low-rimmed bowl, unpatterned dinner plate, or round tray, involves two or three carefully placed groups of related items. For instance, two blushing golden roses and a complementary pair of two furry peaches on a grey ground make a dramatic effect as two pairs grouped round a space (the latter, all important). A fascinating winter version could be pink-edged Christmas roses and miniature bunches of green grapes, perhaps accented by a few tactful dark green ivy leaves placed against pure porcelain white for coolness, or dusky pink for warmth. Equally well one can relate a group of flower heads with a wood carving, a trendy doll, a china figure, or anthing that takes one's fancy.

*To Throw Out and To Balance.* Even if one decides to dispense with rules completely, there are some general points which should at least be considered. One of the most important issues is the amount of material. Selecting appropriate material to put in and to leave out lies at the root of a pleasing floral design. Paradoxically, the less material one has available, often the better is the final design; overcrowding can clutter and drive out all inspiration.

A few branches of foliage selected for their mutual resemblance and contrast look far more elegant and convey far more than the same foliage overshadowed by irrelevant material that happened to be at hand, or that conveniently filled a space. Many people are afraid of space in an arrangement and with images of classical Mass Design shapes of triangles and circles at the back of their minds, fill up the all-important space around the main lines of the design. The effect is

**10** TWO WAYS WITH ONE DESIGN
This arrangement is a simplification of that in *Plate 9*. Often a design can be improved if one checks, before finally completing it, that nothing is superfluous—that it does not appear cluttered. In this case, the rowan branch and berries seemed more striking and suggestive of a diagonal line when left on their own, without further embellishment.

messy: an arrangement that lacks the clear cut lines of Line Design, because of clutter, and that contains too little material to be a convincing Mass Design. Having started to obey the natural flow and line of the material one must continue in the same vein and not get side-tracked putting bits and pieces in here and there.

It is sometimes a good idea when one has completed an arrangement to see if part of it could be removed without disturbing the balance—often one ends up with an improved design (*Plates 9 and 10*). Once a stem has been freed or cut out of its position it is exceedingly difficult to replace; thus it is a good idea to first approximate any new space in the arrangement by holding up one's hand or a piece of paper as a mask when making the decision.

If one is in the situation of relying on roadsides, country lanes, and florists for flowers, it requires great strength of mind not to use up every single piece of precious material. An easy way out of the dilemma, and which avoids waste, is to have a second container at hand for the overflow of superfluous material—not necessarily arranged, but just there, alive, and individually beautiful, a little bit of the outdoors by the kitchen sink or brightening a dark corner.

Of equal importance is the point of balance; obviously, to achieve balance and proportion the arrangement must not be top heavy. The extremities of most designs are sparse and tapered with thinning and diminishing leaves or small flowers and buds, the weight and density being near the base of the design (at the focal point) so the whole does not give an impression of falling over. If this is borne in mind while arranging it is unnecessary to cram one's head with rules dealing with stem lengths and other details.


*Lines Out of Focus.* In the pages that follow the components of a Line Design have been conveniently divided into linear material which gives the shape of the arrangement, focal point material which gives the arrangement a base, and weight, and a point of interest which focusses attention. The split is completely artificial, although it often simplifies arranging to think of the two as distinct but intimately related units. The necessity of somehow relating different parts of the design, through colour, form, or an idea, to give it a feeling of unity and cohesion can not be stressed too much.

Suggestions have been made for materials, orthodox and unorthodox, which easily fit the roles of line and focus. These are first and foremost memory jogging lists, not dogma; lists to trigger a second look at what may seem unpromising materials. Above all the division does not mean that flowers listed under focal point can not be used for making the design shape, and vice versa—it will be seen that many tapering and shapely flower spikes, once trimmed, are ideal for the base of a design, and large tapering leaves, eye-catching as framing shapes, can equally well form part of a radiating focus. The placing of material often largely depends on the size and scale of the design. In short, any material can be used in any position as long as it looks right.

The all important principles are: to keep one's artistic eye open for new material from every day, old and new sources, and to create something that looks right—regardless of lists and rules.

*Lines and Shapes—Hints and Examples.* The linear parts of a design largely determine its character and 'mood'—delicate or forceful, and so on. This has already been outlined on page 41.

A very unified arrangement can be achieved if the essential line and mood of the material is reflected in the overall shape. A curve is more convincing and flows more gracefully if composed of curved stems, such as larch (*Fig S*), than if it is made of sturdy perpendiculars such as heads of reedmace (also known as bulrush). The direction of the tips of things is very important to the overall direction of the line. Create the design round the material rather than force the material into a preconceived design.

There is an important biological point to be remembered when dealing with linear directions. Many flowers such as bluebell, lupin and speedwell straighten and gradually reorient themselves over a period of time, so that one's delicately arched and diagonal extremities become, almost overnight, very positively bent upwards. This natural response to light and gravity can be counteracted by wiring plants, which is a specialised technique, or simply by carefully hanging on weights such as paper clips or safety pins along the shoot or branch overnight. A safety pin is particularly useful as by virtue of its opening one need not touch any of the flowers in order to suspend it. Side branches of flowers like delphinium are often better to use in an outline as these lateral stems are more arched than the main stem. One cannot arrest the movement completely, any more than one can stop a bud enlarging into a full blown flower. The impermanence and changeability of plant life adds to its charm; any living arrangement is always changing, however slowly.

When arranging stems, particularly longer ones, it is important not to cross them over each other, as this very obviously interrupts the smooth line and flow of the design, and it starts to look like a thicket. Clarity in the lines of the design is important—the eye moves easiest, following the line, when there are no interruptions and jerks caused by criss-crossed stems, awkward side branches masking the main stem, etc.

Almost anything with a definite shape can be used as the line of a Line Design: foliage and flower stems of trees, shrubs and small plants, live and dead branches and twigs, driftwood, interesting shapes of rock or wood, dried

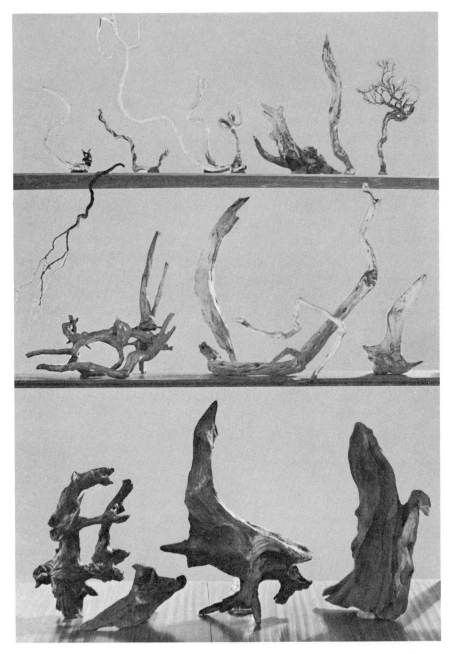

(thoroughly!) seaweed, sea-fan or even part of an interesting container, such as the ornamental handle and rim of a basket. The line can be anything from a suggestion behind a floral cluster (a background), to being right in the fore-ground as the main part of the design, with a minimum of floral or other embellishment.

In the depth of winter, even when collecting material on walks is out of the question, unexpected variety can be found in just a few pieces of stored drift-wood; *Figs A* and *O* show two possibilities with the same piece of driftwood which could look entirely different again when turned round the opposite way to show its greenish-brown side, or when set at an angle to the base. *Figs G, L* and *Plate 38* contain similarly shaped driftwood yet are completely different. Alternatively one can use an ornament as the positive shape and skeleton of a design. In the absence of any such useful props, a single candle or group of candles can set the scene.

In the section on Inspiration from Natural Materials, wild and cultivated material have been listed according to their line and so on (page 32). It is sug-gested that the reader refers back to this section when considering the possibi-lities of line material. Less striking examples which happily lend themselves to line are the following:

## 11 UNIQUE SOUVENIRS OF COUNTRYSIDE AND SEASHORE

Not only can driftwood make attractive cover for pinholders and so on, much of it is beautiful enough to form a major part of the design. Driftwood is a wise floral investment; with a good supply of interesting shapes it is an easy task to make a few flowers and foliage go a long way. The more interesting the form and texture of the wood, the less floral extras are needed—for those without gardens, driftwood is a basic essential.

Far from being old chunks of wood, the variation of colour, texture, shape and 'mood' is endless. No two pieces are ever the same, so an arrangement based on driftwood pieces is necessarily unique; the individuality and distinctive form set the pace of an arrangement.

Gathering wood is an enjoyable habit—on walks along the beach, from streams, or from fields and lanes. The only requirement is that you keep your eyes open, and can recognise a beautiful shape even through a layer of mud.

The piece extreme right bottom row has been scrubbed and washed; the rest is in its natural state. Silver grey shine (see middle row) is the result of years of weathering.

Left to right, top row: the four curving white forms are derived from seaweed 'stems' (*Fig G*, holdfast visible in specimen on extreme left); second from left, a charred heather stem (pruned); third from right, rust impregnated stump from the beach; extreme right, a miniature tree—heather stem. Middle row: antique pieces from a half buried forest (*Colour Plate 2*), and an angular pitted stem of gorse; knotted root on extreme left used in *Figs A, O* and *P*. Bottom row: chunky brown pieces, extreme left used in *Fig O*, second from left used in *Plate 48*.

| CULTIVATED (*material can be preserved) | | WILD |
|---|---|---|
| barberry* | golden rod* | broom* |
| blazing star | hart's tongue fern (underside | catkin twigs* (*Plate 51*) |
| buddleia* | and upper surface, also wild) | gorse* |
| Canterbury bell* | Japanese maple* | hawthorn |
| dropwort | lily-of-the-valley shrub | honeysuckle* |
| eucalyptus* | love-lies-bleeding* | rose hip twigs |
| flowering cherry | montbretia (*Plate 38*) | rushes* |
| forsythia* | New Zealand flax | sedges* |
| (golden bells) | ornamental maize* (corn) | sorrel* (*Fig T*) |
| gladioli leaves | sage* | spring leaves |
| | tulip leaves (rolled *Fig D*) | (forced) |

These are but a few picked at random; as far as the picking of wild materials is concerned, for the benefit of the plant, twigs and branches are best cut with a knife or secateurs. Also, cutting twigs from only one side leaves an unsightly bush or tree; one can easily damage it, stealing valuable growth—only pick abstemiously!

Pot plants from indoors also make good line material, either pieces cut off or large scale arrangements using the whole plant with or without its pot. Interesting shapes are mother-in-law's tongue, anthurium, asparagus fern, kangaroo vine, cordylines, ivy and geraniums. Cut-off pieces of the plant can subsequently be planted as cuttings provided they have been broken off at a node (part of the stem where one or more leaves arise). Arrangements can be made out of a single pot plant (*Fig P*).

Many people fuse the best of the two worlds of Line and Mass Design (the latter is the traditional mass of flowers described in Chapter 3) and concoct a line using lots of flower heads; for example, a group of dahlias arranged so that their faces form an S-shaped line. This type of Line Design, where the materials are organised into a preconsidered form, appears more ordered and contrasts to the type of decoration guided by the nature of the starting material. Different materials lend themselves to different treatments and styles; above all, the most important influence is one's own instinct of what 'looks right' and what does not.

## G FROZEN MOVEMENT

Sinuous swirling driftwood makes a stark three dimensional basis to this design. The continuous enveloping curve round the base was in fact three separate pieces joined and held in position with wire wedged in plasticine. The focus of the shape was provided by autumn dahlias, and chrysanthemum leaves which also covered the mechanics of the arrangement.

The white driftwood was a stark contrast to a midnight blue container, improvised from a small and a large plate secured back to back so that the larger made a wide base holding up the smaller. A circular base was most appropriate for the encircling line of driftwood, and round-faced flowers.

This bone white driftwood is the remains of elastic seaweed 'stems' (page 70), cleaned and bleached by the waves.

*What is Driftwood?* In *Figs G, L* and *Plate 38* very unusually shaped driftwood gathered from the beach has been used. Instead of the customary monumental sculptured pieces of tree wood, the gnarled, contorted knots of intertwined ivy, or the smooth curves of gorse stems, here are swirling serpentine shapes. Suggestive of frozen movement, these loops and curls have been particularly exploited in the arrangement in *Fig G*.

Frozen movement is more than a flight of descriptive fancy, for these strange stems were designed and built for a life of prolonged movement. These are the remains of 'stems' of seaweeds, plants belonging to the most primitive (simple) group in the Plant Kingdom—the Thallophyta which date back to the Pre-Cambrian world of warm seas and the beginning of life (see page 49 for geological time scale). They do not have proper root, stem or leaves, and are less advanced than the mosses (see page 162).

The seaweeds exist by the same means as most other plants: the 'leaves' contain a green pigment (chlorophyll) which catches the sun's energy and harnesses it as chemical energy in sugar which can then be used by the plant. Many seaweeds contain other pigments as well as chlorophyll: brown or red, which masks the universal green pigment. If immersed in warm water, the brown colour is washed out of the plant which then appears green.

There are three big issues in seaweed survival—first, the plant must be kept in the upper layers of water so that it can obtain all possible sunlight; second, it must not dry up when the level of water changes. Lastly, the structure of the seaweed must permit movement with the waves and yet resist being swept away or battered to pieces against the rocks. The seaweed plant is anchored to rocks and shells in shallow water by means of a holdfast: a grasping hand-like extension of the 'stem' visible in one specimen in *Plate 11*. Anyone who has tried to detach a seaweed trophy knows how amazingly efficient this organ is; even after death and decay of all the soft parts of the seaweed stones and shells are still firmly attached. A sturdy cylindrical stem-like portion of the seaweed body lifts the flattened leaf-like extension high towards the water's surface and the sunlight. This leaf equivalent is in some types of seaweed buoyed up at the edges by bladders of gas (these are the tiny balloon-like things that children delight in popping at the unwary).

Particularly in seaweeds of deeper water the 'stem' is long and is subjected to swirling water at one end of the scale, and waves repeatedly beating it against rocks at the other; its vital part in survival demands that it is strong and yet pliable. To protect the plant from drying up it is coated with slime. This also

**12** FOCUS ON RADIATION
Radiating canes of the lid of an old fishing basket form the skeleton of this design. White backed leaves of ragwort continue the shape and lighten the circular outline. The point of radiation of the stems and canes is emphasised by the placing of full blown 'heavy' peonies which draw the eye down to the focus of the arrangement—the largest flower at the base. Bluish-green foliage and a blue container set off the brilliant pink of the peonies.

Mechanical note: the basket lid was supported by stones and Plasticine, and fresh stems were held in a hidden container of Oasis.

allows it to slip over rocks and its neighbours easily, when pounded by waves, without being damaged, any mild abrasions being borne by the slime layer. Wind, sun and waves reduce the dying seaweed plant to its sturdiest structural fibres—the relatively delicate 'leaf' extension and slimy outer skin disappear to leave behind a contorted column of driftwood.

*The Focal Point*

This has already been mentioned in connection with the rules of Line Design and in relation to balance (see above). However regimented and distasteful the term focal point, the very nature of many designs demands the presence of some point of focus, or an equivalent.

First and foremost it is the point from which the stems radiate, giving an arrangement a feeling of being held together rather than of haphazardness. The eye follows the linear parts of the design, such as driftwood (*Fig G*), foliage (*Plate 9*), etc., and is drawn down to the source from which they spring—the point of focus. This point of radiation is emphasised by the placing of 'heavy' full blown flowers, broad leaves and so on, as in *Plates 12* and *20*. Without the point of weight and focus, the whole design can lack depth and look flimsy, the eye wandering all the time.

Essentially, then, the focal point is a solid unit, whose shape is usually rounded (so that the eye is drawn towards its centre) rather than directional (such that the eye travels along moving out and away from the core of the design). Round-faced flowers, particularly those with a central heart, such as the rose or chrysanthemum, make an ideal pivot from which the whole arrangement radiates. The visual weight of the arrangement being at the base gives a sense of balance and avoids any disturbing appearance of top heaviness. For want of a better phrase, 'focal point' is used in a broad sense to cover the lower base point of the design; it is not intended as a clear-cut dogmatic term.

*Focal Flowers.* If there is a choice of material for this part of the arrangement, selection should be influenced by the colours of line material, although in general dark rich colours at the visual centre help to bring it in focus. If a group of flowers is used, a very effective block of colour can be produced by using several of one type. Or for a more subtle effect, related colours could be used or tones of the same colour; unrelated colours can cause a very 'bitty' effect. A further item to be considered when choosing the focal point is that it must blend with the container, which forms the base of the design.

The tables below are intended as a nucleus of ideas for focal point material which could subsequently be used as a quick reference list. Material is grouped according to type—flowers, focal point material other than flowers, and it is indicated if the material can be well preserved for winter (marked with asterisk).

The source of the material has also been considered—whether from wild hedge-rows and waste ground, an ordinary small garden, a specialist's garden, florist, greengrocer, and so on. A note on apparent discrepancies here: plants considered as gardener's specialities in one place are weeds in another, the following classifications are with respect to Britain. Lack of any sort of garden or window box need not preclude having large quantities of material to choose from.

*Exotic flowers*—known from southern climes, florist's window and greenhouses, lend themselves as a dramatic single blossom.

| NAME | NOTES |
|---|---|
| (*material can be preserved) | |
| african lily (agapanthus) bird of paradise (strelitzia) camellia (also leaves) gardenia (also leaves) hibiscus (tree hollyhock) magnolia* poinsettia (growing in its pot) protea* | With so much importance attached to one flower it must be a perfect specimen. Focus can be enlarged and drama-tized if light bloom framed with dark leaves. Several have beautiful perfume. |

*Standard Garden Inmates*—town and country. Just as vibrant as the exotics and more easily obtainable, the larger flowers can be used singly; otherwise, a cluster make a good focus.

| | |
|---|---|
| anemone* | (*Plate 31*), several |
| azalea | several |
| carnations | cluster (*Fig K*) |
| chrysanthemums* | single and large or picked from a spray, (*Figs O and T, Plate 48*) |
| clematis | cut just before petals ready to unfold |
| daffodil* | (*Plate 33*), short stemmed |
| dahlia* | (*Fig G*) |
| daisy* and | china aster, michaelmas |
| daisy type | sunflower. If there is stunning contrast within flower, beware of bull's eye; two or three safer than one |

→

| | |
|---|---|
| geranium | several |
| gladiolus | lower stem or individual open flowers, |
| (corn flag) | top of spike useful as line |
| globe thistle* | |
| hollyhock* | lower stem or individual open flowers, top |
| hyacinth | (*Plate 51*), could be used while growing in pot |
| hydrangea* | single head |
| iris | (*Plate 26*) |
| lilac | one or several spikes, beautifully fragrant |
| marigold* | grouped in a cluster |
| narcissus* | short-stemmed in a group (avoiding bull's eye) |
| pansy* | grouped |
| peony* | (*Plates 12 and 24*), single flower |
| phlox | (*Plate 36*), single head |
| (flame flower) | |
| pink | grouped |
| polyanthus* | one head |
| rhododendron | single or several |
| rose* | single, (*Plate 32*), a sure attention drawer |
| stock* | advantage of dense spike and fragrance |
| sweet peas | grouped |
| tulip* | particularly opened out, (*Plates 20, 27, and 29*) |
| wallflower | grouped, not spectacular, but beautifully fragrant |

**13** (and jacket) MEANINGFUL ROSE—A PERFECT FOCAL FLOWER

A rose looks beautiful in any context—a perfectly sculptured form drawing one's eye to its hidden centre. The open bud, and its tightly closed partner, symbolise, in Ikebana, the present and the future.

A symbol of incorruption, the rose, in the language of flowers, could have been an ambiguous communication to any who did not know their roses. A white rose bud on display meant too young to love; a Dog Rose, pleasure mixed with pain; the Japan Rose, beauty your sole attraction; the Provence Rose, my heart is in flames; and the Moss Rose, voluptuous love. The Yellow Rose left little doubt—infidelity.

The rose may be artistic perfection, but scientifically it is not so. The Rosaceae family, to which it belongs, has one of the less sophisticated floral plans—there are large numbers of separate petals, stamens and female parts; also the flowers are symmetrical.

Sepals remain green and leaf-like and protect the bud rather than become like petals— clearly visible enclosing the bud.

A limited number of flowering plants in the garden need not dictate monotonous arrangements. The same focal flower can look new and different set in a
different design; chrysanthemums have been used in the arrangements in
*Plates 48, Figs O* and *I*. It is encouraging to remember that the possibilities for
different designs starting from the same flowers, a few branches and driftwood are
infinite; a dozen people given the same raw material may produce a dozen
different designs, compare *Plates 20* and *29*.

*From Gardeners' Gardens.* For the keen gardener and those with the space there
are many less commonly grown flowers which are good attention drawers. Here
are a few of them:

| | | |
|---|---|---|
| acanthus* (head) | pyrethrum | love-in-a-mist (group) |
| avens | dogwood* (leaves | megasea saxifrage |
| begonia | frame flower) | mountain laurel |
| blossom of fruit trees, | drumstick primula | (calico bush, |
| almond, apple, etc. | floss-flower | leaves frame flower) |
| campion | flowering cherry (*Plate 3*) | nasturtium |
| candytuft* (group) | freesia | nerine |
| Christmas rose | garland flower (Daphne, | onion (flower) |
| cineraria | leaves frame blooms) | poppy* |
| clivia | globe flower | red hot poker (head) |
| columbine* (heads) | golden rod* | scabious* |
| cornflower* (group) | guelder rose | sea holly* |
| crowfoot | lantana | slipperwort |
| crown imperial | large-flowered | snowball tree (variety |
| cyclamen (sowbread) | mallow-wort | of guelder rose) |
| daisy types*—amellus, | larkspur* (individual | sweet william |
| blue-eyed African | double flowers) | tiger-flower |
| daisy, blanket- | lilies*— candlestick, | tree mallow |
| flower, cape- | enchantment, | tulip-tree* (flower) |
| marigold, | golden-rayed | water-lily |
| chamomile, tickseed, | Peruvian | yarrow* (milfoil) |
| ox-eye daisy, | Scarborough | zinnia* |

Some flowers double as line or edge material as well as focal point blooms,
for example, the tapering hollyhock, larkspur, gladiolus. Individual flowers and

the lower part of the stem, suitably trimmed, can add weight and interest to the base of a design. When placing a focal point flower particular attention should be paid to the direction of the face of the flower: the face is a directional pointer, similar to the tips of linear material. Facing upwards, a shallow flower echoes the horozontal rim and base of the container, and makes less of an absorbing focus than if the heart of the flower were facing outwards towards the observer. The direction of the flower face should relate in some way, or be combined with, the direction of the line material, rather than be popped into a convenient space regardless.

*Without a Garden.* Focal point flowers suggested so far have required either a garden or a purse. However one can still have flowers in profusion without either if one uses one's eyes and discretion. Wild flowers are less flamboyant than their garden counterparts (hence the need for keen observation), are less in number and unnurtured, hence careful picking with discretion. It should always be remembered that by picking a flower one is robbing the plant of its means of making seeds and spreading itself; hence by picking a solitary unusual wild flower one is lessening the chance of survival of the species or variety (*Plate 14*). Only the common wild flowers and so called 'weeds' have been included in the following list, but even among these the less abundant types should not be over picked—the true lover of flowers admires and walks on empty handed! The presence and rarity of flowers and garden escapes varies very much from one part of the country to another according to the climate and soil. Few of the flowers are large or showy enough to be used singly, but a group of common flowers made into a cluster are as eye-catching as any cultivated varieties.

| 'ONLY A WEED' (*material can be preserved) | | |
|---|---|---|
| bindweed | blue fleabane | chervil |
| bird's-foot trefoil | burdock* (*Fig L*) | clover |
| blackberry | burnet rose | common milkwort |
| black mustard | buttercup | common sowthistle |
| blackthorn (lower | candytuft | cornflower |
| stem pruned) | celandine | corn marigold |
| bladder campion | charlock | cow parsley |

| | | |
|---|---|---|
| cowslip (over picked) | meadow sweet* (*Fig L*) | snowdrop |
| crab apple | nipple-wort | stitchworts |
| crosswort | ox-eye daisy* | St. John's worts |
| crow garlic | pansy* | tansy (*Plate 38*) |
| cuckoo-pint | pennywort (although | teasel |
| dandelion | tapered, effective | thistles* |
| dead-nettle | in a group) | thrift* |
| dog rose | pignut | tutsan |
| elder | poppies (do not last) | valerian |
| forget-me-not (groups) | primrose (often over | vetches |
| foxglove (trimmed) | picked) | violet |
| gorse (pruned) | ragged robin | wayfaring tree |
| hardheads (knapweed) (*Fig L*) | red campion | white campion |
| hawthorn (pruned) | red valerian | wild angelica |
| heather* (*Plate 22*) | rock stonecrop | wild chamomile |
| hedge parsley | rose-bay willow-herb | wild cherry |
| hemp agrimony | (trimmed) | wild strawberry |
| herb robert | rowan | wild thyme |
| honeysuckle (*Colour Plate 7*) | scabious* (*Plate 22*) | wood avens |
| hop trefoil | sea holly* | woodruff |
| ivy | sea lavender | wood sedge (group) |
| lady's smock | snakeweek (tapered, | wood spurge |
| large hop trefoil | but makes pleasing | yarrow* |
| mallow | group) | |
| marjoram | sneezewort | |

This list is no more than a summary of the possible variety, as under the names of blackberry, gorse, stitchwort, heather, ivy, vetch, thistle, and others there are many varieties which differ in size, colour, and form. Regional differences spread far beyond obvious scenic changes and different types of woods and hedgerows. Keeping one's eyes open for wild flowers while on a walk has the reward of finding the unexpected and the unsuspected—from a car one sees little of the micro world of the countryside.

Many of these flowers make ideal outline flowers when used in their entirety, such as foxglove or rose-bay willow-herb. Suitably pruned and trimmed these are also good focal point material: flowers are usually closer packed together at the base of the stem and make a compact mass once the upper part of the stem

**14** THE UNTOUCHABLE

If one is using wild flowers for floral arrangements, it must never be forgotten that many wild species are rare and becoming rarer due to the rapid spread of man's building and cultivation. By picking a flower, one is picking its means of reproducing itself and spreading of the species. Wild beauty should be picked only with discretion—a wild orchid is definitely untouchable.

Irregular and asymmetric in form, the orchids belong to an interesting and exotic group of monocotyledons—the family Orchidaceae. In *Plate 27*, a group of more regular and symmetric flowers, also monocots, can be seen for comparative purposes. The most distinctive feature of monocotyledons is parallel veining on long slender leaves—clearly visible here. They are classified into families on page 118. The arrangement of this orchid floral community is in a spike, similar to the cuckoo-pint (*Fig E*).

is removed. Alternatively, if the lower flowers are withering, a pleasing focus can be made from a group of shortened flower spikes; for example, tips of foxglove spikes, or several stems of pennywort loosely held together in a bunch. Here the eye is drawn into the heart of the bunch, achieving the same effect as a large round-faced flower.

## Arrangement Suggestions

*White, Mauve and Green.* Subtle Christmas roses, white, mauve and green tinted, blend well with variegated ivy leaves—cream, dusty bluish and dark green, and the more common rich green varieties. A group of mixed ivy makes a perfect variation on a theme, the tiny lance-shaped mauvish type a crisp shadow of the larger greener varieties. These leaves lend themselves as a 'solid' base to the arrangement and act as frame and contrast to the flowers. Climbing ivy stands on its own, erect in curves and bent angles, ideal for the line and overall shape of the arrangement. Particularly sympathetic with ivy is the patina of silver grey driftwood and light beach pebbles. Once the Christmas roses are finished, a bunch of green touched snowdrops are a delicate contrast to the dark green leaves. Ivy is a particularly useful addition for arrangements as it is amazingly hardy, looking fresh and green after days out of water, if necessary, in a centrally heated room.

*Colour Co-ordination.* A few bright flowers are even brighter when placed in a piece of wood retrieved from the bonfire—the more charred and sculptured, the more dramatic the impact. Different daisy types, anemones, cinerarias, or marigolds, bright vibrant oranges, reds, blues and purples, individually or en masse, look stunning against shining black. For such dramatic effect complementary colours, opposite each other on the colour wheel (*Fig F*) are a first choice. Wild flower choices could be dandelion, poppy, gorse, broom, foxglove, buttercup, daisies, red valerian, thistle, common mallow and the brighter heathers.

Chrysanthemums and autumn leaves are natural partners; yellow, bronze and rusty crimson flowers unite with the graceful lines of beech, leaves turning burnished brown. A single twig of copper beech, leaves of dark burgundy, echo crimson petals, while brass and copper add a final touch to a golden theme.

**15** LINEAR SIMPLICITY
The turquoise shine of the vase shows up the delicate pinks of the apple blossom.
  The two basic lines lead to the large cluster of blossom which balances the design. Although there is a disproportionate asymmetry in the shape, the long twigs are sparsely blossomed and are thus 'light', whereas the focal cluster, though small, is dense or 'heavy'. Balance of the two hinges on the focus being placed off-centre in the vase. The shape of the vase also helps to weight and anchor the base of the upended triangle.

Oatmeal or brown driftwood, pink and golden stones or shells, also fit into the autumn harmony. A single interesting centre is provided by one of the large florist's chrysanthemums with different colours on top and underside of petals so that the dominant colour changes as the petals unfurl and spread out from the tightly packed central spiral. A sprig of preserved oak leaves makes a shiny golden brown frame for a smaller flower, picked from a spray.

*Madame Butterfly.* A single perfect rose rising out of a base of foliage, or a well matched trio of peach and golden coloured roses, portrays something of the Orient when backed by concentric crescents reminiscent of Japanese hair ornaments. The stylised loops can be made of gardener's grass or any pliable thin stem such as weeping willow or cane; these are easily bent into curves when soaked in water and tied. One loop on its own can look sparse; two or three set an inch or so apart, one inside the other gives the crescent body, each line the echo of its neighbour. Placed so that their ends come out of, and return to the focal point (like the angular shapes in *Fig M*), a group of these concentric loops have a great feeling of unity, as the eye is never left wandering off the edge of the design; it is always drawn right around and back into the focal point.

Any exotic flower lends itself well to this contrived yet gracious type of design. Exotics and roses lacking, a trio of bicoloured, double daffodils makes a good alternative. This flowing outline, cradling and framing the bloom, demands a flat and completely plain container. A useful variation of the theme of a stylised rather geometric setting is a canework screen backing the flowers—the semi-circular remains of a fishing basket washed up onto the beach makes an admirable substitute once thoroughly scoured. One is used as a background to peonies (*Plate 12*). A group of wild flowers such as scabious, wild cherry or crab apple could make a centre piece as delicate as any cultivated bloom.

### Focus on Petals

To bring about pollination and thus seed formation: this is the purpose of a flower. Whether this pollination process depends on wind, water, humming birds, snails, bats or insects for the transfer of pollen from the male to the female, the parts of any flower are focussed on this one purpose. The shape, colour, position, and size of each floral structure all have an integral part to play, the whole making an efficient, harmonious unit.

*Insect Pollination.* The basic jobs of the different parts of an insect-pollinated flower have already been outlined in (*Fig E*). Petals, and often perfume, are the advertisement, attracting the insect to the flower. Often, in addition, the petals provide the insect with a landing platform, and cunningly lead them straight into the heart of the flower. Thus they cannot avoid dusting pollen on the stigma (female) and collect new pollen from the stamens (male). The job of the petals (collectively the corolla) is primarily to focus the attention of the insect on the flower and in many cases also to assist the insect's entrance into the flower.

Without the advertisement provided by petals, the insect would possibly not find the heart of the flower and the nectar and pollen contained there, or it would certainly have to spend a long time looking for its prize. The importance of this time factor is more readily appreciated when one realises that a bee can only store enough energy in its body for a matter of minutes of flying time; continual refuelling is vital, and a well advertised flower has a better chance of being visited for refuelling than an insignificant one.

Flowers and insects have a very neat reciprocal arrangement—the flower provides the bee with energy-packed fuel in the form of nectar and pollen. In return the bee benefits the flower and transports and spreads the pollen to the female organs—the process called pollination. Since some insects feed on the pollen which is so vital to the plant's reproduction, the flowers pollinated by pollen feeding insects produce copious supplies so that the mutual benefit continues.

Since all petals are doing the same thing, how is it they do not look the same? In the lists of focal point flowers there are few that are even superficially similar in form. Why are flowers different?


*Insect demands.* Before these questions can be satisfactorily answered, one must picture the insects for whom the floral paraphernalia is designed: these are chiefly beetles, flies, wasps, bees, butterflies and moths. These creatures show important variations in the size of body, their sensitivity to different colours, the length of their tongue, their preference for pollen or nectar, whether they are active during the night or the day, and how plentiful they are at different times of the year, and probably many less obvious points of difference. It is thus important if a flower is to be pollinated and produce seeds that its dimensions, colour, depth and amount of nectar or pollen, its time of opening and shutting, and flowering season are exactly matched to the insect's requirements.

Some flowers have open house and can be pollinated by several of these insects; others are specific and are designed for one insect to the exclusion of all others.

*Honeysuckle—a Fussy Flower.* One flower which is geared to the requirement of a particular insect is the honeysuckle. Several separate petals have fused together to form a long thin tube which separates the nectar at the base of the flower from the outside world *(Fig H)*. The tube is too narrow for an insect's body, and the mouth of the tube curves backwards so there is no platform on which an animal could land to even inspect the tiny opening at close range. This flower is tailor made for pollinators taking food on the wing, and having enormously long tongues; it is for moths. A frequent visitor is the privet hawk-moth which has a longer tongue (30 mm spiralled neatly when not in use) than the average British moth. Other insects visit the honeysuckle for pollen.

Since moths are insects of the twilight and night time they rely on smell more than vision; hence the sweet night smell of the honeysuckle and its rather humble unobtrusive flower. White or light coloured petals render nocturnal flowers more visible for moths. The sense of smell in moths is so pronounced that

### H HONEYSUCKLE—MOTH CO-OPERATION

In the sophisticated flower of the honeysuckle five petals have joined together forming a long tube at the bottom of which is the insect's prize for visiting the flower—nectar. The narrowness and length of the tube exclude all insect visitors except for the specific pollinating agents—moths. Moths are ideally equipped for extracting nectar from the base of a long tube, their tongue is extremely long, as much as 30 mm, and when not in use is neatly coiled like a clock spring beneath the head. To suit the night flying visitor the honeysuckle is light coloured, and heavily perfumed in the evening and dispenses with any petal landing platform which would be superfluous for the hovering moth. The honeysuckle and the moth have, over a long time, become perfectly matched for each other.

The special moth-orientated shape of the honeysuckle makes an interesting comparison to the bee-orientated shape of the sage *(Colour Plate 5)* another sophisticated flower in which petals have joined to form a tube. Similarly the differences between the tongues of the two insects are worth noting. The same numbers have been used in labelling corresponding parts in the moth and bee. For easy comparison, the labelling numbers of the floral parts are kept the same throughout the book, see *Fig E, Q, I* and *J*.

*Flower Parts* (for name explanations see *Fig E*)—one flower opened out.
2—*sepals*; 3—*petals*, joined most of their length to form a tube (3a), separate at the end (3b); 5—*style*, here elongated to bring the stigma in contact with the moth; N—nectary; 6—*stigma*; 7—*filament*; 8—*anther.*
*Insect Parts*—moth—front view of head.
15—large *eye*; 14—*antenna*, used for sensing the surroundings—touch and smell—and enlarged in the smell-dependent moth.

Instead of having one tongue, insects have several pairs of mouthparts, like small legs surrounding the mouth, which are exclusively used for, and therefore modified for, feeding; the sizes and shapes of the various mouthparts differ with the type of food. 11—*paired mouthparts* (not involved in forming the sucking tube therefore small and insignificant); 12—*several mouthparts* modified for sucking up fluids, greatly elongated and grooved to fit together making a suction tube.

# Honeysuckle flower

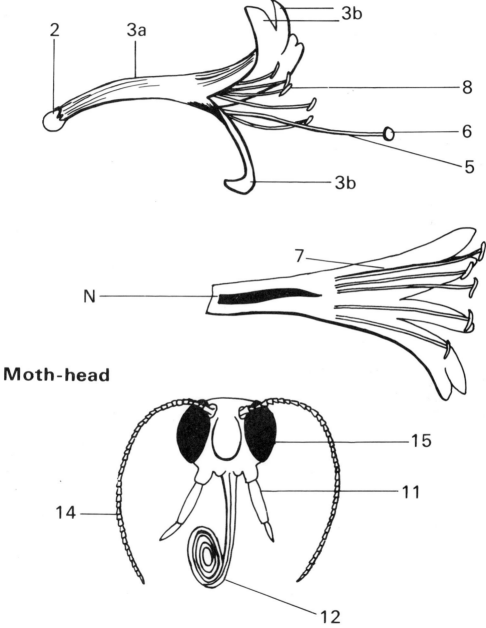

## Moth-head

some male moths can detect the presence of a female up to five miles away. The sense of smell is fully exploited by the Madonna lily, the lily of the Annunciation, so often featured in the religious paintings of the Italian Renaissance. The majestic flowers send off a heady evening perfume and the pure whiteness of the petals almost luminesces into the night. Evening primrose, privet, white campion and tobacco plant are less dramatic attractors of night moths.

*Mix and Match.* At the other end of the tongue scale are the flowers which rely on the visits of short-tongued insects (3 mm or less) for pollination. In some the nectar is completely exposed on the surface of the flower, as in the ivy; others are shallow and open, such as the saxifrages, attracting beetles and some flies.

In between the two extremes of honeysuckle and saxifrage are flowers with the nectar partially covered—stitchwort, buttercup, and strawberry. Even deeper flowers have the nectar well concealed—gooseberry, geranium, rose-bay willow-herb and figwort; these need the longer tongued flies, the smaller bees and wasps. These insect types are, in turn, excluded from visiting the daffodil, larkspur, nasturtium, lilies, and irises whose long tubes of petals or sepals, or spur-like nectaries, demand the long tongues of butterflies and moths, or the larger bees. Many irises further guarantee attraction of bees by their blue and purple hues, colours which have been found to be particularly attractive to bees. The long petal tubes particularly associated with butterflies are red: pinks and red campion. Furthermore, the butterfly perches as it feeds, a feature which is reflected in the petal arrangement of these flowers, the edge curving out to form a landing platform.

The perfume, appearance and habit of flowers is thus linked very closely with the insect which pollinates the flower. Each cannot exist without the other, and so each offers what the other needs. The insect requires a constant supply of food: pollen or nectar or both, which the flowers provide. The flowers advertise the food's whereabouts in a way which will be easily perceived by its insect. On the other hand the flower needs a carrier that can easily pick the pollen, made sticky and clinging for this purpose, and transport it far away to another flower. This is what an insect can do as it flits from flower to flower; butterflies, moths, flies and bees are covered in small hairs to which the pollen clings and all are efficient fliers.

Since flowers are so closely associated with insects, the effects of changes of climatic and physical conditions through the ages have been very complex.

Changes, large (outlined in Table 1) and small have affected the plants and thus their dependent insects, which in turn have influenced other plants, and vice versa—the whole situation is like several interlocking chains. One sees today the success stories of this insect-plant cooperative; however, since the emergence of flowering plants during the Cretaceous (120 million years ago) there must have been much trial and error in partnerships and many flowers left to die by the wayside without ever producing seeds. Unfortunately little is known of the early pollinating insects as fossils. Perhaps one can see a little into the past by looking at one of today's very primitive flowers, the magnolia (*Plate 16*). This is pollinated by beetles, which eat the flower, and have smooth bodies, and cumbersome slow flight.

The mutual dependence and assistance has developed a long way between the simple magnolia and the intricacies of the sage flower, described in the next section.

*Special Devices—Pedals and Levers.* Another difference between petal arrangements in different flowers lies in the level of efficiency they have reached in bringing about, with the insect, effective pollination, i.e. guaranteeing that the visiting insect actually brushes against and takes some of the pollen. From one viewpoint the most efficient pollination involves the least amount of wasted material: a kind of floral time and motion study.

Sage, a member of the advanced mint family (also including thyme, dead nettles, lavender) is a particularly efficient bee-pollinated flower, which, having developed a sure method of transferring pollen to the insect, produces only a bare minimum of stamens (male parts) and pistils (female parts). The bases of the petals have fused together to form a tube, and one large lip petal forms a prominent landing platform as well as advertisement. Above this is a petal hood, protecting the stamen and pistil. Thus there is only one approach and path into the flower. The rows of bright spots (honey guides) within the throat of the flower lead the insect down towards the well protected nectar.

Attached to the wall of the petal throat is a strange hinged arrangement of the only two stamens which actually move and clamp down on the back of the bee when it pushes against a stamen lever. The bee cannot fail to trigger off the stamen movement as it crawls into the flower, guided and funnelled towards the nectar at its base. When pollen production ceases in the sage flower, the stamens recede and the stigma, which has been neatly tucked against the uppermost

## Sage flower

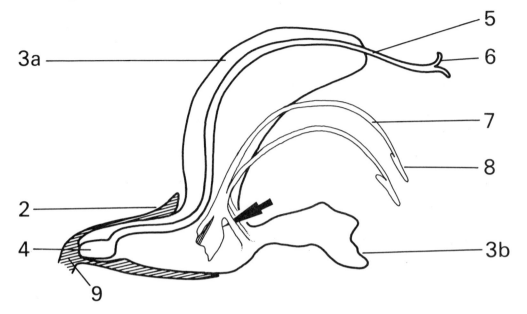

3a — 

5
6
7
8
3b

2
4
9

## Bee-head

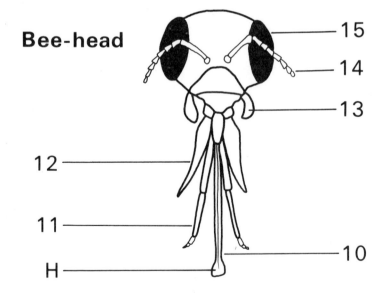

15
14
13
12
11
10
H

hood-like petal, now grows down and droops from the hood. As the insect proceeds along its predestined route the one stigma cannot fail to rub against the bee's back. The apparently incongruous shape and position of the petals and stamens is intimately related to the size and weight of the bee and thus to the success of this particular method of transferring pollen. Some robber insects (beetles and ants) are excluded by the narrow tubular base of the throat, but this is most effectively done in those flowers with a ring of protective hairs, visible in *Colour Plate 5*—cultivated sage from the herb garden.

The specialised efficiency of the sage flower can be fully appreciated when the situation in the simply designed buttercup is considered. In the latter, the flower is like an open bowl with the pockets of nectar at the base of the petals, and the pollen unprotected from the elements and insect marauders. A pollinating insect, such as a bee, can alight from any angle, with its head in any direction; its approach and landing are not assisted, and there are no directives such as spots or lines indicating the whereabouts of the nectar. The insect crawls about tracking down nectar; the flower produces lots more pollen on its many stamens to cope with that robbed and wasted.

The buttercup relies on the bee crawling over the pollen by chance—it has a spiral spread of stamens producing quantities of pollen and bears many spirally

I 'WHERE THE BEE SUCKS'
(see *Colour Plate 5*)
Like the honeysuckle-moth arrangement (*Fig H*), the sage-bee co-operation is efficiently designed. The advanced tubular form of the joined petals excludes short-tongued insects from reaching the nectar at the base of the flower. The bee is the invited visitor; a landing platform is provided (3b) and the insect is attracted by the petal hood (3a) the size of which varies in different species.

As the bee pushes into the tubular throat of the flower (part cut away to show interior), it pushes against pedal extensions (arrow) of the filaments (7), causing the pollen bearing anthers (8) at the other end of the lever to swing down and clamp on the bee's back, dusting it with pollen for the next flower it visits.

The mouthparts (specialised 'eating legs' around the mouth) of the bee are modified for inserting into a shorter tube than those of the moth.

> *Flower Parts* (as in *Figs E* and *H*). 2—sepals; 3—*petals*; 4—*ovary* ('seed box'); 5—*style*; 6—*stigma*; 7 –*filament*; 8—*anther*; 9—*receptacle*. Arrow represents position of the bee's head thrusting into the base of the flower.
> *Bee Parts* (as in *Fig H*). 15—large *eye*; 14—*antenna* (shorter than in moth, as bee more dependent on sight; it is a day-flier); 13—*mouthparts* shaped like a wax moulding tool (used for cell construction in the hive); 10, 11, 12—*mouthparts* when held together these form a tubular structure for sucking up nectar; H—mobile honey spoon, a specially expanded portion of mouthpart 10.

### 16 A VERY PRIMITIVE FLOWER

Sophisticated flowers demand sophisticated insects: those with furry bodies to which pollen can cling, once it has been brushed from the anthers, with fast flight for rapid pollen transport, and with specialised diets of nectar rather than flower petals. The magnolia is anything but sophisticated; it is pollinated by beetles, the primitive robber insects of the plant world, which eat the flower itself, and fail to pick up much pollen on their smooth bodies during their destructive visit. Any pollen that does adhere to their legs and bodies suffers slow transport as their flight is cumbersome and tardy.

The magnolia is primitive for the following reasons: its construction is on the basic unspecialised floral plan, the early flower model. The parts of the flower are arranged spirally on a club shaped axis (visible in the centre of the right hand flower) and there are large quantities of these—lots of petals, stamens (male organs), pistils (female organs) which remain completely separate from each other, rather than fusing together as in sage and honeysuckle (*Figs H, I* and *Colour Plate 5*). There are no insect directions as to the whereabouts of food, the flower's side of the pollination bargain; guide lines, spots, colour contrasts, and so on are absent. On the other side of the coin there are no insect barriers; robber insects are not excluded by hairs or a narrow constriction.

placed pistils; thus a large amount of material is used to produce a few seeds. The sage, on the other hand, produces a few seeds, but only requires a small amount of material such as stamens and pollen as its method guarantees that the pollen and later the stigma reach the insect target without wastage. The buttercup is considered by most to be a primitive flower, the sage belongs to what is considered to be a more advanced flower family (see Chapter 3).

*Special Devices—Triggers and Pistons.* Although the honey-bee is one of the best pollinators, it cannot penetrate the trigger flowers, such as the pea family, monkshood, or the tightly closed toadflax or snapdragon. These flowers have an opening mechanism which demands forceful heavy pressure of a bumble-bee, another long-tongued insect. In the lupin or the sweet pea, the upper large 'banner' petal attracts the bee which lands on the two lower landing petals. The insect's tongue touches the base of the honey guide (stripe or spot of colour contrasting to the rest of the petal), and the keel (i.e. the lower) petals are depressed. This releases the stamens and pistil from their tightly sheathed wrapping of petals which have hitherto protected them. The stigma acts as a piston ejecting pollen onto the insect's body. The toadflax, monkshood and red clover flowers are so tightly closed, and thus dependent solely on the bumble-bee, that they only grow in areas where the insect lives. Monkshood has become very modified in order to achieve its intricate trigger shape; the showy parts are really sepals, the two upright nectaries being petals.

The roles of petals and sepals in the flower are very interchangeable—many of what are usually called petals are in fact sepals which have taken on the role of the petals and thus taken on a petaloid appearance. This occurs in iris (*Plate 27*), bluebell, marsh marigold, Christmas rose (relative in *Fig D*), daffodil (*Fig E*), lilies (*Plate 27*) and others. It has already been seen, in Chapter 1, that bracts behaving as petals come to look like petals.

*Flower Gazing.* Watching insects and flowers could be called a child's occupation, but it is only by first-hand observation that one can begin to appreciate the intricacies of floral anatomy and to understand these masterpieces of functional design.

One should spare a thought too for the insects—with a brain the size of a pin head, they recognise the colour and perfume of a particular type of flower, and visit several individuals in succession, lessening the mixing of pollen from

different species. Having recognised a flower they judge their distance from the flower's landing platform and 'land' themselves accurately, recognise and follow honey guides, finally navigating their way directly back to their hive or nest. Bees then pass on information of their last food source to the rest of the hive by means of their 'dance language', the other bees respond to the message, leave the hive to seek the latest food supply, and the whole incredible process starts again.

*Focal Points Without Flowers*

Many flowers once past flowering produce intricate and delicate seed heads. These are often ignored due to their lack of bright colour and humble size in comparison to the preceding flamboyant flower. Ignore a few fading flowers and soon there will be a multitude of forms and patterns—green, brown, pointed cusps, globular spheres, contorted twists, large, minute, symmetry side by side with assymmetry.

*After the Flower.* Once the flower has been pollinated, the only important part of it is the ovary (*Fig E*). The sepals, petals and stamens wither and often disappear, having served their purposes of protection, advertisement, and pollen production respectively. A grain of pollen having been brushed onto the receptive female stigma, a tube grows out from the tiny grain and penetrates down the style (stalk part of the pistil). It grows downwards until it reaches the ovules inside the ovary. The female unit from the ovule fuses with the male unit from the pollen grain and it is the fertilised ovule which is the seed. The enlarging ovary containing the seed is called the fruit.

Thus the term 'fruit' is slightly different in its biological sense from its everyday sense. Most of what one usually loosely calls seed heads are in fact fruits—columbine, poppy, bluebell. For instance, an apple is not a true fruit. The true

**17** FLOWER GAZING
One cannot admire a group of flowers without seeing evidence of the close insect-flower relationship. Here, a group of crocuses attract an early bee.

Aptly, the bee is the symbol of industry. A few minute's pause for scrutiny of one insect on its hunting expeditions more than justifies the ancient symbolism.

fruit is the core, i.e. ovary walls and enclosed seeds. The edible part of the apple and the skin, far from being the fruit, are formed from the upper part of the stem (receptacle) which held the flower in a cup-shaped depression. Biologically the apple is a false fruit; that is, parts other than the ovary are involved in forming the fruit, other examples being pear, strawberry, fig, pineapple, hawthorn, cotoneaster, rowan and quince.

As well as protecting the developing seeds the fruit assists in dispersing the seeds. Obviously if the seeds are not efficiently scattered, well away from the potentially competitive parent plant, the very raison d'etre of flower formation, pollination and fertilisation, is lost. Upon the fruit and the seed lies the responsibility of dispersing the next generation.

Seeds are exploded from the fruit as in many of the family Leguminosae (*Fig Q*): gorse, broom, and lupin. In honesty, geranium, stock, shepherd's purse, and evening primrose various parts of the ovary or remaining style dry unequally, causing a sudden violent splitting. Other fruits shake out their seeds: columbine, snapdragon, foxglove, monkshood, lily and iris.

Many seeds are not freed from the fruit before dispersal; the whole fruit with its precious cargo is transferred from one place to another.

In some fruits, the ovary wall is extended to make a wing which is blown on the wind, such as ash, elm, birch and maple. The lime achieves the same end by means of an enlarged bract (leaf). Flying seeds as well as fruits use 'wings'— Scots pine and gladioli. Rose-bay willow-herb and cotton seeds rely on plumes to achieve buoyancy.

As well as being blown to a new area, seeds are floated away from the parent plant, hooked onto passing animals as in burdock, or casually dropped once the fruit is eaten. Some are even designed to be vomited into the world before being irretrievably digested. Cherry, apricot and almond seeds are dispersed by virtue of the fleshy edible ovary wall. In other edible fruits the flesh of the nut is not the ovary or flower remains, but is part of the seed. Survival of the seed thus often depends on the squirrel's bad memory! The ovary wall becomes hard and protective in hazel, oak, beech, sweet chestnut. More will be said on the clever ways in which fruits and seeds have adapted themselves to their roles in Chapter 7, *Fig Q.*

Variety extends far beyond the suggestions opposite; in the wild there are many different species of plantains and fir cones, there are all the cultivated varieties of wild plants, and a glance in a gardening shop will reveal many exciting varieties of gourds and corn which can be grown from seed.

# FRUITS, BERRIES, AND SEED HEADS
*(most can be preserved)*

| WILD | | CULTIVATED *(Garden and Greengrocer)* |
|---|---|---|
| alder *(Fig A)* | honeysuckle | apple |
| barberry (berberis) | *(Colour Plate 7)* | *(Colour Plate 7)* |
| beech | hornbeam | ash |
| bilberry | ivy | astilbe |
| blackberry | lime | barberry (mahonia) |
| black bryony | maple | castor-oil plant (pods) |
| bladder campion | marsh mallow | catalpa (clustered, |
| bluebell (bunch) | mistletoe | Indian bean tree) |
| buckthorn | nightshade-woody | cherries |
| burdock | oak | Chinese chestnut |
| *(Fig L)* | old man's beard | Chinese lantern |
| caraway (whorled) | (traveller's joy) | eucalyptus (gum) |
| chervil | plantain (grouped) | fig |
| cinquefoils | *(Plate 39)* | grapes |
| common toadflax | poppy | gourds |
| cow parsley | *(Colour Plate 10)* | grains (wheat, barley) |
| *(Fig C and Plate 26)* | reedmace (bulrush) | *(Colour Plate 10)* |
| crab apple | rose hips *(Plate 50)* | hollyhock (trimmed) |
| cranberry | rowan | honesty |
| crowberry | *(Fig A, Plate 10,* | horse-chestnut |
| crow garlic | *and Colour Plate 3)* | iris |
| cuckoo-pint | scurvy grass | lemon |
| dandelion (lacquered) | sea campion | lilies |
| dogwood | sedge (grouped) | lotus seed head (florist) |
| elder | sloe (blackthorn) | magnolia |
| elm | *(Colour Plate 10)* | marrow |
| fir cones | sorrel *(Fig T)* | melon |
| *(Fig S, Plates 49 and 51)* | sycamore | nuts (walnut, peanut) |
| guelder rose | teasel | orange |
| hawthorn | thistle (lacquered) | peppers (and chillis) |
| hazel | white bryony | pineapple |
| *(Colour Plate 7)* | wild angelica | plums |
| heath bedstraw | wild cherry | pumpkin |
| herb robert | wild strawberry | privet |
| holly *(Fig U)* | winter aconite | pyracantha |
| | | satsuma |
| | | scabious |
| | | sweet corn (maize) |
| | | tulip *(Colour Plate 10)* |
| | | tulip-tree |

**18** GLISTENING FRUITS
Clusters of berries and seed heads make ideal focal points for almost any sort of design ; .
berries are not only a bright colour and a simple solid form, but their brilliant glistening adds
a texture which is not to be found in flowers, except perhaps in exotics such as anthurium
which looks almost plasticised. Berries have been used as focal material in *Fig A* and
*Plates 9* and *10* and as line and filler in *Colour Plates 3, 7, 10* and *Fig R.*

The poisonous berry spike of cuckoo-pint corresponds to the female flowers of the
community (*Fig E*). The ovaries of the flowers become swollen after pollination by the
insects trapped inside the sheath.

*Useful Hints.* As with flowers, many fruits and seeds lend themselves first and foremost as line material; however, with stems suitably shortened and heads grouped together, a point of focus can be improvised, for example alder, bluebell, columbine, plantain, reedmace, certain types of sedge, sorrel, teasel.

Large berries, fruits and cones should be placed low in the arrangement: apart from their focal qualities, there are the mundane mechanics to be considered—all of these are heavy and, particularly if mounted on a stalk, false or otherwise, could topple bringing the entire arrangement with them if set in a top heavy position.

Another practical detail which should not be ignored is the attraction of berries to children: many succulent and gloriously coloured berries are poisonous. Positioning of the arrangement and use of berries at all must be considered carefully if there are small children in the house.

Seed heads and fruit are particularly attractive to those without a garden, as these materials lend themselves to perpetual use. Lush and green, reminiscent of the harvest festival when fresh, once dried they are a wonderful standby. Seed heads of bluebell and poppy form delicate filigrees once weathered down to the skeleton, and require no further attention. Others, such as cow parsley, once past their prime become grey-brown and rather uninteresting. These can be transformed by a dip in paint. Fluffy seedheads, such as dandelion and thistle, can be kept under control by a quick spray of hair lacquer. Many fruits have a more interesting texture when dried than when fresh: for example, gourds, orange, lemon.

If one is completely reliant upon wild material there is often the problem of lack of variety; in a particular locality one might find that the only colourful plant for three weeks or more was rowan trees. Lack of variety in raw material need not dictate similar arrangements; branches of rowan berries have been used in completely different designs in the following (*Fig A, Plate 10 and Colour Plate 3*). (Complete lack of vases did not detract from the variety, either.)

*Imaginative Leaves.* Leaves are most frequently used as a frame and foil for flowers, but they can also form an attractive point of interest on their own. The appeal of variegated leaves is immediate, but the beauty of the plainer ones is less apparent until they are contrasted with their opposite. For example, the steely blue of sea holly can be featured by grouping it with glossy green laurel and mat grey dusty miller or yarrow, or intricate coloured begonia leaves, metallic

### 19 LEAF TAKEOVER

Protection and advertisement of a flower are usually provided by its sepals (usually green leaves closely cupped round the petal base) and petals. Like the cuckoo-pint, poinsettia flowers are economically reduced to their basic essentials—sexual organs, and these are grouped in a community for maximum efficiency and least wastage of plant material. Petals having been discarded, the community uses specialised leaf-like structures called bracts for carrying out the work of absent petals.

Bracts used for petal purposes, not surprisingly, come to look like petals—large, showy, and coloured. In poinsettia, the bracts are a brilliant beautiful red—the uppermost layer have a smooth outline, those beneath more closely resembling the usual leaf shape of the plant. In the centre is the insignificant looking, but all important, flower community or, to be more accurate, community of communities, for each pollen tipped cluster (three in the photograph) is not one flower with lots of stamens, but a community of flowers with one stamen. In this picture there are thus three communities of flowers. Very many flowers are advertised by the one set of bracts, instead of each bearing its own colorful banner.

A similar situation was seen in the cuckoo-pint (*Fig E*) in which one bract took over on behalf of the community. This single bract, enlarged to colossal proportions, is called a spathe. Where not used for advertisement and show, bracts and spathes are usually small, as in the bluebell and the daffodil.

Poinsettia belongs to the very strange family of Euphorbiaceae, which also includes spurges and the castor-oil plant.

and crinkle-edged, contrasted to smooth striated hostas, with their parallel veins accentuated by a few wispy leaves of cream striped spider plant. Contrasting leaves have been exploited in the arrangement in *Plate 44*. The more exotic tropical leaves such as glossy green fatsia with its intricate outline and indentations, or bright red bracts (leaves) of poinsettia (*Plate 19*) can hold their own without a contrasting partner.

Many shoots have enough variation of form and colour to focus attention when used singly, for example kale. A sprig of holly is naturally arranged in a fairly tight and concentrated configuration, however something like variegated ivy sprays would make a better focal point if the leaves were stripped from the stem and arranged in a loose rosette shape, otherwise the eye wanders along a scattered line of leaves rather than being drawn to the centre.

*Leaves Galore.* The leaves of plants listed below have distinctive and interesting surface texture, veining, colour or outline, and have been grouped in the Table according to their source. Many can be preserved with glycerin treatment, pressed or dried naturally (for details, see Chapter 6); those marked † dry particularly well in beautiful colours.

Many of these seem very ordinary at first sight—just another leaf—until partnered to make an eye-catching combination. Although so commonplace that they usually fail to cause notice, leaves are well worth a second glance. Many leaves of herbs are attractive when dried; for example, fennel.

| WILD | GREENGROCER | GARDEN OR FLORIST |
|---|---|---|
| alder | asparagus shoots† | aralia† |
| arrowhead | (real luxury) | azalea (autumn) |
| barberry† | beetroot | begonias (*Plate 44*) |
| copper beech | brussels sprouts | box |
| cuckoo-pint | cabbage† (gone to seed) | camellia† |
| dock | cauliflower† | caster-oil plant† |
| fir† | celery | coleus† |
| foxglove | chard (gone to | cordylines |
| fumitory | seed) | cyclamen |
| guelder rose | chicory | dusty miller† (*Plate 8*) |
| herb robert | endive | eucalyptus† |
| holly† | globe artichoke† | euonymus |

| WILD | GREENGROCER | GARDEN OR FLORIST |
|---|---|---|
| horse mint | kale (gone to seed)† | fatsia† |
| ivy† | leeks | geranium (variegated |
| oak† | lettuce | grape vine |
| plane† | marjoram | hop vine |
| plantain | parsley | hosta |
| poplar | parsnip | Japanese maple† |
| poppy | rosemary | joy-weed |
| roseroot | spinach | laurel† |
| sea holly† | sweet corn | lavender |
| sea purslane | watercress | magnolia† |
| silverweed | | mimosa |
| thistle† | | plum |
| white bryony | | rhododendron |
| white mullein | | saxifrage |
| willow | | virginia creeper |
| winter heliotrope | | woolly lamb's ear |

*The Indoor Gardener.* There is yet another source of foliage—pot plants, the standard favourites, tradescantia (wandering jew), spider plant, or the more exotic anthurium, peperomia, African violet, or poinsettia (several pot plants (*Plate 31*)). Any prunings, or the entire plants, are useful, the latter obviously suited to larger decorations and can be placed, pot (suitably camouflaged) and all in the arrangement; the more hardy plants will stand careful removal from the pot for the occasion. More will be said of this in the Chapter on Mechanics.

**20** SPRING CURVE
Natural curves of pussy willow make the austere line of this arrangement—interfering twigs having been removed. The solid curves of tulip leaves echo the line and provide a dense base for the arrangement. The highest leaf was placed lower side uppermost to achieve its upward curve. The three bright red peony tulips follow the main sweeping curve, the largest at the focal point.

When the tulips died, substitution of more tulip leaves, still radiating and following the curve, made an even more elegant and clean cut arrangement, the smooth bold shapes making an interesting alternative to the fussy pattern of flowers.

The soothing effect of smooth water can be readily appreciated in this design—stones cover a large pinholder. The patterned glass dish was given a coat of black paint before entering service as a flower container.

On a smaller scale there are rosette succulents and small cacti from an indoor cactus garden. Many of the succulent plants have attractive patterns on their bulbous leaves and can be grown easily from a single leaf cutting. For people without even an indoor garden, succulents tinted yellow and orange can often be found wild on the rocks in quarries and on cliffs, and have the added advantage that they last well in water.

Fungi can also be used; the colours of many toadstools are dazzling, that used in *Fig C* was a brilliant shining scarlet and lemon yellow. Many of these plants are very poisonous; if in doubt, wash your hands after touching them and keep well away from children. Less hazardous are lichens; the bushy varieties growing on trees detach easily, have interesting texture and shapes, and are a subtle bluish green which remains once dried (*Plate 48*).

*Why Stick To Plants?* For those who like the unusual and are confident of their sense of balance and design, inanimate objects are a further source of focal material—stones and minerals, fossils, sea shells, shells of birds' eggs and feathers (reminiscent of the old masters), or suitable man-made ornaments and objets d'arts. In *Fig C* the convoluted monumental forms of a horse's tooth have been used. These were found beautifully polished and blue tinted, washed up on the beach.

*Arrangements Without Flowers: Green Themes.* For a cool elegant effect of shade in tropical summer, leaves are unbeatable: fresh lime green leaves caught before summer hardening, white and creamy variegated patterns and white vein skeletons, light spring spathes of cuckoo-pint and tiny dusty textured green grapes, languishing grey driftwood forms, shiny and sleek. Set in front of a blue-green shot curtain, the colours are quietly soothing even in soft spring sunlight.

Autumn leaves from the wild are pretty enough to make an arrangement on their own. Yellow and brown edged reedmace leaves bend in smooth curves to varying degrees, a radiating group making a pleasing assymmetric triangle, with a note of interest from intermingled stems of grasses in flower. The focus could be a smaller triangle of contrasting leaves—delicate lemon and green celery tops and heavily veined leaves slashed with autumn colours, yellow, orange, red, magenta and crimson.

*Seed head Doubles.* Teasels, prickly brown and globular, contrast with elongated thorny twigs of gorse with twisted pods and yet they are two of a kind. As a background, tall elegant reedmace contrast with curving leaves; in front, set low, a pitted lotus seed head echoes the rich dark brown of the velvety heads behind. The patterned lotus head also echoes the repetitive pattern of a bunch of grapes; vivid bright orange of Chinese lanterns add panache to bronze of barley heads, and an ideal pair for light relief are flimsy silver fluff of traveller's joy and shining satin discs of honesty—alike, yet unalike.

*Berries of Autumn.* The smaller wild fruits, such as acorns, rose hips, rowan, dogwood, hawthorn, not to mention cones, such as larch (often attractively encrusted with green lichens) are easily interchangeable with flowers and present little design difficulty. With autumn leaves and warm coloured wood, sparkling orange, red and yellow berries are as natural and appropriate as the most expensive chrysanthemum. The variations of size, shape and colour make a random mixture of berries an interesting and well matched group. Berries combine well with flowers and so can be used to make a few flowers go further.

*Fruit and Vegetables.* Everyday fruit such as gleaming oranges, shiny green, pink and red apples (plain ones helped by a touch of lipstick), look rare and beautiful once polished and intermingled with light green waxy apples, brown gold pears, mat yellow and brown mottled bananas, and of course grapes with bloom, green and black. An occasional seasonal luxury of cherries or satsumas add to the variety of colour, texture and shape. As far as focal points are concerned, one's choice is largely affected by the size of the decoration; generally, the smaller the fruits the better if combined with foliage and berries, and early wind-fall apples are ideal.

The bold colours of fruit are splendidly contrasted with glossy green laurel leaves, variegated geranium and ivy leaves, and begonia. An even more un-expected source of bright colour lies in the vegetable basket. Glistening succulent tomatoes, bright radishes and carrots make a gaudy splash (*Colour Plate 3*), foiled by dark textured nut shells and leaves. Purple damsons or mat skinned sloe berries beautifully complement lemon yellow, or on a larger scale, shiny blackish aubergines with grapefruit.

Fruit and vegetables with foilage still attached make for interest—rhubarb, apples, carrots, celery, radishes. The 'foliage' vegetables form an intricately patterned centre piece—cabbage, red, green or white (preferably still with loosely packed outer leaves), a handful of sprouts, or white and green leeks. The close packed leaves of a red cabbage heart make a fascinating pattern of crinkled convoluted stripes if a section is cut out at an angle.

Many vegetables have become standard decoration material and can be easily grown from seed—ornamental kale with mauve or green and white centre, brilliant green or ruby coloured chard, sweet corn or ornamental maize with pink, yellow and white kernels, flower-like sheath and plumes, castor-oil plant pods and leaves, dried blue-grey, orange or red. After a few years of neglect in the garden cabbages and kale look exotic and carrots and parsnips provide yet another source of attractive foliage. For those without a garden, celery tops cut from a stick from the greengrocer can be kept for long periods in water, and apparently dead beetroot tops sprout fresh lime green leaves with bright crimson veins after a few weeks in water.

*Important Points*. The focal point above all must have interest and involve the eye; therefore it is important that care is taken when using the simple bold shapes of fruit and vegetables. One must be on guard against having a large area of monotonous colour and texture; ears of wheat and barley overlapping an uninterrupted expanse can add interest. In *Colour Plate 3* heads of marram have been used in the absence of any cereal stalks and serve the same purpose.

As always the selection of material is vital; the choice must be an appropriate one—a large grapefruit does not marry happily with the delicate line of maiden-hair fern, nor does a small bunch of cherries rest well in a frame of outsize hosta leaves. Sizes must mix without jarring. In a predominantly vegetable and fruit arrangement, if pebbles and stones look out of place, a more relevant choice might be a heap of lentils, dried beans, or sunflower seeds borrowed from the pet hamster! Container selection should also be appropriate—the everyday vegetables and colours in *Colour Plate 3* team well with the frying pan.

Most of us cannot afford to leave this category of arrangement material un-eaten, and although one has the triple enjoyment of discovering new beauty, creating a fascinating arrangement, and finally eating a square meal, there are disadvantages. The longer the food is in warmth and light, the more nutritional value is lost, and it takes a strong mind to remove the perfectly positioned grapes before they age and wrinkle, deteriorating beyond appetite. A vitamin conscious compromise is to select the best sized and coloured items for show (and not too distant consumption) and firmly stow away the rest in a cool dark place or a refrigerator. For those who place aesthetics before nutrition, there are on page 129 suggestions for the traditional massed fruit arrangements with foliage and flowers, harking back to the still life paintings of the Flemish and Dutch old masters.

CHAPTER THREE

# Masses of Flowers

An armful of beautiful flowers is inspiration enough for a traditional arrangement. This style shows off the myriads of forms, colours, and perfumes of the
plant world to perfection. A thoroughly British style, it is based on classic shapes
such as the triangle, circle or rectangle. It is an interesting point that the triangle
makes a very satisfying composition in painting: many old masters placed
figures to fit into a perfect triangle. As well as making an attractive one-sided
display, these shapes make an all-round floral design which can be viewed from
all sides.

In common with Line Designs, a mass of flowers looks far more pleasing if
the edges of the shape are tapered and sparse and the central part of the design
is made up of round shapes forming an interesting core or focal point. Thus the
eye is drawn in towards the centre of the floral picture. Plants in the lists of
linear material (see page 32), and many of the lines and shapes of Chapter 1
are ideal for edging mass arrangements. The round-faced focal flowers, fruits
and leaves listed in Chapter 2 are equally absorbing placed centrally amongst
lots of flowers.

*Rules in Practice.* Various rules have evolved concerning the relationship of plant
material to the container. The highest point of the arrangement should not be
less than one and a half times the height of the vase. This sort of size ruling is
self evident: if one has the tallest stem too short, the container dominates the
picture, and the overall effect is squat and dumpy, or to use a gardening phrase,
there is an appearance of stunted growth. Having placed the highest point of
the design, the next dimension to be considered is width. Rules have it that this
should be two-thirds of the height.

From the practical and artistic point of view, it is best to place first these long
stems forming the outline of the design. By making the outline first one can

**21** THE IMPORTANCE OF BALANCE
An arrangement can easily be spoilt by lack of balance, particularly a Mass Arrangement based on a geometric shape such as this one. Even the appropriate choice of materials (warm coloured dahlias, copper coloured lustre vase on a highly polished honey brown table) cannot counteract overlapping flower faces and lopsided distribution of 'light' leaves and 'heavy' full blown flowers.

A feeling of balance in a mass of flowers is best achieved by mentally bisecting the outline shape and checking that where there are one or more round-faced flowers, there is an equivalent amount of volume or visual weight on the opposite side, not exact symmetrical placing of flowers to achieve a mirror image.

immediately rectify errors of size and shape in relation to the container. By starting at the back and sides of the design, one avoids leaning across and touching any of the flowers in the front ranks. Having got a skeleton of the design shape, one can then work on placing flowers and foliage within the shape and concentrate on the placing of different sizes, shapes, and colours without fear of ending up with a basically unsatisfactory outline.

Obviously, the graduation from tapered spiky shapes at the edge to round-faced flowers at the centre will require lots of different stem lengths. Rather than cutting the raw material into lots of different lengths so start with, as some people do, it is wiser to hold each bloom in its probable future position and try the various possibilities before making the cut. This has the advantage of trial and error, and lessens the number of stems unnecessarily shortened. If closed buds, such as rose buds, are used as the edge material, it must be remembered that their shape will change as the buds open into full blown flowers. Flowers in the central part of the design give a more three dimensional and pleasing effect if they have different stem lengths, making different levels in the arrangement.

More than any other, Mass Designs need a focal point, a point low in the arrangement, from which all the stems radiate. This impression of radiation from a central heart cannot be achieved if stems are allowed to cross each other. The point of radiation of the stems is often emphasised by the placing of round-faced blooms. The heart of the arrangement can also be accented by reserving the deeper colours for this part of the design, keeping the lighter colours to the outside, as in *Colour Plate 4*.

*Weight and Balance*. As with line design an important issue is the quantity of material in the arrangement; flowers are not happy packed too close together, and overcrowding can look messy. Not only are flowers disturbed by tight packing, but also the appearance of the whole decoration. Overcrowding smacks of old-world arrangements before the advent of stem holders, when a vase was packed full in order to keep the flowers in place. In *Plate 21* the overlapping dahlias make for a jumble of bisected and incomplete flower faces jostling together, as opposed to each flower retaining its identity within the arrangement. For a more delicate arrangement, light flimsy flowers and foliage can fill awkward gaps between larger key blooms without giving an effect of overcrowding. Ideal fillers of this type are baby's-breath (gypsophila), forget-me-not, and love-in-a-mist.

Also, the whole arrangement needs to be balanced without any disturbing hint of top-heaviness or lop-sidedness. If the overall shape of a mass of flowers is an oval, there should be an equal weight of flowers on each side of an imaginary central perpendicular line—this does not mean an equal number, nor that one side should attempt to be a mirror image of the other. Flower for flower symmetry

# 1 THE OTHER WORLD

Not a flower in sight, but other plant materials make a beautiful design in nature of fresh spring leaves, lichen, and fairy-tale toadstools; in the background, weathered chunky rock.

Are toadstools really plants? Many people think of plants as only the flowers, shrubs and trees grown in gardens, together with non-flowering mosses and ferns, but the Plant Kingdom contains many surprises. At the bottom of the plant scale there is a large and varied collection of primitive plants—the Thallophyta (without stems, leaves or roots), which besides bacteria, benign as well as dangerous, includes tiny microscopic globules, possibly similar to the first plants that appeared more than a thousand million years ago. Seaweeds (page 70) share many features with these microscopic plants and are also included in the same group, the algae.

As well as bacteria and algae, the primitive collection includes the fungi—toadstools, mushrooms, moulds, yeasts and so on. They lack the green coloring (chlorophyll) which is so typical of other plants, and are therefore unable to make their own food; they are mostly parasitic, or feed on decaying matter. Individuals of tiny algae and fungi associate together in a co-operative existence in the shape of lichens, which are therefore dual organisms.

From this stage on, plants begin to look like plants, with green leaves or leaf-like parts, and so on: the flat prostrate liverworts and mosses (page 161), then the ferns (page 48 and *Fig B*), the horsetails (page 161 and *Plate 6*) and lastly the varied and most familiar group, the seed-plants which include the less sophisticated conifers (page 48), and the highly efficient and most recent group, the flowering plants.

## 2 DRIFTWOOD RELIC OF THE PAST

Two thousand years ago the scenery in many places looked very different. In the British Isles much of what is now grassland and moor was then luxurious forest, deciduous in the south-east, and coniferous in the north. Man's own activities and those of his animals have caused the gradual change. In the moorland peat of the Pennines and Scotland, remains of birch lie buried, proving the former extent of the forest.

The photograph shows a relic of a lost forest—now sunk beneath black, sticky peat, sphagnum moss, ling, heather and sedges. By the edge of a loch, peat recedes, exposing tree trunks and roots glistening silver grey where the wind and sun have buffed and polished. The splintered broken trunk is now smoothed, undulating and sculptured, but the roots retain their knotted contortions. Pieces of this antique wood are shown in *Plate 11* and have been used in arrangements in *Figs A, O, P* and *Plate 49.*

## 3 ORANGE KITCHEN THEME

A design in a frying pan, jug, or other asymmetric container must be largely governed by the handle in order to achieve balance and make the plant material and container union look convincing. In this arrangement, the very long handle has been incorporated into the design by means of a low flat curve of rowan branches, and the unequal distribution of gleaming berries.

The length of the handle is offset by berries being concentrated towards the middle of the pan, and the focal point not being dead in its centre, but towards the handle. The point of weight of the central cluster of red and yellow berries is emphasized by bold focal forms— an onion and a tomato. The large onion has had its skin torn and pointed shoot bent, in order to break up a large monocoloured surface. Its solid round shape echoes the round form of the pan and the berries, also the tomato and carrot top. The carrots act as a transition of shape and colour between the onion and the tomato. Also leading the eye into the focal point is the handle, and heads of marram (used in the absence of more appropriate wheat and barley).

As well as roundness of shape, another factor in selection of materials was colour. The starting point of the arrangement was the matching colours of frying pan and rowan, so warm colours of yellow, brown, orange and red were called for. The choice of vegetables also made the frying pan a more convincing container to use. The red berries overhanging the wooden handle were chosen in preference to yellow, as they picked up the red enamel lower down the handle. Yellow was kept for the centre of the design—the low-set yellow berries meet the uppermost yellow band on the frying pan. The bright red of the tomato at the front was vital to the design. Without picking up the brilliant red of the pan the arrangement would have been dull. Mental substitution of an orange for the tomato will prove the point. The warm colours were flatteringly contrasted by the cool bluish-grey inside the pan.

Mechanics—an inner container with a pinholder and plasticine. Such an informal arrangement is ideal in a kitchen dinette or a farmhouse style kitchen—light natural wood makes a perfect team with yellow and orange.

## 4 RED TO VIOLET-BLUE

In this traditional Mass Arrangement related colours, red, through magenta, violet and violet-blue are used to give an impression of depth to the centre of the triangle and to accent its diagonal lean. A fairly intense coloured perpendicular—a foxglove—makes a stable backbone and high point to the shape, and a light edge is made by pale colours leading into intense colours at the centre and at the base of the triangle. The diagonal sweep is accentuated by the graded intensity of the four roses placed in a flowing line, with the lightest pink near the edge of the design. The red-magenta theme is set off by a complementary tint of green in the container. Such bright colours demand a light plain background, certainly not a dark corner.

Spike shaped flowers are used for the outline of the arrangement; bulkier spikes are kept for the main body of the design, and round-faced flowers for the centre of the base for emphasis and focus. The radiation of spikes from one focal point is high lighted by the roses being placed at this point.

The shallow serving dish makes a plain wide base for the design. Long stems were held in place with wire netting in an inner container.

COLOUR PLATE 5
See caption to *Fig 1*.

## 6 ECONOMICAL WEEDS

Dandelions and daisies are abundant from mountainside to city or sea shore and, often to the gardener's dismay, on well nurtured lawns. The dandelion and the daisy are not, strictly speaking, flowers. As their family name, Compositae, implies, they are massive communities of miniature flowers on one stalk with one root—the consequent economy of plant material and growth is enormous.

In the dandelion all of the tiny flowers have their five petals joined in a long strap. In a mature flower an elongated curling tipped stigma (female) emerges through a close packed ring of stamens (male), this is visible against the black background. The tuft of white hairs at the base of the flower becomes the familiar parachute once a seed is formed and is ready for dispersal.

There are two types of flower in the daisy community. Outer strap-like female flowers are enlarged for advertisement, and the inner tubular shaped flowers contain both sex organs.

## 7 AUTUMN FRUITS

Wild and cultivated fruits of autumn combine with the beautiful red rose, laurel leaves and honeysuckle. The asymmetry of the shape is accented by careful placing of the apple and hazel nuts near the base of the container. Tapering and small shapes are kept for the edge of the design, and solid shapes placed near the centre. The brass candlestick brings out warm autumn bronzes and reds.

A candlecup has been used to secure the arrangement.

## 8 COLOURS FROM BENEATH THE EARTH

Environmental change is a continuous process; the surface of the earth is in a perpetual state of flux, however small, whether manifested in the obvious form of volcanic eruptions (*Plate 40*) or as a beautifully coloured geyserite formation at the brink of a hot spring.

The white deposit in this geyser encrustation is silica (a combination of silicon and oxygen). Colours around hot springs can be due to minerals crystallized from hot solutions, and compounds associated with the springs breaking down to give colourful results. Also simple forms of life, such as specially adapted algae (primitive plants, described in *Colour Plate 1*), can grow in hot springs and add characteristic brilliant blue-green hues.

This crystalline waterfall was photographed in the Yellowstone National park, Wyoming— an active earthquake area where the lie of the land in the near future is still being determined by forces underground.

## 9 HUMID GREENS

Water is the stuff of life, not least for plants. In many plants the leaves have no specialised protection from excessive water loss. The primitive mosses in particular are imperfectly adapted for life away from dampness and shade.

Whether one has a moss garden in miniature indoors, or a Japanese style outdoor land-scape featuring thirty species of moss like that of Saihoji Temple, the Moss Temple (also known as Kokedara Temple) large surfaces of water and a protecting leaf canopy are vital to the lush growth of the luminescent green. Almost all plant material benefits from a surrounding blanket of water vapour. As well as the beneficial humidity for the plants one has for oneself a peaceful expanse of shining water to contemplate, an integral part of the Japanese approach to flower and landscape arrangement.

## 10 PRESERVED COLOUR

A charred piece of tree root lends itself as a container for dried fruits, seed heads and flowers, and dictated the diagonal line of the arrangement.

All of these materials were dried naturally without any demand of time or materials other than hanging strawflowers upside down in the airing cupboard. Their bright red is shown off against the dull black of the wood and the bluish tints of blackthorn (sloe) berries.

The round-faced flowers and a heavy tulip seed head have been placed low in the arrangement to give weight. Delicate barberry stems, a larch twig, bracken, and barley make a wispy fan shape about more solid perpendiculars of poppy and columbine seed heads, which all frame the focal flower heads.

can be very boring. The effect of lack of balanced weight in a basically symmetrical shape is demonstrated in *Plate 21*. The leaves and bud are too light in relation to the round forceful shapes of the flowers in the corresponding position on the other side. Thus the decoration is slightly disturbing.

*Shapes and Containers.* The choice of the container is as important as the placing of the flowers. The most vital thing to remember here is that the container is an integral part of the design and the two must fit together in a pleasing appropriate way; they must not compete with each other. As one plans the outline of the arrangement it is helpful if the line of the container is taken into account as well as the natural flow of the flowers or foliage to be used.

Essentially straight perpendicular stems and flowers can look out of place if involved in a contrived curve, just as a curvacous classical urn looks strange containing a straight-sided column of flowers. The natural stance of the materials and the container should be important considerations in deciding on a design. A very flowing effect can be achieved using asymmetrical outlines such as a triangle or curve, a C or a sloping S, the latter being called a Hogarth curve.

It is largely a matter of personal preference and whether one has the luxury of a prolific garden that decides whether one chooses a container to fit the flowers, or picks the flowers to fit the container. Container possibilities and selection are discussed in Chapter 4.

The division between the orientally inspired Line Design and classic British Mass Design is difficult to make once one considers designs of lots of flowers arranged in a linear shape. This type of line treatment of lots of flowers has been mentioned earlier (Chapter 2). It is particularly useful if one is without the classical pedestal vase or urn, and relies on improvised containers. Containers with definite line and flow such as baskets, bottles, or jugs look very well if this characteristic is echoed in a linear shaped array of flowers.

Massed designs can be dazzling, whether composed of one type of flower, such as roses or sweet peas, mixed flowers, flowers and foliage, foliage on its own (cut or still growing in a pot) or with fruit. From the pretty posy to an exotic tropical pot-et-fleur, Mass Design is as emotive as any linear simplicity—geometric, casual, multicoloured or tones of one hue, grand, informal, flowing, static, patterned or plain.

*Arrangement Ideas*

*Rhapsodies in Blue and Gold.* Dusky pink tulip buds, solid-shaped and slightly tinged with blue, make a delicate contrast of form and colour to the spring blue of majestic iris crowns. More fragile are freesias, pink, white and mauve with striped mouths and fresh perfume; their tapered bud tips making a gentle edge to a classic triangular design. Weight and focus can be added with solid simple shapes of tulip leaves (some rolled previously for extra curvature). One or two opened tulips, with petals gently smoothed and arched backwards to expose centres make a round faced contrast to high positioned tapering buds.

The step by step arrangement of developing gladioli spikes are a must for shapely outlines. Majestic, golden and flame, gladioli flowers answer warm-hued dahlias, round and patterned and brash. A dark brown echo of the notched flower spikes can be suggested by including a few larch twigs, and the patterned form of the dahlias can be reflected with a few cones, larch, cedar, or pine.

Blue and gold make a truly regal combination on a magnificent scale with blue delphinums, larkspurs, and cream and gold gladioli providing a spiky frame for perfect gold roses. The sculptured form of roses contrasts with the fluffy edges of a few cream and dainty carnations. Intricate gold chrysanthemums gild the heart of any arrangement beautifully, a contrast of form and colour with intermingled agapanthus, and the pyramid is complete.

*All of a Kind.* Curves of bowing bluebell stems and leaves make a pretty posy in a glass goblet. Smaller still, and falling in tiny droplets, lilies-of-the-valley make a fragrant triangle arranged in a glass, or a fan-shape. Arrangements in the shape of an open fan radiating from a central point look particularly effective in a similarly shaped or patterned container (such as an up-ended scallop shell). On a grander scale, but still with heady lily perfume and presence, Madonna lilies rise beautifully in a mass from any tall vase.

*Wild and Improvised.* One of the commonest shells on any beach is the shell of the whelk, with the beautiful spiral marred by a great gaping hole (*Plate 46*). By closing the mouth of the shell with foil, filling it tightly with Oasis and using the broken opening for a living pin cushion of flowers, one has a pretty little minia-ture vase. By using the 'back' of the shell for the flowers, rather than the natural

**22 MASS IN MINIATURE**

A handful of wild flowers and an ashtray can make a traditional Mass Arrangement of flowers. In the small white ashtray, pink, mauve, and purple flowers have been arranged in a circle. The spike shapes—common persicaria—were arranged first in the outline shape. Persicaria spikes were also placed here and there nearer the heart of the arrangement, pointing towards the observer to give depth and add variety.

Within the pretty pink outline, light pinks and mauves of heather and pink tinged devil's bit scabious led into the deeper colours of bright purple heather, blue heads of scabious and the reddish purple tint of red clover. As well as the centre of the circle being given weight by means of graded colour intensity, round-faced flowers were placed at the heart of the arrangement.

A tiny inner container was used—an upturned lid full of Oasis. Miniature designs are always fiddly, particularly where delicate stems are used. When space was getting too limited for fingers, tweezers were used to grasp and place stems. Miniature designs are not ideal for those in a hurry, but are well suited to awkward corners on shelves and dressing tables.

mouth, it is very much easier to capture the flow of the shell in the flower arrangement.

The curvy feeling of the shell is well emphasised by curved and delicate filigrees of foliage—yarrow and leaves of the family Umbelliferae, occasionally a beautiful intense magenta colour. Set at a lazy S-bend angle with a few echoing dwindling curves of wild carrot foliage there is a perfect frame of blend and contrast for a theme on pink—from pink to white and cream and from pink through mauve and violet to blue (colour wheel).

Tiny flowers are fitting for tiny designs: thrift, delicate pink, found hanging on to windswept cliffs, and from the same habitat the multiple heads of devil's bit scabious, mostly blue, but a few blooms of pink and white. Still by the sea, one finds delicate mauve sea stocks from sand dunes, and by a trickling brook white heads of watercress, lilac Lady's Smock, and the abiquitous shepherd's purse (those having relatively large and bold flower faces must be carefully placed so as not to overshadow other tinier blooms). From moor and hedgerow there are rich purple pansies, mauvey-pink ling, fluffy powder puff balls of creamy meadow sweet and crowded heads of yarrow, and a range from pinkish-mauve to brilliant purple magenta heathers.

Such a group of related colours looks very pleasing if a merging, moving effect is created, one colour leading in to the next. The cream and light colours placed around the upper edge of the design lead gently and naturally through the pinks and mauves to the blues and purples set low in the front of the design near the darkest, near-black burgundy foliage.

Wild flowers are usually small, but one can quite easily have a large traditional mass of flowers picked from hedgerows and waste ground. Still on a mauve theme, there are foxgloves and rose-bay willow-herb for the outline, and the more solid blooms of thistle, hardheads, and burdock, with lighter textured and coloured flowers as fillers, such as meadow sweet, cow parsley and heather. Obviously one's combination of wild flowers depends on the locality; the above combinations occur together in the north of Scotland. Further south, there are wild teasels, old man's beard and mallow to fit the colour scheme.

If one lives near deciduous woods, there is nothing to surpass the delicate lines of spring catkins and furry tufts of pussy willow. From the floor of the wood and meadow there are primroses, sometimes daffodils, and bluebells, but they are becoming more scarce—be content with the tiniest posy in the vase and a carpet still growing for next year.

## Masses of Flowers: Telling Them Apart

In Chapter 2 the different forms of petals, their colours, spots and stripes were explained by reference to pollinating insects. It will be shown how floral form has a quite different emphasis in flowers which use wind rather than insects to transfer their pollen. But all flowers, however different in appearance, have in common the single purpose of producing seeds, and all have a form and arrangement to perfectly match their function.

In spite of the colossal differences between flowers, some seem to be more alike than others, and it is on this sort of basis that flowers are sorted into the families so familiar to gardeners or to anyone with an interest in flowers.

*Flower Families and Family Trees.* The grouping of similar flowers into families is not done for catalogue convenience. The grouping or classification, as it is called, reflects the relationship of one plant with another, and reveals something of the history and ancestry of a flower species.

The variety of living flowers presents a fragmented, incomplete jigsaw to the botanist and represents only the tips of the branches of the family tree. Incomplete because, through millions of years since flowering plants emerged and flourished, the species slowly changed to better suit the ever changing conditions (the sort of changes and conditions are summarised in Table 1, page 49). Fortunately along with the more successful 'improved models' of flowers living today, a very few older styled ones survived without radically altering in spite of the outside changes. It is these surviving primitive flowers, and fossils of their extinct relatives and predecessors, which provide one of the pointers to understanding the relationships of the flower families.

Thus, from the hotchpotch of ancient and modern remnants, a sequence of differences between groups of flowers emerges, reflecting a sequence of changes and evolution during flower history—another twig in the family tree.

*What is a Flower Family?* Flowers which are very closely related are classified in the same group or genus and have recently diverged from a common ancestor. For example, the affinity of the primrose and the cowslip is obvious at a glance —they are in the same genus, Primula (a genus name starts with a capital letter). The slight differences between the two flowers are reflected in their being in

**23** GENUS PRIMULA

In the classification of plants, similar species are grouped together in the same genus (genera pl.). Genus Primula includes the primrose, cowslip, and polyanthus as well as the bog species of primula in the photograph. The similarity of these plants reflects a relatively recent divergence from a common ancestor; they are thus closely related. Easily recognisable features of the group are the low growing herbaceous habit, the floral form, and clustered grouping of flowers in an umbel (i.e. like the spokes of an umbrella, see also *Plate 26*).

Similar genera are grouped together in the same familiy. The primrose, cowslip, primula and polyanthus have characteristics in common with yellow loosestrife and scarlet pimpernel, genera Lysimachia and Anagallis respectively. All of these plants are in the same family: Primulaceae. They all shared a more distant common ancestor.

separate species: the primrose is species vulgaris, the cowslip is species veris (the species name does not have a capital). When referring to a plant by its scientific name, the genus and species are quoted, hence the primrose is Primula vulgaris and the cowslip is Primula veris. Apart from being universal and therefore unambiguous, the latin name refers to a particular feature of the plant: the name vulgaris means the flower was common when named. As all plants closely resembling each other are in the same genus, it is not surprising to find another of the spring flowers, polyanthus, belongs to the genus Primula.

The Primula genus (*Plate 23*) has many shared characteristics with other genera (plural), such as Lysimachia, Cyclamen, Anagallis; examples of which are, respectively: yellow loosestrife, cyclamen, scarlet pimpernel. These all have in common the following features: the plants are non-woody, the flowers are symmetrical, the five petals being joined at the base. The five stamens are always opposite the petals, and all of this group of plants produce the same sort of fruit after fertilization. These genera are therefore grouped together within the same family, Primulaceae. As a group these plants have more in common with each other than with any plants from other families. All the plants in Primulaceae are distantly related; far back in geological time there is a single common ancestor.

*Old Style/New Style.* The similarity of flowers closely related enough to be in the same family is fairly easy to appreciate; within the group the flowers and fruits share a basic plan. Relationships between the different families are controversial and depend a lot on botanical intricacies, but one view of the positions of the more common families in the family tree can be appreciated without resorting to details tedious to all but the specialist.

The flowers which are closer to the ancient original flower plan are said to be primitive. These old-fashioned flowers carry many stamens and pistils (as in peony, *Plate 24*), only a few of which will be fertilized. Parts of the flower are arranged spirally and remain separate from each other. Also, as explained in Chapter 2, in primitive flowers, the pollen and nectar is not well protected, hence the need for their copious production. Insect directions, such as guide lines and spots are often absent or unsophisticated, so pollination is an altogether chancy affair.

Advanced flowers economise on the amount of pollen, number of stamens and pistils, and also petals. In primitive flowers the petals are separate from each

other; however, advanced flowers have joined petals which do the same tasks more effectively and economically. Stamen economy is such that not only are there very few of them, but extra height for a stamen is not achieved by lengthening its stalk (filament), but by shortening it and joining it to a nearby petal so that less material is used. In order to increase the possibility of fertilization in spite of the lessened amount of raw material expended, ingenious devices are formed which guarantee the insect comes into contact with pollen or stigma and which make the flower asymmetric. The efficient mechanism of the sage has been described in Chapter 2.

*Female Efficiency*. Wastage can be considered to be primitive. Many separate petals, a lot of pollen and large numbers of stamens are typical of the less specialised flowers. Another important item to look at is the pistil, the female organ of the flower. A group of separate pistils, as in the buttercup, is a primitive feature. In the more advanced flowers, the pistils fuse together to make what appears to be one. The give-away that the 'single pistil' is in fact a descendant of five pistils which have joined, lies in the presence of five compartments inside the ovary, which represent their ancient predecessors. Many flowers have tell-tale compartments which can be seen whan a mature ovary is cut across at about its half way point with a sharp knife or razor, e.g. iris, lily, tulip.

The fusion process often involves the ovaries without progressing as far as the stigmas; thus the style appears to bear a branched stigma (*Plate 27*). In fact the number of branches to the stigma is a sure indicator of the number of

**24** OLD-FASHIONED BEAUTY
The peony is a flower of the old style—symmetrically shaped (bisected on any radius, the two sides would look the same), lots of petals which are separate from each other, and without nectaries, myriads of stamens (male organs), several separate pistils (female organs). These are features of the primitive flower, which has been least modified from the original basic flower design (*Plate 16*) of millions of years ago.

Lots of flower parts, and copious pollen production by the many stamens of the peony, are unnecessary for guaranteed pollination—compare the sage flower which has a single tube of five joined petals, and only two stamens (*Colour Plate 5* and *Fig l*). These types of variation in structure of different flowers give important clues of plant relationships and family trees, reflected in their classification into families and orders. The peony belongs to family Paeoniace ie, one of the more primitive groups of flowering plants.

The round face with lots of petals and pronounced centre of pollen laden stamens makes the peony, particularly a double variety (*Plate 12*) a valuable focal flower.

ancestral pistils which have only incompletely joined. In the geranium, five pistils have fused to make one large five compartment ovary, but the stigmas remain separate. In the primrose the join is complete and there is one club-shaped stigma.

This fusion of several female organs to make one is more practical than it at first seems. If the stigmas of several ovaries are fused together as a club-shape or held close together by virtue of joined styles, one insect visit can easily scatter pollen to reach each ovary. However if the five stigmas were separate, it may well take five visits to dust pollen on each one, or at best would take a long extended visit. Separate pistils must therefore be considered primitive if one holds that there is a relationship between primitive flowers and efficiency of seed production. Some botanists do, some do not.

*Family Organisation*

Positioning of the flower parts is also important in the classification of flower families: whether the ovary is above or below the sepals, the placing of the stamens and so on, but those details will be by-passed in favour of looking briefly at the relationships of some common wild and cultivated flowers. Only a few classification notes have been included.

| |
|---|
| *Dicotyledons*—large group, net-veined leaves, flower parts in fours and fives or multiples of. |
| ORDER I    Many flowers have parts arranged in spirals rather than concentric circles, usually many stamens and pistils (rarely fused together). |

| | |
|---|---|
| *Ranunculaceae*—a family of old-fashioned flowers, often inefficient. | meadow rue (wind pollinated in some types), anemone (some species have nectar only partly concealed); buttercup, marsh marigold, Christmas rose, love-in-a-mist, traveller's joy and garden clematis are pollinated by a variety of insects; |

## 25 RELATIVE TO A ROSE

At first glance prunus blossom and roses seem poles apart, but their similar floral structure and type of fruit betray a closer relationship than one might expect. The botanical similarity of genera Rosa and Prunus is reflected in their both being in family Rosaceae, the most obvious distinguishing feature of which is the prominent receptacle or enlarged tip of the stalk which bears the flower parts.

|  |  |
|---|---|
|  | columbine, larkspur and monkshood are most specialised with long protected nectaries demanding large bees. |
| ORDER 2<br><br>*Cruciferae*—(cross-bearers) four petals in shape of | mustard, cabbage, water-cress, cauliflower, |

→

| | |
|---|---|
| cross, fewer stamens and pistils than Ranunculaceae, usually two short stamens and four long. | wallflower, honesty, candytuft, sea rocket, shepherd's purse—in many of these the sepals are stiff and hold petals in tube shape demanding pollination by long-tongued insects; dame's violet, some species of stocks pollinated by moths hence flowers large, light-coloured, evening-scented (see page 84). |
| ORDER 3<br><br>*Papilionaceae, Leguminosae*—pea family, often called trigger flowers. As names imply, petals often arranged in butterfly shape—a modification of the traditional all-round symmetrical flower plan. Pollination works in a trigger fashion (see page 91). | Mostly bee flowers, many interesting pollination mechanisms: clover - petals return to original position; kidney vetch, rest-harrow, lupin, bird's-foot trefoil—stigma acts like a piston pushing out pollen; Pea, bean, vetch, sweet pea, wisteria, broom, gorse, peanut. |
| ORDER 4<br><br>*Rosaceae*—Rose family, receptacle flat, bowl, or cup-shaped in middle so ovary often lower than petal bases, receptacle often enlarges to form fruit after fertilization (*Fig Q*). (Receptacle is top of flower stalk bearing the flower). | rose, raspberry, blackberry, apple, cherry, rowan, hawthorn, strawberry attract many sorts of insects with their nectar; meadow sweet, dog rose, agrimony do not produce nectar, but pollen for insects. |

| | |
|---|---|
| ORDER 5<br>*Umbelliferae*—parsley family, economy of material, lots of stalked flowers on one stem (advantages of which have been described on page 112), radiating like umbrella spokes (*Plate 26*). | parsley, carrot, parsnip, celery, fennel, Queen Anne's lace, hemlock, sea holly (flowers packed tightly together), earthnut and many others. Pollinated by many short-tongued insects; frequently petals of outer flowers of cluster are enlarged assymmetrically so that the community is edged by larged showy petals like an individual flower; only outer flowers are involved in this advertisement, inner ones concentrated on reproduction. |

| |
|---|
| ORDER 6 Flowers usually unisexual, the simple flowers are considered to be the result of more complex flowers having been reduced to their basics. Catkins. |

| | |
|---|---|
| *Betulaceae*— | birch, hornbeam, alder, hazel |
| *Fagaceae*— | oak, beech, sweet chestnut |

| |
|---|
| ORDER 7 Trees or shrubs, flowers in catkins, flowers unisexual. |

| | |
|---|---|
| *Salicaceae*— | willow—insect pollinated<br>poplar—wind pollinated |

| | |
|---|---|
| ORDER 8<br>*Scrophyulariaceae*—have become asymmetric, many are tubular. | snapdragon, foxglove, speedwell (veronica), eyebright, monkey-flower, slipperwort; open flowers pollinated by hover flies, rest by bees, in particular bumble-bees. |

→

| | |
|---|---|
| *Labiatae*—Mint family, have changed old symmetrical flower plan and petals have joined to form a tube with lip and throat; there is a reliable pollination device (see page 87) and economy of material (see page 89). Highly advanced, 'improved model' flowers. | catmint, sage (*29*), ground ivy, peppermint, thyme, lavender, bugle, dead-nettles, rosemary; most British members are bee flowers. |
| ORDER 9<br><br>*Compositae*—in this family what appears to be one flower is a cluster of tiny flowers grouped together for economy and efficiency (*Colour Plate 6*). | dandelion, chicory, chrysanthemum, dahlia are in one sub-family, as all flowers have petals joined in a strap shape and contain both sex organs. Thistles, hardheads, burdock, cornflower (neuter outer flowers) are in a second sub-family, as all flowers have petals joined in a tube which is long; therefore pollinated by bees and butterflies. Within same sub-family, a second group with outer flowers strap-like for advertisement (usually female) and inner flowers tubular and both sexes, usually: daisy, yarrow, wild sunflower, tansy, groundsel. |

→

**26** FROSTED SILHOUETTES

In the family Umbelliferae the characteristic grouping of a community of flowers on the stem is in an umbel; that is, the individual flower stems radiate out from the tip of the main stem like the ribs of an umbrella turned inside out. This arrangement is clearly visible on the upper seed-bearing stem in the picture. The basic umbrella shape is a simple umbel.

Most commonly members of this family have a compound umbel, in other words an umbel of umbels—or the handles of several umbrellas clasped together so that the umbrella sticks themselves make radiating umbrella spokes, thus an umbrella of umbrellas.

In *Fig C* a stem skeleton of a compound umbel and a lengthened single umbel have been used in an arrangement. Parsley, carrot, Queen-Anne's-lace and cow parsley are members of this family. Other arrangements of communities of flowers on the main stem are to be seen in *Fig E* and *Plates 14, 19.*

*Monocotyledons*—plants with leaves with parallel veins and flower parts ususally in threes, smaller group than Dicots.

| ORDER I | |
|---|---|
| *Liliaceae*—sepals and petals usually alike, flowers regular and symmetrical. | agapanthus, aloe, leek, onion, wood garlic, common fritillary, lilies, tulip, bluebell, hyacinth. |
| *Amaryllidaceae*—as above. | daffodil, snowdrop, narcissus. |
| *Iridaceae*—sepals and petals can be different. | iris, crocus, freesia, gladiolus. |

| ORDER 2 | |
|---|---|
| *Orchidaceae*—many weird pollination devices, irregular and asymmetric flowers. | spotted orchid (*Plate 14*), butterfly orchid. |

ORDER 3   Grasses and sedges—mostly pollinated by wind not insects, showy flower parts (sepals and petals missing), *Fig J*.

| *Gramineae*—*grasses*, one of largest families. | couch-grass, perennial rye-grass, false oat grass, sugar-cane, bamboo, wheat and other cultivated grains. |
|---|---|
| *Sedges*—distinguishable from grasses by solid, triangular stem (grass stem hollow), rushes not closely related as sepals and petals present as scales. | common cotton-grass, hairy sedge. |

There is little variation within families such as the Compositae and Orchidaceae, i.e. the genera and species do not differ greatly from the basic plan. In the more primitive families, however, such as the Ranunculaceae and Rosaceae the family characteristics can only be very generalised as there is so much variation between genera, and even within a species plants can look deceptively unrelated.

## Other Than Masses of Flowers

*Catkin Combinations.* Delicate light lime green hazel catkins, draping and fragile, make an airy outline, intermingled with tangled tusseled spikes, of winter willow-herb, contorted and dried and severe dark twig shapes, bare and dormant. At the core of the design, regular patterning of brown beech leaf ovals and silver honesty moons, make an unusual combination with tiny sprigs of light brown bracken tips. For the base, either delicate fresh spring leaves to bring out the tiny crimson clusters of female hazel flowers, or preserved bronzy magnolia leaves to emphasize the wintry browns.

There are many other catkins tinted lightly with colourful overtones; green and yellow pendulous catkins of hornbeam in early April, elm flowers tinged with purple, and the rare golden blaze of sweet chestnut in July. All of these look beautiful teamed with pinks or mauves—tradescantia trimmings, begonia leaves, mauve kale, red cabbage, or subtle purplish tones of dried cauliflower leaves—garden flowers are superfluous.

*Appetising Arrangements.* The praises of fruit and vegetables have already been sung (see page 103)—their incomparable bold bright shapes and textures lend themselves to every type of display. Heaped high and luscious they make a splendid Mass Arrangement, whether on their own or with suitable foliage and flowers.

In a low plain trough or a sleek boat of smooth carved wood such an arrangement automatically fits in with a starkly contemporary room. The same arrangement could look mellowed and inseparable from an antique setting if placed in a beautifully engraved silver pedestal vase or a punch-bowl. And again, in the warm wooden hues of a farmhouse-style kitchen, the very same fruit and vegetables could look rustic and part of the décor in a wicker basket. Massed

fruits are not just for harvest, but make adaptable material at all times and in all settings.

Strong positive forms and colours are needed if flowers are to be happily united with the less dainty fruits. For example, bright vibrant colours, intermingled with dark glossy leaves, are enough to make oranges, lemons and mandarins look exotic. Ideal are flowers like French and African marigolds frilled with gold, bright annual chrysanthemums, dazzling pot marigolds, rich dark and velvety purple pansies, warm hued zinnias, geometric gold and brown venidium and black-eyed susan, ursinia, dark centred amellus with deep purple-blue rays, orange, yellow and bronzey-red blanket-flowers, cape marigolds, polyanthus, intense crimson or purple edged with yellow, and cinerarias in every shade of puce to purple. Blue-purplish tints can be echoed with a few black large grapes among the citruses.

To compete or darken vivid brightness with an all too negative container would be disaster. Whiteness lightens: for example a contrasting antique white and gold porcelain basket (or jazzed up modern wickerwork), or a high stalked

**27** 'SIGHT AND SCENT ALIKE INSPIRE'
'Iris, crocus, amaryllis,
Tulips red as Nimrod's fire,
Roses, violets and lilies
Sight and scent alike inspire.'     *Kushhal Khan Khatak.*

Iris, crocus (*Plate 17*), amaryllis (now often listed as hippeastrum), tulips and all lilies not only share appeal of sight and scent. They all belong to the same order—Liliiflorae, within the group of monocotyledons in plant classification.

In the photograph visible characteristics of monocots (the usual abbreviation) are long slender leaves (parallel veined), and the flower parts are in threes—that is, one circle of parts is either three or six. For example, the opened out tulip has three sepals (which resemble petals), three petals, six stamens (male organs, in two rings of three) and a stigma with three points, showing it is made of three joined pistils (female organs). (For explanations of flower parts see *Fig E.*)

Characteristics of the order Liliiflorae are that the sepals and petals are usually alike—differences between members of the order are reflected by its subdivision into three families: Liliaceae, Amaryllidaceae and Iridaceae. The solitary tulip belongs to the former family, amaryllis to Amaryllidaceae, and iris and freesia to Iridaceae.

In the iris (*Plate 8*), the petal-like sepals and petals stick out and up, while the end of the style (part of the female pistil) is like a petal, enclosing a stamen between itself and the sepal. The two thus form a long petal tube shape.

One can see the guide lines in the freesias, amaryllis and iris. Advertisement of pollen whereabouts by contrast of pollen to petals is visible in the pink and white tulip with purplish pollen.

bowl basically white with formal pattern of pure cobalt blue, salmon reds and orange.

*Old World Designs.* One has only to open a book of reproductions or visit an art gallery to appreciate the inspiration afforded by massed flower and fruit arrangements through the centuries. Not only were tulips, irises, roses and sunflowers massed in circular or triangular display, but also flimsy catkins and grasses and meandering sprays of grapevine leaves. Fruits were often included— in 'Flowerpiece' by Jan Davidsz de Heem, fruits are strewn about the base of the vase, some of them with sections enticingly removed or even nibbled, all adding interest and variety to the design! He included items of zoological interest as well: butterflies, a bee, dragonfly, and caterpillar fly and wriggle over the arrangement. For the unsqueamish the old Dutch idea is fun to copy; insects, once dead, dry out very quickly without odour and retain their shape (caution—the legs break off very easily once the body becomes brittle). Another useful idea is the use of the fascinating glimmer of water droplets on fruit and vase stand, catching the light and glinting like the blue glass vase.

Jan Davidsz de Heem's flowers were arranged in a large circle radiating from a narrow necked bulbous vase. A more delicate triangular arrangement was painted by another Dutchman, Balthasar van der Ast. Fruit tumbles out of an upturned basket about the foot of the vase of spring flowers and a few beautifully patterned shells have also been included. As well as the darting insects, there is a note of animal humour as a parrot perched on the upturned basket and a more than sinuous lizard exchange meaningful glances. Acquire a gaggle of Victorian stuffed birds and the possibilities are endless!

In earlier and modern times, the division between fruitful flower arrangements and still life compositions is a slim one. Foliage, usually of the grape, fruit and impeccably chosen accessories and objets d'art have been painted as 'Still Life' by Abraham Hendricksz van Beiferen (hams are probably best excluded in these hygiene conscious days), Jan Jansz van de Velde, Caravaggio-

**28** THE CLASSICAL TRIANGLE
Often the form of plants growing inspires a design. Here a climbing rose in full bloom makes the perfect asymmetric triangle so often used in Mass Arrangements. The arrangement of roses, delphiniums, lupins and foxglove in *Colour Plate 4* is based on the diagonal triangular shape.

'Bacchus' and many others. Less elegant and sumptuous but more modern are the still life arrangements of the Impressionists, for example Claude Monet. Art books hold a fund of ideas for the keen flower arranger.

*Airborne—Catkins and Grasses.* Gracefully bowing grasses and catkins were recognised centuries ago as ideal for edging a massed arrangement of spring flowers, and today although fashions have changed they are both still dependable as elegant additions in any design shape.

Can one really include grasses and catkins as flowers? They lack petals and do not always attract insects, yet have found their way into floral classification (see pages 83 and 121): the answer lies with pollination.

Attracting insect visitors is one way of transferring pollen from one flower to another. Simply dangling in the wind is another, only the mechanisms for dangling with maximum efficiency are far from unsophisticated. Just as the forms of insect-oriented flowers are geared to advertisement, insect guides, levers and booby traps, so are the wind-oriented flowers shaped for gusts and breezes. As one would expect, bright colours, nectar, spots, stripes, scent and even petals are absent, and the flower is small.

In wind-pollinated flowers the stamens are large and hang loosely and pendulously, exposed to the air and unmolested by petals, so that the way is clear for pollen dispersal, *Plate 30*. Pollen is light, dry and smooth so that it is easily freed from the stamen and borne high on the wind. Stigmas moulded for the wind-borne pollen are frequently feathery and large, dangling freely to present the biggest possible net for catchment and styles to raise the stigmas high are not needed. In short, the whole flower is the exact opposite to the insect pollinated design where stamens are compact and protected for maximum retention of

**29** ARCHES OF PUSSY WILLOW
Outward curving catkin twigs make a flimsy edging material to a Mass Arrangement or if placed curving inwards form a pretty frame for more flamboyant flowers. Here, a bunch of pussy willow has been used to make a hollow shape, tapering at the top, fuller towards the base. The tulips and leaves accentuate the framed space, rather than fill it, and continue the curved shape drawing the eye down to the focal point.

White silky pussies of early spring give way to a mass of pollen polka dots as male catkins mature. Twigs of male trees are lightly dusted with golden (left-hand arch) while trees bearing female catkins become studded with silvery green (right-hand arch).

Are catkins really flowers when they lack petals and the accustomed floral form? *Fig J* proves the point.

pollen from the wind, pollen is heavy, sticky and spiked, and stigmas are rather small, protected, and sticky and ridged.

The stature of the plant is also related to the pollination mechanism—many wind-pollinated trees flower in spring before the leaves appear so there are no leaves blockading in the freed pollen or the waiting stigmas in the catkins. Smaller plants such as grasses, plantains and sorrel bear their flowers on high stems well above the leaves (*Fig 30*).

Stamens produce copious amounts of pollen as the very nature of wind transport involves massive waste. Economy of pollen is impossible with this method of pollination. The incredible miracle of wind pollination is that it should work at all, when one considers the volume of air, the thousands of species casting their pollen to the wind (3,500 species of grasses alone), and the more than remote possibility that pollen of one species is caught by the stigma of a flower of the same species as opposed to one of the other 3,499. The amazing fact is proven by the abundance of grasses, plantains, and sorrels, and trees such as the pine, poplar, hazel, sweet chestnut and others. Wind pollination may appear wasteful of pollen but is highly economical on sepals and petals; above all it is certainly successful.

*Masses of Greenery?*

Foliage, ordinary and exotic, makes exciting line material and dynamic and unusual focal points. Given a variety of texture, shape, and colour, foliage alone can make anything from a riotously colourful mass display to an austere design of variations on green. If the variety of fresh greenery seems less than is practical for a Mass Arrangement, dried grasses and seed heads swell the bunch without looking out of place and add a new dimension of oatmeal muted tones and interesting sculptured and wrinkled textures to contrast with smooth leaf surfaces. Also dried foliage could be used—beech, ivy, bracken from the wild, or some of the cultivated silver foliages such as shrubby ragwort.

**30** and **J** (see page 135) BLOWING IN THE WIND
Flowers which rely on wind pollination have no need to be visually attractive—large bright petals, perfume, and nectar are redundant. Wind-oriented flowers are grouped together and hang pendulously. The male organs, stamens, hang free to expose their copious pollen. The female organs, the stigmas, are long and feathery as in grasses, or are erect and prominent as in poplars, to guarantee catching pollen from the breeze.

→

Apart from making a bunch of fresh leaves go further in an arrangement, the addition of seedheads and grasses can make an interesting attractive arrangement out of an otherwise rather monotonous boring one. Birch, beech, alder with winter catkins, fir and pine with small cones provide plenty of variety of shape, but provide no colourful inspiration at all, not even when a few sprays of autumn rowan are added, giving orange, yellow and russet brown and bunches of sparkling red berries. The rowan looks and acts like bull's eye targets and the overall effect is stark and uninteresting. Add oatmeal, cream, dark brown, touches of white, and a variety of pattern, form and texture in the shape of lots of differently shaped dried grasses from the solid cylindrical heads of marram to delicate cascades, rounded bladder campion seedheads, skeletonised bluebell fruits, patterned plantain and fluffy thistle heads, grey thistle leaves, heads of sorrel and burdock, and the display is fit for a banqueting table.

Ornamental indoor plants yield prunings of beautifully coloured leaves, every shade of lime green, blue-green, emerald green, gold, cream, white, grey, crimson, purples and browns. With patterned leaves like those of the aptly named peacock plant and zebra plant, one need never use a garden for a striking Mass Design.

*Pots and Pans.* In fact, what better for a flat-dweller—an arrangement of growing plants, complete with pots, as an extra in a more traditional arrangement, or an arrangement exclusively of potted plants. At one end of the scale one can make a Line Design arrangement with a single pot plant with additions of artistic container, driftwood, and material such as moss, pebbles, shells, seed heads, fungus, and lichen for camouflage or contrast, with perhaps a cut branch of

Comparison of wind and insect pollinated flowers (*Figs E, H, I* and *Colour Plate 5*) illustrates how structures initially very similar have gone their separate ways, depending on the conditions. Pussy willow catkins (previous Plate) differ from those of the poplar in that they are erect, and individual male flowers have fewer stamens; stigmas of female flowers are less prominently branched; and both sexes contain nectaries. The differences stem from the willow attracting insects rather than relying on wind.
C—a grass flower from a spike (*Plate 30*).
D—flowers of poplar, from male and female catkins.
*Flower Parts*
1—bracts (compare *Plate 19*); 2, 3—reduced sepals, petals; 4—ovary, 5—style and 6—stigma, making up the female pistil; 7—filament, 8—anther, together making the stamen (male).
a—male flowers; a'—female flowers.

# Wind Flowers

## C-Grass

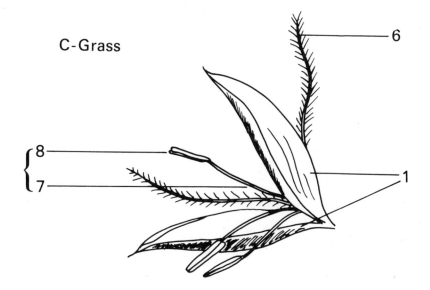

## D-Poplar

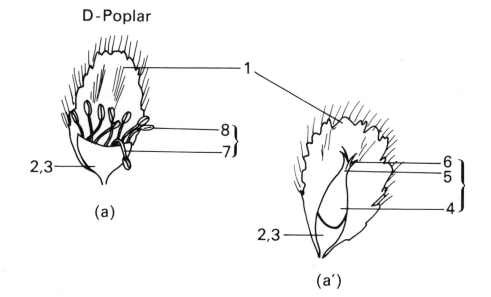

(a)

(a')

**31** BRIMMING BASKET

This Massed Arrangement of pots was not the result of extensive planning and financial outlay—it was made within the strict proviso of 'making do'. The poinsettia in flower, the one expensive and difficult indoor plant, the other plants are standard indoor varieties—total cost less than a pound with pots. All of the plants were growing separately in different parts of the house, not very successfully, in a dry centrally heated environment. It was therefore decided to plant them in a group to create a humid atmosphere around them.

The shopping basket was the only available container and was duly lined with thick plastic before propping the four pots, kept separate to allow for different watering requirements. The pots were tilted at angles to give the impression of leaves and stems radiating leaves or catkins (*Plate 51*). On medium to enormous scale, potted plants en masse look well in any large wide-mouthed container: a bowl, log-basket, preserving pans, old washing copper, footbath or specially made modern trough, standing high on a pedestal, low-set for smaller and upright plants, or suspended in a basket for trailing ivies, tradescantia, spider plant and any cascading flowers or foliage.

As with any Mass Design, the tapering and delicate forms such as asparagus fern, mother-in-law's tongue, ladder fern, aralia are ideal at the extremities of the arrangement. Tall plants such as poinsettia, rubber plant, amaryllis, gruyère cheese plant, stand high at the back, while focal forms and well defined leaves such as succulents, house leeks, begonia, bird's nest fern, stag's horn fern, African violet, cyclamen and cacti draw attention to the base of the design.

To give unity, the forms should radiate from the focal point, and in front, elegant leaves of spider plant, trailing ivy, tradescantia, Christmas cactus drape beautifully over the rim of a high standing container. Particularly while plants are becoming established, in the early stages of such an arrangement, any obvious design absences can be substituted with cut branches, twigs, trailing stems and leaf posies, depending on the scale of the design. It is very important that while planning such an arrangement the scale of the whole thing be kept firmly in mind so that the design is well balanced: a colossal focal plant would look ridiculous within a small overall shape.

Apart from the added effect of massed pot plants in a large design, as opposed to a military line of pots or plants isolated round the room like small islands, there is the beneficial humidity effect. Water in the air is vital to the survival of

from a central point. The spider plant, a very focal form, was best in a front position. The height of the poinsettia was offset by the slightly lower placed mass of ladder fern and the tall slim fronds of the variegated fern.

Although the selection of plants was random, there was a good contrast of leaf shapes and colours. Left-over foliage was used as a filler (on the right) to complete the round shape that was largely dictated by the basket. A cut trail of ivy and a catkin twig were used to break the rim and give the impression of spilling out of the basket. The bright red poinsettia was matched by low placed gleaming red and purple anemones held in individual bottles. The space in between the pots was filled with potting material and covered with stones and moss to hold moisture. The basket was tilted forward and propped with a stone to allow more of the plants to be visible.

By grouping several pot plants, one achieves a pleasing focal point to the room, very much healthier plants (the poinsettia remained in flower more than four months) and months of pleasure and variety, as different flowers in season are added for colour and interest among the plants.

both cut foliage and house plants (see Chapter 6). By placing all of the plants together, a high level of humidity, or water in the air, is held in pockets in between the leaves, and strategically placed moss and stones around the base of the arrangement help to retain water. Obviously pots cannot be immersed in water, so the best way of providing a water source for the atmosphere is to sink the pots in potting material, moss, oasis or some similar water retaining substance. These sorts of materials also keep the pots firmly held in any desired position. Special arrangement media such as Oasis or Florapack are particularly suitable if a few fresh flowers are to be included with the plants. Also sunken bottles and jars keep posies and branches well watered. More will be said on the mechanics involved in potted plant arrangements in Chapter 4.

*Bits and Pieces Make Plants.* Any excessively clumsy or excessively lazy gardener knows full well that healthy plants can sprout from battered remains of severed leaves, and scraggy pieces of obstinate dandelion root. Many succulents reproduce themselves at an almost alarming rate from leaves accidently broken off from the parent plant: a juicy leaf laid on the surface of some soil within a few weeks has a miniature shoot showing at the severed end and fine strands of roots attached, extending several millimetres down into the soil. Begonia can also be reproduced by means of a leaf cutting—either by splitting the edge of a leaf placed flat on the soil, by planting the leaf stalk, or by cutting the veins on the underside and placing on the soil surface.

The efficiency of root cuttings has reduced many a diligent gardener to his lowest ebb—a mere two inches of tenacious dandelion root left in the ground is sufficient to sprout once more into yet another dandelion. Blackberries spread by means of ordinary stems which bend over in magnificent arches. As the stem grows towards the soil the tip swells and tiny roots appear intermingled with leaves. Shoots develop at the bases of these leaves and once rooted break away from the parent and start life as a new individual. Carnations, chrysanthemums, dahlias, lupins, delphiniums can all be grown from root or stem cuttings.

Many indoor plants produce miniature plantlets which later detach from the parent. Bryophyllum has fleshy leaves with serrated edges; in the indentations bulbous swellings appear which are soon discernible as small leaves below which dangle tiny roots. Once these are an inch long the plantlets fall to the base of the parent. Spider plant sends out long stems of white flowers at the extremities of which miniature plants develop, which later start life independently.

In all of these examples the plants have reproduced from small pieces of themselves—called vegetative propagation. This method of reproduction has the advantages of speed and reliability. It neither depends on time-consuming flower production nor upon the risky process of pollination. Also mechanical damage to the plant, far from being deleterious, is turned to positive advantage as has been seen in the case of leaf cutting of succulents.

To balance the advantages there are disadvantages; there is no variation in the young plant—it is an exact replica of its single parent. The nurseryman turns this to his own advantage and can rely on producing a pink carnation from a cutting taken from a pink parent. Reliable propagation of plants by means of cuttings is not a result of modern investigation; two thousand years ago the Greeks were using the same method.

Although many of the offspring plants are produced on the end of long stems and suckers as described in the blackberry and the spider plant, they still become rooted very close to the parent plant. This is a disadvantage in that the new and old plants compete for water, minerals and sunlight. No new areas are colonised by means of vegetative propagation.

This type of reproduction, which is asexual, is not exclusive to the higher plants (flowering plants). Some mosses can also reproduce from parts of themselves, and the lowliest plants, such as the green slimy strands of algae (see *Colour Plate 1*) one sees in ponds and ditches, form new strands from broken pieces.

Although man has known for so long about the regenerative capacity of plants, it is only in the past thirty years that the nature of the mechanism has begun to be understood. Chemical compounds--plant hormones—are responsible for stimulating growth of roots; the hormones act as messengers carrying 'orders' from one part of the plant to another. It is also known that another compound, vitamin B, is concerned in the process. This vitamin is present in some green parts of the plant and may be transported from there to the site of root growth. Vitamin B has also been shown to be present in some seeds in which it may affect growth of the embryo. One thing is certain: the relationship of plant hormones and other active chemicals to each other, to the leaves, stems, and roots is exceedingly complicated.

*Wayward Greenery.* Mechanical damage such as broken stems and detached leaves is only one of the many environmental influences which steer the growth and form of a plant. Trees growing on exposed coasts are weird, lop-sided and malformed ghosts of their inland sheltered counterparts; by the sea, driving winds are continually moulding the plant shape. Availability of light also prescribes the shape of a plant—where light is one-sided shoots and leaves twist and become aligned to it (this happens to plants on window-sills if they are not regularly turned round). Where there is little light available, stems elongate rapidly upwards to reach it and the result is an elongated plant with extra long leaf stalks and yellowed leaves.

Other vital conditions to any plant are water, minerals and temperature and so on, which all affect its pattern of growth. Since the environment varies from one area to another, within one area, even within one field, or up the side of one hill, the size and shape of the leaves and the overall appearance of one species of plant will vary accordingly, however slightly. Thus there is no standard infallible pattern of leaves, stems or roots for any species which could be used to classify plants. It is for this reason that it is the form of the flower and fruit which determine plant grouping, while the general appearance of any family is only stipulated in very vague terms. Two leaves from the same plant can look as if they come from completely unrelated species; fortunately flowers and fruits are more constant and predictable.

CHAPTER FOUR

# Containers and Mechanics

*Container Choice*

*Pattern Versus Plain.* A plain container is easier to deal with than a patterned one, otherwise one is continually having to watch for the arrangement becoming confused with the pattern. In some cases one can successfully combine patterns of flowers and container, each enhancing the other as in *Plate 32*. Container and plant life can be related by means of a common feature, for example real oak leaves in the arrangement linking with painted oak leaves on the container. A patterned container has a limited use, however, and can be a positive restriction.

*Shapes and Colours.* The size of the container is also vital to a successful design. Neither plant life nor container should dominate; there should be a feeling of harmony between the two.

   If a very wide-mouthed container is used for a Line Design it should be fairly shallow so that a single bloom or cluster is not overshadowed and obscured by the rim. Very simple containers are usually used in Ikebana, allowing every item to be visible and, by sheer simplicity, giving accent to the colour and form of the plants used. If there are several containers to choose from, the choice should depend on the colours in the arrangement so that the two form a pleasing whole as opposed to two separate identities. Also it must not be forgotten that the plant-container unit should look pleasing as a whole within the surroundings by means of matching or toning with the overall décor or accessories.

   White, grey and black look well in a room of any colour scheme. A white container emphasises the freshness of the floral colours, but also seems to absorb some of the colour. Greys are very quiet and restful, while black makes a striking contrast to brightly coloured flowers, and a dramatic effect with white alone. Black can also enrich subtle dark colours but the latter combination should not

be placed against a dark background for obvious reasons. A green container is a good standby, guaranteed to match or tone with any fresh foliage. Even in the absence of foliage, green looks very natural. Deep green has the added advantage of contrast.

Picking up a colour in the plant material with the container has a great unifying effect as in *Colour Plate 3*. Similarly the shape of the container can relate to the type of line; for example, a predominantly spiky line looks appropriate in a straight sided container, smooth sleek shapes look well together (*Fig D*), and round shapes happily unite (*Plate 15*). A slender bottle demands an elongated and smooth curved line; feathery, flowing lines unite beautifully with an oval or curve.

On the other hand, for effect one might want a dramatic contrast of line; whatever the container, it should be planned rather than picked from a heap at random. Linear design is very inspirational, one shape leads to another, one colour leads to another; and from an initial suggestion of a line a harmonious variation can be evolved.

A shallow container does not have to be a bowl or trough. A wooden bread board, or slice of barked tree trunk, or hollow or bark replies beautifully to woodland flowers, to soft autumn hues of dried material, to the brighter berries and fruits, or to a single element of driftwood in a fresh decoration. Many containers and household items lend themselves to improvisation.

In the following pages container suggestions are grouped according to whether shallow or tall. This is followed by the mechanics of fixing material into these two types of container and comments on hiding the mechanics from view.

Rectangular baking tins, particularly old or once rusty, take on new lease of life when painted with enamel inside and out. Alternatively the outside edge can be neatly disguised with a narrow length of plain material or ribbon, or heavy paper quickly pinned or stuck with plasticine—these add an interesting texture to the design. Also smooth or crinkled kitchen foil, or in keeping with a particular room, an off-cut of curtain or cushion material, or matching Fablon.

**32** (and jacket) AN UNUSUAL PATTERNED CONTAINER
The dominant colour of this quaint junk shop candlestick is a pure light blue painted on the stem and base. The pattern is echoed by round-faced flowers: light pink rose buds, still with petals furled tight, accentuating their circular form, and white shasta daisies with yellowish tints at their centres. The blue of the container is picked up with blue spikes of speedwell. The form of the design centres round the form of the container. The handle is balanced by a single rose floating at the base of the candlestick. The tall spikes of speedwell echo the stalk of the candlestick, without making an over-formalised outline.

| IMPROVISED CONTAINER IDEAS—SHALLOW | |
| --- | --- |
| *From outside—* | |
| seed tray from garden<br>trug from garden<br>shells, whole or broken | lined with plastic.<br>lined.<br>use of broken whelk<br>described on page 110. |
| dried fungus<br>flat stone<br>wooden slice | hollowed out.<br>in *Fig A*.<br>most effective if bark still<br>attached and polished with<br>furniture or shoe polish,<br>after sanding. |
| hollow log or curled bark | in *Plates 9 and 10*—a<br>natural trough effect. |
| *From the kitchen—* | |
| casserole dishes or lids | in *Fig B and Colour Plate 4*,<br>earthenware, stoneware,<br>china, or enamel. |
| cane bread basket (used<br>in *Plate 47*)<br>wooden pastry or cheese<br>board. | good for reflecting natural<br>oatmeal colours of dried<br>material or drift wood, |
| chopping board<br>cake base | in *Plate 35*. |
| baby's cast off eggcup<br>cum plate | built in asymmetry. |
| plates, large or small<br>wooden bowl | in *Fig G and Plate 33*.<br>reflects wood and dried<br>material. |
| frying pans or saucepans,<br>ancient and modern | for modern example, see<br>*Colour Plate 3*, ancient<br>copper has an inimitable<br>warm glow, ideal for<br>autumn colours. |
| preserving pans | for large growing<br>arrangement, (*Plate 44*). |
| glass pie dishes<br>oval meat dish<br>hors d'oeuvres platters | *Plate 38.*<br>*Plate 48 and Fig T.* |

| | |
|---|---|
| tin trays | camouflaged with foil to give watery effect, moss, a sea of small stones or shells. |
| gravy boat and ladle | an unusual pair. |
| baking tins | in *Fig L*, ideal trough for orientally styled arrangements with large expanses of water; for camouflage see below. |
| shopping basket | lined with plastic, ideal for mass arrangement of potted plants (*Plate 31*). |
| *From the dustbin*— | |
| ham and sardine tins | painted, or covered with laminated cloth (*Fig C*). |
| *From living room*— | |
| fruit bowl | |
| ashtray | in *Plates 22 and 37*, copper and brass have a warm glow, whereas pewter or glass are cool contrasts to plants. Pewter helps keep water clean. |
| bulb bowl | for cut or growing arrangements, (*Plate 51*). |
| *Oddments from auction rooms, junk shops and antique shops*— | |
| knife tray | |
| dinner plates | |
| soup bowls, shallow or stalked | |
| soup tureens | good for planted arrangements. |
| old pearly glass light bowls | used as a bowl, or suspended containing hanging foliage and flowers. |

→

| brass or copper trays | often beautifully patterned, art nouveau or oriental. |
|---|---|
| warming pan | makes an interesting wall arrangement. |
| sugar shovel<br>bowls made from gourds | native art examples and junk shop oddments shown in (*Plate 34*). |

*Unusual Fruit Containers*. Other possibilities are fruit shells, which demand a little preliminary effort prior to use, but once in a while make a change. Fruit salad looks most attractive heaped into a gouged out pineapple shell, with its greenery still attached, and perhaps topped with meringue for a very special occasion— but why not use the skin for a few more days more with flowers and leaves tumbling out of it?

On a less festive occasion, an empty grapefruit skin neatly cut with a straight edge, or wavy, or to be outrageous zig-zagged, lined with bright daisies makes an amusing piece on its own or as a focal point within a modernistic design. The juice of fruits is acid, so fruit shells should be lined before use.

A more lasting base can be concocted from two half coconut shells set at 100 to 120 degrees to each other with their openings facing; their bottom edges could touch in order to portray them as one unit. They can be fixed with plasticine or glue to a rough flat piece of wood (echoing the texture of the coconut), or sturdy cardboard, preferably cut in a round or oval shape. The well rounded form of the coconut lends itself to rounded plant shapes and curved lines or creeping vines. The shape can be reflected in minature with something like a few well placed walnut shells round the base, giving harmony of forms. Gourds and citrus fruits would also look in keeping in this context. Spare coconut shells hanging from trees are encouragement for wild birds.

**33** SPRING IN A SALAD DISH
A curved salad plate makes a smooth outline for a few spring flower heads. The shape of the main perpendicular piece of latticed prickly pear skeleton (a holiday souvenir from a beach) was echoed with the hyacinth leaves, the tips of which were smoothed back the wrong way to mimic the curling tip. Hyacinth heads made a patterned transition between severe straight lines and round focal flowers. The tulip petals were gently smoothed back to show the centre.

Fresh materials were held in place with Oasis in a small container hidden behind a piece of smooth bark. The prickly pear skeleton was supported by plasticine and kept dry.

*Tall Containers.* Tall containers, particularly straight sided ones, can be very difficult to unite happily with a line design. Mass designs, on the other hand, can be created to fit the container without much difficulty. Tall square slab vases and cylinders usually present most problems. These have been expertly overcome in *Plate 39*. Tapered and flared shapes are easy to follow; for example, single or double gourd shapes, bottles, globular or trumpet shapes.

| IMPROVISED TALL CONTAINERS | |
|---|---|
| *Second-hand miscellany—* single or grouped candlesticks | a variety in *Plate 34*. arrangements can be made in florist's candlecup with or without candle, or around the base; beware of putting water in unlined brass bases, otherwise a more or less permanent water line results; used in *Plate 32 and Colour Plate 7.* |
| woven staw cylinders pot pourri baskets compote dishes old decanters stone cider jar old 'witchy' boiling pots | as suspended over open fires in bygone days. |
| *Commercial containers—* well shaped wine bottles | tapered or contoured rather than the ordinary 'bottle-neck' shape. In *Fig U* a bottle has been used for a Christmas arrangement. |
| fruit squash bottles dimpled bottles elegant cosmetic bottles | e.g. whisky. |
| straight sided jars | e.g. chutney. |
| hexagonal jars | e.g. honey. |
| large chemical bottles | also ideal for indoor gardens, once nature of |

## 34 UNUSUAL CONTAINERS FROM UNUSUAL SOURCES

It is not necessary to spend lots of money on vases and hand thrown pottery in order to have a good range of containers, although of course such luxuries are very useful. One can buy a container of any shape, size or vintage from a junk shop or in a part lot at an auction sale very cheaply. One of a pair fetches a ridiculously low price (such as a candlestick) and occasionally one comes across something exotic and unique quite by accident. The individuality of an unusual container can so often trigger off a beautiful design.

Against the white background are unusual containers from far-away places. The pair of African clay figures demand related but not twin designs, one is a hollow vase, the other supports a shallow bowl; the round shapes are carved-out gourds; the patterned cylinder is made of straw, and the others are wooden.

The containers against the dark background are more conventional finds—the tarnished silver tea box (it cost next to nothing as its lid was missing) will be transformed once energetically polished and filled with bright flowers.

| | |
|---|---|
| cylinders | previous contents checked and thoroughly removed. modified and painted washing-up fluid containers, need weighting. |
| *From the dining-room—* | |
| coffee pot<br>tea pot | carefully placed lid, with or without flowers at base of arrangement adds interest to the design. |
| jug | lip and handle best featured. |
| modern stumpy tumblers | heavy based ones have the advantage of being very difficult to overbalance. |
| classically shaped wine glass | as long as it will not be top heavy. |
| brandy glass | has almost become usual vase, ideal for floating single bloom. |
| tankard | pewter can mark easily. |
| cane wine bottle holder<br><br>coal hod | water holding container inside. |
| *From outdoors—* | |
| watering can | sturdy garden variety or long spouted for indoor plants. |
| upended hollow log or bark | hiding old can retrieved from the dustbin. |

Pleasing and cheap containers can also be made from other curios: laquer-work tea boxes (often to be found slightly chipped at auction sales, but retrievable with shoe polish or enamel paint) plain or with attractive oriental designs, cigarette boxes (with smell of nicotine removed), miniature chests of drawers, snuff boxes, and confiture dishes. For a naturalistic arrangement, a group of

**35** EVEN THE CHOPPING BOARD

An ordinary kitchen chopping board makes a plain base for a complex sculpturing of a tree trunk relic. Potted coleus plants and a geranium cutting form a coloured focus and complete the triangular outline. The deep velvet texture and regular pattern of coleus intensify rough irregularities of wood, stones and lichen.

 An arrangement such as this is completed in a matter of minutes—the utility chopping board surface does not demand careful cushioning of sharp edges of stones nor protection from stray drops from the watering can.

textured and attractively coloured stones hiding a small water bottle is very eye catching (these should be placed on a protecting surface to avoid scratches).

Obviously where bottles or jars are used, thickened rims and screw threads should be hidden by foliage or flowers. Similarly unsightly broken hinges or lid props should not be apparent.

If there is time to spare, a permanent and artistic container can be made by attaching a shallow bowl shape onto the rim of a contoured bottle or upturned wine glass or goblet (obviously the components should be cheap or chipped as they are to be sacrificed), making a container suggestive of a fountain. The success of this improvisation depends very much on the choice of well balanced partners.


*Any Container.* A container can be given extra height and isolated from surrounding clutter by using a stand. Improvised stands can be made from tiles (ceramic and polystyrene, a piece of smoothed painted wood, an upturned tray or trough, a tea pot stand, or a heap of table mats given a smooth perpendicular edge with a length of insulating tape. The stand will, of course, become part of the overall composition and must be selected accordingly. Using stands also protects furniture. Many Ikebana designs incorporate stands.

In short almost anything can be used providing it has a pleasing shape; something as improbable as a bird cage or an old lantern frame can look stunning holding cascades of foliage, fruit or flowers. The most necessary facility for a wide choice of containers is not finance, but kleptomania for oddments and plenty of shelf space!


*Mechanics: Fixing to the Container*

Having chosen material and an appropriate container, one is faced with the problem of fixing it all securely together. One can only make a good design if one is confident of the mechanics of the arrangement.


*Props for Shallow Open Containers.* If one is arranging a few flowers in a very shallow open container, it is more than likely that much of the floor of the container will be visible and therefore means of supporting the design must be compact yet effective and above all invisible. Well tried means of fixing material in this type of container are:

| | |
|---|---|
| pinholder | for impaling medium and thick stems, and heavy material. |
| pinholder + wire netting ball | for heavy stems, diagonal or horizontal stems in particular, or for thin delicate stems which cannot fit over needles of pin holder. |
| plasticine + wire netting | as for pin holder and netting. |
| plasticine alone | for dry driftwood, twigs, branches, grasses. |
| small inner container of Oasis | for all but thick woody stemmed twigs, or excessively heavy or flimsy stems. |
| small inner container of wire netting. | Florapak is a good addition here for stem stability and water retention. Type of material dependent on amount of wire netting inserted through Florapak. |

*Pinholder.* A selection of round pinholders from miniature to large sizes are available from florists. O-Shaped ones for use with candles can also be obtained. Metal ones have the advantages of a heavy stable base and the brass pins are really sharp; however, some corrosion may occur. This can always be reduced somewhat by adding a pinch of borax to the water (this does not harm flowers).

For supporting large twigs and branches a large pinholder is vital. Plastic holders do not, of course, have the rust problem, but it is more difficult to impale tough stems on the pins. The type one uses is dependent on the plant material and one's personal preference.

All pinholders, even the large heavy-based metal ones, must be securely attached to the container. The holder and the container must be perfectly dry, before joining them with three or four small balls of plasticine, pressing these onto the underside of the holder and pressing it firmly into the desired position. Unless the container is very heavy indeed (and valuable), one should be able

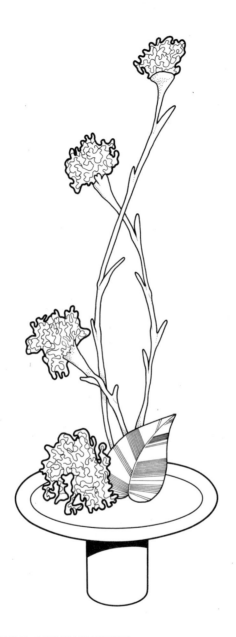

**K** JAPANESE FREE STYLE ARRANGEMENT
Three carnations make an elegant curve, balanced by a mass of nine carnation heads. The kenzan or pinholder holding the flowers in position is covered by the flower mass and the money plant leaf. The stalk of the container is an integral part of the design.

to pick it up by means of the holder. Time spent at this stage is well spent and avoids the heartache later when a lovely arrangement comes to grief due to bad mechanics as the final stem is added. Plasticine should not be used with silver containers.

There is no right or wrong way to use a pinholder, except that the stems at the back of the arrangement should go to the back of the holder to allow space for the rest. Similarly edge material should be placed at the edge of the pinholder. This also ensures that there is no disturbing crossing over of stems. Straight-forward placing of material is best achieved if stems making the outer form of the design are placed in position first, and the shorter stemmed central material is placed later. If some point of focus is decided on right at the beginning, stems will radiate naturally and not jostle together in a lattice: simplicity and elegant design are very dependent on the integrity of the line of each stem radiating from the focus.

Diagonal stems are very easily impaled by fixing one side of the stem and then gently pushing the stem at its base in the required direction, thus impaling the opposite side of the stem at an angle. Alternatively a small perpendicular piece of cut stem will hold a diagonal in position.

Thin stems can be propped up by small pieces of cut stem packed in between the surrounding pins. Very thin delicate stems can be held in a pin holder by means of a false stem—their own stem is inserted through the bore of a hollow stem such as a daffodil or even a straw.

*Pinholder and Wire Netting.* When unwieldy tough stems need support further up the stem than the pinholder can provide, or if the stems are to be held at extreme slants or horizontally, a ball of crumpled wire netting (two inch mesh) can be impaled on top of the pinholder, cut wire ends sticking upwards for further impaling stems or encircling them. The wire netting should be cut so that its dimensions are roughly twice the width and depth of the final required shape, and then crumpled so that the stems will just fit through the holes.

In the cases of delicate stems or light material, a ball of netting can be used as an extension of the holder, say, in front of the holder. The back of the ball can be impaled by the front pins. In order to further support delicate stems and for water retention Florapak can be enclosed in the ball of wire netting, provided it is not so crumbly that it will float out and be visible on the floor of the container.

**36** A SPLASH WITH FOUR HEADS OF FLOWERS
The strong horizontal line of the basket is echoed in bands of summer colour—clipped flag
leaves frame bright orange Peruvian lilies and pure white phlox. The orange and green add
a bright note of contrast to the phlox and the cream cane. Leaves and flower stems are held
firmly in Florapak and crushed wire netting.

*Plasticine and Wire Netting.* Wire netting on its own can be fixed to a container
with plasticine. Plasticine makes a fairly deep base in which the shaped crumpled
wire can be embedded, with raw ends sticking upwards for extra support.
Plasticine in conjunction with wire netting together make a particularly flexible
set-up, as the improvised holder can be made to any shape: long and thin, a
solid triangle or circle, a crescent, or even a hollow ring which could surround a
pin holder.

*Pools of Water*. All of the supports so far described require that the container is full of water if fresh material is being used. In the case of the pinholder, the pins must be submerged in order that the stems are thoroughly in contact with the water. Where it is not desirable that all of the materials in the design should be standing in water, as in the case of some driftwoods, a second container can be used inside the design container.

This hidden container can either enclose the wet part of the design so that the main container is dry, or vice versa. Considerations here are: does a sheet of shining water in the main container add to the design? Clear areas of water are an integral part of Japanese designs; apart from the visually relaxing qualities of water, evaporation from its surface keeps the air humid round the plants, thus reducing their water loss by transpiration, an important factor in preserving cut flowers (described in the following Chapter).

*Plasticine Alone*. Some types of driftwood, particularly the loose packed fibrous type such as derives from seaweed 'stems', absorb water which quickly seeps through their entirety, becoming slimy and brown. This can also happen with cork. If the dry texture and colour are desired for a particular effect, these materials must be kept quite dry in the arrangement.

Woods too hard to be spiked on pins, dried stems, coral, shells, rolling pebbles and fruits can be wedged firmly and cheaply with plasticine. Where the adhesive shows, it is advisable to choose a colour close to that of the container or the stem; otherwise, other putty-like substances such as Bostik are useful.

For particularly unwieldy pieces, stones wedged around the base keep things stable. For securing flimsy brittle stems, holes can be made in the plasticine first and the plasticine squeezed snug to the stem afterwards, or the stem can be pressed in by its very base—in tight corners, stems are easiest held by tweezers.

*Small Inner Containers*. As long as no heavy items are being used, a pinholder can be dispensed with and a small container of Oasis or Florapak can be used. The inner container must be firmly fixed to the main one with plasticine.

Examples of small, useful containers are pill bottles, fish paste jars, cosmetic jars, deep lids for very light flowers, plastic cartons such as yoghurt or cream pots which have the advantage of being cut down easily with scissors. Oasis holds its own shape and can simply be enclosed by a cupped shape of kitchen

foil to retain moisture. Small blocks of Oasis support surprisingly tall stems.

Oasis has the advantage of being stiff, and stems keep their exact position once pushed into it; however, for fresh arrangements, it must be watered regularly once a day, particularly in a heated room. Florapak has the advantage of being more retentive, but needs something to contain it as it is loose and crumbly.

Both Oasis and Florapak are bought in blocks and can be used wet or dry. Oasis can be cut with a knife straight off the block into the approximate shape of the container. The shape can then be trimmed and should be thoroughly soaked through before being squeezed into the container. One can test whether it has been waterlogged by piercing and checking there are no air bubbles. Off-cuts of Oasis can be packed into small containers such as egg-cups rather than thrown away.

Florapak is best dampened and then crunched up until it is pliable enough to fit into the container. Sturdy stems usually need the added support of wire netting enclosing the Florapak. It is a good idea to get the small container ready with the filler inside it prior to fixing it to the outer container. This avoids making the latter messy (thus contaminating the sheet of clear water) and wet (which would make adhesion between the plasticine and containers difficult).

In Mass Arrangements the floor of the container does not often show once the arrangement is complete, so Oasis and Florapak need not be enclosed in a

L WILD FLOWERS IN A KITCHEN CONTAINER

A baking tin masquerades as a trough under a coat of black enamel paint.

The sinuous curves of white textured driftwood demanded curving lines of plant material— the smooth curves of reedmace leaves (montbretia an alternative) were used, and the available wild flowers were arranged such that the flower heads formed a curve.

The tips of the three driftwood pieces and two leaves and container make a balanced outline of a triangle. The tips of the two small driftwoods pointing towards the observer make a line drawing the eye into the focus of the design. At the focus purplish tinted barbs of road-side burdock, red clover flowers and crimson and brownish red autumn leaves form the one point of weight in the design, pin-pointing the radiation of the stems. The line of purple hardheads follows the curve of the tall driftwood and reedmace leaf, and their paintbrush form links with that of the burdock and clover, giving the design a feeling of unity. Fluffy full blown meadow sweet makes a pretty scented filler and lightens the purple theme; here and there solid little ball-shaped buds add variety.

The black baking tin makes an ideal contrast of form and colour to curves and the startling white driftwood.

Mechanical note: seaweed driftwood becomes slimy when wet; therefore, these were fixed in plasticine in the base of the tin, and fresh flowers held in an inner container of Oasis.

small container unless one is introduced towards the back of the arrangement to give extra height to short stems. Oasis or Florapak and wire netting (which must be firmly secured to the sides of the container by bending single wire strands) can equally well be used to fill the entire shallow trough shape.

*Camouflage.* Whatever the means of mechanical support, it must be invisible (*Plate 37*) so that it does not interfere with the design and look clumsy. When the design is standing in water and the dense focal point material does not cover the pinholder or netting, lower leaves in the arrangement often lend themselves as cover-up without disturbing appearances.

In simple designs with few items, extra leaves can be sparingly introduced at the base, less sparingly for Mass Designs. Care must be taken when allowing leaves to dip into water—many types of leaves, particularly those of chrysanthemums, decay quickly when wet and pollute the water. Evergreens do not disintegrate or become slimy as quickly as other leaves and so make useful submerged camouflage. In Ikebana no leaves are allowed to dip in the water or touch the rim of the container.

Less bulky covering material, but just as effective is moss, which naturally grows in wet places. Moss, being of very fine texture is less likely to spoil the composition of the arrangement; it also has the advantage of lasting for long periods indoors. There are other camouflage possibilities: stones, shells, coral, bark, or wood (types unaffected by water), in fact anything which will fit the requirement and not look awkward in the overall design.

*Camouflage Scrutiny.* The study of one tiny patch of moss can be fascinating: at first sight a velvet green carpet, at the second myriads of miniature shoots with tiny leaves arranged around flimsy stems. Colours range from spring fresh lime green to dark holly or reddish tints. Their form can be that of a miniature palm

**37 CAMOUFLAGE IS VITAL!**
This little triangle of golden rose buds in a metallic grey ashtray would have been a pretty design but for lack of camouflage allowing gleaming brass pins to be seen. A container with a dipping lip like this one must be scrutinised carefully for any disturbing pieces of wire or pins. It is easy to get carried away with one's design and not to notice a piece of mechanics staring one in the face. An objective outsider will most probably notice the mechanical fault at first glance.

tree or a minute fern (*Plate 51*) complete with 'leaflets', others spread creeping branches over pebble boulders or stand upright free and blowing like pampas grass; may have miniscule plants packed so tightly together that one individual cannot be picked out singly with the fingers. Mosses present the diverse plant world all over again, only on miniature scale. An opportunity not to be missed is to peer down a binocular microscope (one with two eyepieces giving a three dimensional effect) at a 'field' of different mosses—for a glance one sees into another world. . . .

In the world of 300 million years ago in Carboniferous fern forests there were primitive ancestral mosses growing, dying and decaying, some leaving a few fossils behind them. The mosses represent a stage in the plant effort to leave the ancestral protective home of water and emerge onto dry land. Contrasting to the seaweed stage doomed to imprisonment in water, mosses do not rely on water to support them; the definite leaves and stems (also contrasting to the structure of seaweeds) contain some supporting tissue. However, the ancestral mosses lacked true definite roots, the proper water carrying system and the sturdy and extensive supporting structures possessed by the ferns and their kind, therefore they were limited to a miniature damp existence for ever.

There are 14,000 different kinds (or species) of mosses, a figure which is less astounding once one has scrutinised several mosses. Before looking at the moss plant itself, there is its habitat to consider; there is a wide range, from very wet boggy ground to slightly damp crevices almost without soil. Growing up from the main moss plants there is often a prominent long thin stalk bearing a knob which varies in size, shape and colour according to the moss type. This knob is in fact a special capsule containing spores which will be released when they are ripe and weather conditions favourable to dispersal.

There is infinite variation in the shape of the leaves—pointed, oblong, narrow, wide, smooth-edged, serrated, to name but a few. Leaves are sometimes hairy, or have a thickened middle line along the leaf length. Their arrangement may be spiral around the main stem or in separate rings, or leaves may be organised into close packed groups which look at first glance like a single leaf. These finer details require a microscope or powerful magnifying lens and time and patience to separate leaf from leaf, one by one, using two pins, but there are as many unexpected discoveries to be made with an observant naked eye.

*Supports for Tall Containers.* Narrow Necks: This type of container does not usually need mechanical aids for keeping plant material in place. The arrangement will probably be self supporting. Often it is a good idea to tie stems together before putting them through the narrow opening; this keeps them in set positions relative to each other. With the narrow neck and no water retaining filler, the water level can change alarmingly quickly—bottle shapes should be topped up with water more often than other containers.

Where there is not enough bulk of stems to fill the opening, pieces of short stem and plasticine can wedge the design stems apart. Alternatively the stems can be held together with wire, the two loose ends hooking over the back facing rim of the container. If a filler is vital, Florapak is the best choice as it can be easily fed in to the container through the narrow neck—although it will not be so easily removed!

The Japanese use pieces of wood or stick wedged at right angles to each other across the mouth of the container, dividing it into four small spaces. Another method uses a Y-shaped piece of split wood or pruned twig (*Plate 39*). This is ideal for a solitary stem. Rules of Ikebana have it that the stems in the arrangement cannot rest on the sides of the container. Similar in principle, but more mundane, an ordinary clip clothes peg wedged in the neck of the container holds stems well.

If one is using a tall bottle for a broader design, such as a Hogarth curve, a wide-mouthed container must be fitted into the bottle's mouth so that stems can be placed at diagonals. Either a candlecup can be used (*Colour Plate 7*) (a small bowl on a foot which is inserted in the candle space or bottle neck), or the original cork or lid from the bottle can be glued firmly on to a suitably sized light plastic bowl. A pinholder or piece of Oasis firmly holds stems set at oblique angles. Candle cups are designed to still hold a candle if required, in a bottle or a candlestick; a candle can look very elegant incorporated in the design.

Tall Wide-Mouthed Containers: When few flowers are used, not all of the mouth will be filled with stems; this must be borne in mind when deciding upon the method of fixing the arrangement. Also, the type of holding device depends very much on whether the container is made of glass. If a glass container is used, particularly a transparent or light coloured one, volumes of wire netting, Oasis and Florapak filling the container will demand massive awkward looking camouflage. The following ideas can be used for glass containers with fairly wide mouths.

Tell-tale Glass: If the flowers have a good long drink in a deep container of water prior to arranging, the stems need not reach right down to the bottom of the vase or glass. A column of perpendicular stems has overpowered many a beautiful glass contour.

If ferns or evergreens, such as cypress or box, can be successfully incorporated into the overall design, these can rest across the rim of the glass, just skimming the water surface thus forming a network through which stems can be placed. For extra stability, one or two narrow U-shaped pieces of wire can clip a leaf or two onto the rim; even a widened paper clip would do, so long as it is covered in the final design.

Avoiding the introduction of lots of foliage, strands of clear Sellotape can be latticed, sticky side down, across the mouth of the dry container, sticking on to the outside of the rim. This method is only useful for delicate plants and is certainly not transportable.

For sturdier stems, a length of thick wire can be looped round the stems and the free ends twisted for tightness and strength, then bent in a hook over the rim of the container. A more sophisticated version of the same idea is the T-shaped holder. This can be made from a scrap of sheet metal such as sheet aluminium. The metal should be cut (with metal cutters) in a T-shape and the top arms of the T bent round until they nearly meet in a circle. The remaining straight piece is then bent back on itself to form a hook which will hang

### 38 WILD FLOWER IMPRESSION

A summer arrangement in reverse: the tonal scale has been reversed for artistic effect. Wild flowers from the sand dunes and wayside are combined with driftwood and cork from the sea-shore and a kitchen container.

Strong curving driftwood shapes (seaweed driftwood, page 70) are held in place with discreet plasticine mounds. Montbretia foliage and flowers (a garden escape), tansy, marram grass, and scentless chamomile are secured with a pinholder, which has been carefully hidden with foliage as the container is transparent—a glass pie dish.

The ribbon-like driftwood was the basis of the design, the smooth outlines shared by the montbretia leaves. Straight spikes of marram contrast to the smooth curves, and bright orange montbretia flowers add colour and act as a filler. The eye is drawn to the point of radiation of the stems by a cluster of bright golden tansy. At the focal point itself, the clustered balls of tansy are echoed and amplified by four yellow centres of scentless chamomile; the ray 'petals' (really flowers, described in *Colour Plate* 6) have been removed.

The delicate foliage of tansy softens the rim of the container and its fussy outline links with that of the montbretia flowers. A pitted round piece of weathered cork placed opposite the plant material, linked via a driftwood base, balances the arrangement, adds textural interest and at the same time echoes the smoother round plant shapes. The colour scheme of the arrangement is white and cream, graded through yellow to bright orange, and green.

over the rim of the container, with the curved arms inside the glass ready to support the plants. For small amounts of material the two arms of the holder can be pushed to overlap each other, making a smaller circle for the stems. As always these mechanical devices should be meticulously hidden within the design.

If the whole mouth of the container is to be covered with a mass of flowers, and there are to be overhanging pieces, a double layer of wire netting, slightly squeezed in on itself to reduce the size of the holes, can be very satisfactory. The netting can be hooked over the rim by means of snag ends. Children's marbles, plain or coloured, stones, washed sea shells, or beads are useful for holding stems in place, wedging them firmly in an interesting base.

*Containing Secrets.* A container that is not transparent is very much easier for the novice and those with little time to spare. Stems and driftwood can be secured by the following means: Oasis, wire netting, alone or with Florapak, used in the same way as above. If cracked crockery is being used it is safest to line it with plastic or foil before filling with Oasis or Florapack. Plasticised insulating tape can mend small cracks and holes very successfully, and it is less cumbersome than plastic sheet or foil. If the outer container seems beyond salvaging, several small jars secreted inside can hold the water. Rush baskets can be water-proofed with plastic, foil, or an inner container. These can also be used to protect the inner surface of valuable containers; screwed newspaper placed inside silver ware or pewter prevents wire scratching. Better still, wire netting can be bought which has a hygienic plastic covering, also preventing any deposits from clinging to the wire in between uses.

Two-inch mesh should be cut twice the diameter of the container, omitting

**39** TRADITIONAL FIXTURE
This is a Japanese flower arrangement (Ikebana) in which stems have been fixed in position by means of a Japanese fork holder, basically a Y-shaped piece of wood in which stems can be wedged.

The arrangement is striking through its contrasts of line, colour, texture and forms. The sharp angles and dull surface of the branch contrast with the straight-sided glossy black vase. The yellow chrysanthemums are ideally contrasted with the bright black container, dull golden berries on the branch and at the vase base acting as a transition between the two extremes.

This dynamic arrangement by Mrs. Rehana Savul won first prize in a flower show in Pakistan.

the thick selvedge. This square can be squeezed into a cup shape, keeping the snag ends uppermost, for hooking over the rim and piercing and encircling wayward stems. Care taken in wedging the wire against the sides of the vase gives a tight fit. The whole container can be picked up by means of its wire netting filler if the latter has been packed in securely. Once you can do this, the mechanics of the arrangement are almost over. The netting should rise above the rim of the container if there is a mass of flowers to cover it, not when only a few flowers are being used.

One can buy at florists' special packs of plastic covered wire and suction stickers—these get over any worries of not being able to secure the wire firmly to the container. The long snakes of wire can be twisted into any shape, and are ideal for bending into someone's initials for an arrangement for a special personal occasion.


*Making Growing Arrangements*

A Line Design with only one growing plant was described in Chapter 2; the important point with making a pot into an arrangement is that it should not stand in water.

In a Mass Design most plants are happier left inside their own pot within the arrangement container, but the more hardy and less fussy ones can survive with roots enclosed in a plastic bag of water (for a limited time), or being planted in an awkward space between pots. If one has plants without pots, the container filler must be soil or potting material, otherwise water retentive peat, old bulb fibre, old Oasis or Florapak, or sand can surround the pots.

Pots are held at any angle by Oasis and Florapak, but need wedging with stones and wire in soil and the other materials. Decorative driftwood can be supported in the same way.

When planning the arrangement, the individual requirements of the plants must be taken into account, particularly if several are to be planted straight into the container and will receive the same amount of moisture. The type of pot holding the plants is important in this context—earthenware pots absorb water all over their surface, while plastic ones only take it in through their base. Plants to be kept drier than the rest are best in plastic pots.

It is important not to over-water such an arrangement—stones and moss over the surface help to hold moisture as well as enhancing the appearance. Occasional twigs or posies of flowers can be planted direct or in small bottles depending on the filler material.

*Mechanical Memoranda.* Tender stems bend easily over the rim of a vase if florist's wire is inserted up a short way—fibrous and woody stems are more difficult to deal with.

Knitting needles and skewers make ideal false stems for fruit and vegetables, and stick well in plasticine.

Skewers inserted up hollow stems keep dubious perpendiculars under control, and the circular eyelet is easily supported by plasticine. This has been done in *Fig C* with horsetail stems. Straightened hair pins are ideal for narrow bore stems.

Candles are easily and painlessly impaled on pinholders or in wire netting if warmed first.

Two stems can be joined, or a stem may be strengthened, with florist's tape.

Thorns are ideal for impaling awkward stems in position (surreptitiously, of course), or for suspending bunches of berries. In the absence of thorns, dressmaking pins can secure bunches on foreign stems and twigs.

In a Massed Arrangement, light grasses, dried foliage and light seed heads can sometimes be supported in position by neighbouring foliage and flowers, although care should be taken not to give an appearance of cluttering as a result. Light stems can also be held in the forks of sturdier branches with discreet pieces of plasticine.

Shells can be held in an upright position by filling with plasticine which is then wedged onto a piece of bent wire. This has been done in *Fig C*; also in this Figure, toadstools have been impaled on short pieces of bent wire.

There are also the artificial aids of old: bunched reeds, straws, peat, glass blocks with stem holes (very limiting), and metal mesh tops for rose bowls which work on more or less similar principles to modern versatile wire netting.

Small heavy items, such as pieces of lead and stones are useful for weighing down light containers.

Wood shaving flowers sold by gypsies at low prices are a bright and attractive investment. They look almost real if mounted on leafy stems, and add a very real splash of colour in winter.

**40** PLANTS COLONISE A NEW VOLCANIC ISLAND
In the centre of a sea-filled crater, possibly the one whose violent eruption wrecked the almost legendary city of Atlantis, a new volcano appeared in 196 B.C. A sequence of eruptions continuing in present times have thrown up islands formed by solidified lava— basalt. The old parts of the island have been harassed by the elements for over a thousand years, and have eroded into smaller more mellowed rocks and a gritty soil, which are visible in the photograph. Around the island shores, new and angular chunks of completely unweathered gleaming basalt defy any existence of life.

*History in Stone*

Chunks of rock, pebbles and stones present a fantastic variety of colours: opalescent, white, cream, yellow, orange, terracotta, beige, pink, mauve, greyish-blue, silvery, charcoal, green and black. Dormant colour emerges pure and beautiful under water or varnish. Some are plain, others are striped, mottled, veined, or spotted; in regular shapes, jagged masses, often almost hand-moulded. Almost every texture of the plant world is repeated in stones—smooth, rough, granular, shimmering and dull with a bloom.

Why are there so many different types of rock? Why are there different rocks in different localities—flint in Sussex, serpentine in Cornwall, ammonite fossils in Dorset, sea-urchin 'pound stones' in Gloucestershire limestone? Are rocks important to plants?

*Volcanoes and Soil.* When one picks up a stone, one is holding a fragment of the earth's history. Way back near the beginning of history the surface of the earth was molten and from this liquid all rocks have been ultimately derived, even if by a round-about route. Some of the molten mass solidified directly to granite and basalt—called igneous rocks as they have a molten or volcanic origin. The faster the molten lava cooled, the finer the grain of the resulting rock. Basalt is a dark coloured, fine-grained rock formed by rapid cooling. Lumps of basalt are visible in *Plate 40*. Cooling occurs slower underground, and consequently coarse-grained igneous rocks are formed at depth, later emerging on the surface due to erosion of overlying rock and earth movements.

Once the igneous rock is exposed to the elements its destruction begins—wind, rain, frost and waves beat it, and pound it, seeking out faults and cracks, breaking up the rock. Softer minerals give way first, harder ones follow. Eventually the rock loses its raw chunkiness, is mellowed and rounded; centuries of weather and the destructive agency of lichens form fine particles which go to make up soil. Frost is one of the chief weathering factors forming soil; also, water carrying carbon dioxide in solution makes a weak acid.

Life would not seem possible on ground that is still warm underfoot and composed of yellow and grey sulphurous powder and stones, but it is. On a soil that is still forming from volcanic lava and the elements, grass and flowers are growing, visible in the foreground.

Basalt does not occur very widely in Britain, but there are other more common types of volcanic rock which make an equally dramatic form and texture in a design; a table of their distribution is given on page 174.

The nature of rocks is thus more important in determining vegetation in an area than one might imagine—rock underlying soil affects drainage which in turn influences waterlogging, soil movement and nutriments. Soils over chalk and limestone are alkaline. Since the skeleton of the soil is derived from eroded rocks, the hardness of the rock is important because this largely determines particle size which is a vital factor in the water holding capacity of the soil.

Eroded rocks contribute mineral salts taken up by the roots of the plant. These do not on the whole influence the distribution of plant species (except in extreme cases such as lime and pure quartz sand—for composition of these, see below).

Different stages in the weathering of igneous rock are visible on the Kaumene Islands, in *Plate 40*. The dark islands one sees rising menacingly out of the sea have been thrown up by a sequence of eruptions separated by hundreds of years. The first appeared in 196 B.C., and subsequent islands have formed during eruptions between A.D. 726 and 1870. This century there have been four disturbances, the most recent upheaval causing an earthquake in 1956. The old rock is mellowed, almost 'ordinary' and reassuringly familiar, and fine particles and ash have formed a sort of dry stinking, sulphurous soil which is visible in the foreground of the picture. Life has already infiltrated the new land—small hardy plants can be seen growing (an interesting point to note is that the flowers are a sulphurous yellow).

The new rocks present a totally different aspect. Thrown up from a molten inferno only a few hundred years ago or less, the rocks are grotesquely contorted, faceted and sharp, gleaming crystalline—almost unreal, an awe inspring insight of the untamed violence of a raw earth—the past and the future.

*Build-up and Change.* Eroded particles of igneous rocks are carried to the sea by rivers and laid down as sediment. Gradually the sediment accumulates and the pressure from above forms the particles into sedimentary rock (see *Plate 7*). Layers of clay and mud under pressure form the familiar light grey shale. Sand particles—tiny grains of quartz—packed together become cemented by other minerals to form sandstone. In the sea, shell-covered animals and plants (primitive ones called diatoms) die and disintegrate, leaving their hard shells behind them. The shells, made of calcium carbonate (compound of calcium, carbon and oxygen) are pounded into a powder. The closely packed particles of calcium carbonate form yellow-grey limestone or white chalk. The laying down of the sediments takes a very long time; remains of plant and animal life become trapped between layers—it is ancient trapped remains that are today's fossils, such as sea-urchins and ammonites.

All through the history of the earth there have been great movements (see Table 1) which form mountain ranges, folding the sedimentary layers as they slide over each other and pile up. One can sometimes see this folding in exposed striated rocks. Below the mountain range there is a build up of heat and pressure, one of the outcomes of which is an outbreaking onto the earth's surface as a volcano, pouring out volcanic lava and ashes. Another outcome is that all the sedimentary and igneous rocks at the base of the range are subjected to an intense heat and pressure. These physical forces cause the old rocks to recrystallise and form new minerals. The changed igneous and sedimentary rocks are called metamorphic rocks. Metamorphosis involves a hardening of the rock, for example carbon under intense heat and pressure metamorphoses into diamond.

A table of the different types of rock, constituents and localities is given at the end of this chapter.

*What is the Difference between Minerals and Rocks?* So far, rocks have been talked of in general terms, but rocks are made up of solid chemical compounds—minerals. These compounds are built up out of two or more chemical elements: carbon, oxygen, silicon, calcium are examples of the chemical elements. There are approximately ninety natural elements in the earth's crust, most of which are contained in the 2,000 minerals reported so far. Different types of rock contain different types of minerals and elements; minerals containing copper are often blue or green, and others have typical colours (*Colour Plate 8*).

A few of the most common and best known minerals are listed below:

quartz— a mineral composed of the elements silicon and oxygen; transparent or white crystals several inches long can be found in granite; related to opal, chrysoprase, cornelian, onyx, agate—all contain silicon.

felspar— another mineral containing silicon, also potassium, aluminium; white or flesh coloured, in granite.

mica— also contains silicon, and aluminium often; the small glittering scales in granite, and also occurs as large crystals which can be separated into thin transparent plates.

→

TABLE 2

| ROCK | MADE OF: | FOUND IN: |
|---|---|---|
| *granite*— greyish, granular, crystalline | quartz, mica, felspar | Dartmoor, parts of Cornwall, parts of Scottish Highlands and Islands, parts of Wales, round coast of Ireland except in South. Calfornia, Massif Central, Brittany. |
| *basalt*— fine particles, dark | lava which has solidified on surface, containing silica, and usually iron and magnesium | Isles of Mull and Skye, parts of Southern Scotland, Farne Islands, Northumberland coast, parts of Northern England, North East Ireland, Lizard Head, Cornwall. Immense masses in Washington, Oregon, and Idaho. Auvergne, Vogels. |
| *shale*— light grey and laminated | mud or clay | Wales, most of Central and Southern Ireland, parts of Northern England and Midlands, Scottish lowlands, West Country. Widely distributed. Colorado, Utah, Germany. |
| *limestone*— dark grey, yellow or white depending on whether it was formed during the Carboniferous, Jurassic or Cretaceous. (see Table 1) | calcium carbonate derived from marine life | Wales, some southern uplands of Scotland and North East Scotland, Ireland, most of West Country, Northern England and Midlands. Cevennes, Tarn, Kentucky, Grand Canyon. |
| *sandstone*— yellow | small grains of quartz cemented together. | South East and South England, West Country, Midlands, North of England, Scottish Lowlands, South East Wales. Grand Canyon, Ardennes. |

| METAMORPHOSES TO: | WHICH IS: | FOUND IN: |
|---|---|---|
| *gneiss* | greenish-mineral grains of felspar, quartz, and a dark mineral arranged in roughly parallel lines. | Scottish Highlands and Islands, Northern Ireland. Areas of Canada. Northern Quebec, N.W. Territories, Switzerland, Austria. |
| The metamorphosis of basalt is very complex and a subject of research—it is rare in Britain, occurring in Highlands and Islands of Scotland and Northern Ireland. | | |
| *schists* + *slate* | dark grey and black minerals arranged in roughly parallel layers which split into thin irregular plates. | Highlands of Scotland, Southern Uplands of Scotland, Wales, Lake District, occasionally in South West England. Central Alps, Scandinavia, Ardennes. |
| *marble* | crystalline and granular, variable colour (white/ pink), patterned. | rare in U.K. France, Northern Italy. |
| *quartzite* | hard, quartz cemented together by silica. | Welsh Boarders, Midlands of England, North West Scotland. Grand Canyon, Alps, Scandinavia. |

iron pyrites—
fool's gold, beautiful gold crystals, very heavy, compound of iron and sulphur.

malachite—
bright green compound of copper, carbon and oxygen, used as decoration when polished.

topaz—
contains fluorine, aluminium, silicon and oxygen.

sapphire and ruby—
mineral containing aluminium and oxygen.

emerald and aquamarine—minerals of beryllium.

diamond—
metamorphosed carbon, hardest mineral known.

pumice—
perforated rock formed from solidified froth of lava.

Silicon minerals and quartz in particular are the most important minerals forming the rocks. Some beaches yield semi-precious stones such as garnet, and around some of the disused mines and quarries in Devon and Cornwall one can find dazzling pieces of iron pyrites and malachite, and many less colourful ores such as cassiterite (tin-stone). Chunky minerals and geometrically shaped crystals, fascinating pieces in their own right, make an eye-catching focus or camouflage, or when not in an arrangement, an unusual paperweight.

CHAPTER FIVE

# Flowers Through the Centuries

*Past, Present and Future*

Through the millions of years of plant history, land and weather conditions have been changing—large changes such as those outlined in Table 1, and small localised changes—a particularly dry season, an extended time of frost, a sudden scarcity of pollinating bumble-bees. Apart from plants produced asexually (by vegetative propagation) individuals of a species differ from each other—some bloom a little earlier than others, some are taller than others, or have thicker stems than others, and so on. Usually the differences are irrelevant; however, in a particularly dry season, or under some other changed condition, they may render some plants at an advantage over the others.

To take an example, individuals blooming and making seeds slightly early will have a marked advantage if the middle of the normal blooming season is a continual downpour of rain. The early flowers will have produced seeds, the late blooming flowers will not have the opportunity as flowers are battered, pollen washed away, and insect visitors deterred. The early flowers will leave behind the seeds which will produce more early flowers, the normal and late flowers will die and leave nothing. If this continued for many seasons the species will have few normal and late flowering individuals left: it will have changed into an early flowering species.

Thus changing conditions caused the species as a whole to change—the advantageous variation was there in the first place, only it was the exception rather than the rule. The changed environment caused the exception to become the rule—those with the advantage left progeny for the next generation, those without it did not. Changes are not sporadic; they are going on all the time, however slowly. This is the mechanism of evolution by natural selection, discovered and explained by Darwin and Wallace in 1858. The idea of a relationship between extinct life of the past and all present day species was not new;

Aristotle had envisaged a ladder of life of ever increasing complexity.

Since the discovery of the relationship of the living thing to its environment and the mechanism of evolution there have been vast changes. Up to the time of neolithic man the changing environment held the reins of evolution and the pattern of future species. Then man emerged—plundering, planting, building, grazing his animals, cutting down trees—man, the desert-maker. Unknowingly man and his activities were pulling at the reins. Then, with Darwin's discovery and the study of heredity, came knowledge of what was happening and how it was happening. Men actually saw the pattern of living things changing as a result of their activities—light coloured insects disappeared from communities in industrial areas, and the species were seen to change to a sombre soot brown to match man's new surroundings.

This century man has seized the reins and dictated change at a galloping pace. In the last two decades the difficulty of steering has gradually dawned, and man, the first creature to control his own environment, and now in possession of many of the facts, has a decision to make—which New World to create?


*The Distant Past—The East.* Before the emergence of neolithic man, the insects and the wind dictated much floral progeny; the bee's flight determined whether pollen from flower A fertilized ovules of flower B or C. Then man became an agriculturalist, artificially planting and transporting food plants, selecting plants for his own purposes rather than for the good of the species; plant life made the transition from the wild to the cultivated state.

In 2000 B.C., irrigation was practised in several civilisations. There was even artificial breeding of plants, limited, but nevertheless practised: the Assyrians and the Babylonians in 700 B.C. recognised two kinds of date palm, and artificially pollinated them. As civilisation extended and men migrated, the plants they used for food, clothing and medicine went with them. The Madonna lily owed its transport from southern to northern Europe to its medicinal value for the Roman legions.

Then as now, plants were useful to man, and also in common with modern man, flowers were symbolic and a source of pleasure: the ancient Egyptians enclosed rose buds in their tombs, the Persians cultivated beautiful gardens, Greek mythology was packed with idyllic gardens and floral garlands; many flowers and trees were dedicated to heathen gods, such as the laurel to Apollo, narcissus to Ceres, and the oak to Jupiter. The Romans practised topiary, and painted gardens of orange trees, firs, daisies, and sweet-scented jasmine on interior walls.

In the Far East, the Chinese were the first to make miniature gardens and it was from north-west China that the tree peony, flowering peach, chrysanthemum, and peony came to the gardens of Asia. Ornamental trees have always been favoured in China and Japan. After nearly 3,000 years of Chinese civilisation, the sensitivity for living things was at a peak. During the Tang Dynasty, about A.D. 800 (when Europe was dominated by Charlemagne), landscape, flower, and bird painting flourished in China. Paintings of this age and later can be seen today at the British Museum, London: 'Bamboo' (attributed to Wu Chen) and 'Bird on a Branch' (attributed to Emperor Hui Tsung). Seventeenth and eighteenth century pictures of China and Japan show elegant branches set on low tables as a natural feature of life and surroundings, as in the art of Ch'ên Hung-Shou in Cleveland, Ohio, and 'Moonlight Revelry at the Dozo Saganu' in Washington D.C. All of these capture the ancient sensitivity for the beauty of plant life and the balancing of natural forms and space.

Feeling for natural beauties was shared by the Japanese. Buddhism was introduced from China before A.D. 500 and the practice of Zen Buddhism brought out a rejection of the artificial, an outlook of simplicity and appreciation of nature unembellished. The Japanese, then as now, saw beauty in everyday things—a stone, a piece of weathered wood, an arched branch of a tree. The Japanese tea ceremony epitomizes this outlook—friends meet in quiet austere surroundings, drink a special kind of green tea according to rules of etiquette, and talk of mutual aesthetic interests. Restraint, discipline, and simplicity of outlook create the ability to escape from mundane troubles and enjoy beautiful things.

Withdrawal into natural beauty is an attitude manifested in Ikebana—The Arrangement of Living Plant Materials (usually loosely included as 'flowers'). Since early times the Japanese have shown a special interest and aptitude in arranging flowers. It is said that the Samurai, fighters of great ferocity, contemplated arrangements of branches and flowers, in order to restore peace and serenity to the mind after the horror of the battlefield. The art, in the form of floral offerings, appears to have been first associated with the Buddhist priests and was later developed in schools attended by noblemen and priests. It is recorded that the first rules on the arrangement of flowers for shrines were written in about the eleventh century. The bronze urns in the temples were filled with flowering shrubs, grasses, and flowers grouped around largish

branches. Appropriate styles of Ikebana were created for specific circumstances, for example the tea ceremony. The ancient sensitivity for balance and harmony can be seen today in modern Ikebana.

The Japanese art lacks fussiness and clutter; their simplicity could have been in Bacon's mind when he wrote 'Beauty is like a rich stone, best plain set'. The arrangement depends on line, and relationships of components, giving a feeling of motion, force, or static eloquence. Poetic ideas are often portrayed in arrangements—the seasons are interpreted in terms of sensitive displays of forceful spring growth, stark withering winter, and so on.

The state of mind while creating the arrangement is of the utmost importance, the handling of materials giving spiritual enlightenment, and the positioning of the materials being symbolic. There are various schools of Ikebana, which classically abide by rigorous rules of proportion and selection of material. For example the Sogetsu Ryu, School of the Grass Moon, adopts the following names: there are three basic lines in the arrangement, the shortest, 'hikae', which means literally 'earth'. 'Shin' is the longest element and means literally 'heaven', and 'soe', the middle element, stands for 'mankind'. The angles and directions at which these three elements are placed in relation to each other and the container are strictly bound by rules in the classical styles; 'jushi' or filler material can be included as well. Water is an important part of an arrangement, particularly in 'moribana' arrangements in low shallow containers.

Traditionally a flower arrangement was stood in a recess built in to one wall of a room which is largely empty of furniture, thus the beauty of the outside world—trees, shrubs, water, moss and flowers are brought inside. By the end of

**41** GARDEN HARMONY
'. . . green lawns and murmuring waters
Glad the eye and charm the ear, . . .
Shalamar with all its fountains
Cannot rival these cascades.' *Khushhal Khan Khatak.*

The poet was ranking Shalamar second to a Persian garden, but the present day Shalamar Gardens cannot fail to 'Glad the eye and charm the ear'.

Harmony of architecture and gardens was the essence of Japanese country villas and tea-houses. While the masterpiece of the Katsura Imperial Villa was being created in Japan, Shah-Jahan's reign in India saw similar creations—the Taj Mahal in the years between 1631 and 1645, and in 1642 of the Shalamar Garden, Lahore in Pakistan. This was an imitation of the original Shalamar Gardens of Kashmir and consisted of several terraces, with pavilions, summer-houses and fountains set in gardens, sweet with scented flowers.

the ninth century, this appreciation of natural beauty was part of Japanese culture and country villas with tea houses were built for the tea ceremony, and flower and moon-viewing. The architecture of the tea houses was simple; the focus of the interior was the flower arrangment in its recess or tokonoma, while the view outside was of beautifully landscaped gardens. During the fourteenth and fifteenth centuries the art of creating these impeccable surroundings, for the simple appreciation of flowers, summer evenings under a cool moon, and exhibitions of skills, was flourishing.

The peace of mind created by quiet expanses of water was not limited to flower arrangements, but extended to the garden landscapes. Idyllic gardens included ponds dotted with islands (*Colour Plate 9*) and stepping stones; side by side were miniature landscapes planned for an effect from a certain viewpoint, and severe geometric straight lines and shapes. The views were planned down to the last rock and seasonal detail. In the Katsura Imperial Villa, an unquestioned masterpiece, completed in 1658, the Pavilion for Enjoyment of Flowers is placed on an island, with unmatched views of spring cherry blossom, summer azaleas and autumn maples. In the words of a Japanese proverb: 'In the hum of the market there is money, but under the cherry tree is rest'. Ornamental trees were introduced from China, and the Japanese also bred their own native plants. By the seventeenth century there were Japanese varieties of azalea, camellia and tree peony.

While this beautiful fusion of architecture and landscape gardening was being completed in Kyoto, garden pavilions surrounded by scented flowers and trees, and quiet sheets of water, were being constructed in other parts of the East. The Emperor Shah-Jahan of Mogul India was building a classic of architectural landscape, the Taj Mahal. This was built in the years from 1631 to 1645. Shah-Jahan's years have been called 'the reign of marble', for he built many beautiful buildings set amidst gardens and pools with fountains. Not least was the Shalamar gardens, where paths cross still lakes with cascading fountains, and one can still sit in summer pavilions and withdraw to a quieter world (*Plate 41*). Not only were real flowers used as part of the setting of buildings, but stylised flowers and leaves appear all over Muslim mosaics and carved into screens and marble walls.

In the Orient, certain plants and animals have religious significance, in particular the lotus. The name was given to different plants by various religions and nationalities—the Egyptians, Greeks, Hindus, and Chinese. In Ikebana the lotus signifies purity as its flowers rise up above the mud and the water.

According to the Egyptians (who called a water-lily a lotus), God sat on a lotus above the mud; thus the flower's habitat had much to do with its symbolism. The significance of the lotus was also marked in India during the ninth century; it was the symbol of the universe, and a beautiful hand gesture, (or mudra) depicts the flower (called ala-padma) which figures prominently in Indian classical dancing, which has its basis in Hindu philosophy. Mohammed brought the lotus into Islam, and told of a lotus tree in the seventh heaven.

*The Recent Past—The West.* In the west flowers were not introduced from the north as they had been in the East, but came from the south. Until modern times all of the main plants of European gardens stemmed from Mediterranean countries. Two very critical species in cultivated plant history were Rosa sinensis and Dianthus sinensis from which modern roses and carnations were developed.

The European garden was quite different in concept and layout from the gardens of Asia. The plan was strictly geometric, but East and West shared the tranquillity created by lakes and ponds. Symmetry and formality can be seen in many British gardens; often European garden planners were imported, as for instance in the planning of Greenwich Park in London. Often, as in that park, the garden plan has not been kept up as trees and plants died and needed replacing; however, many formalised layouts and Tudor gardens have been preserved in historic palaces and stately homes. Viewing these in the summer can while away many happy afternoons. The natural landscape style is, however the most typical of English gardens.

Christianity involved many floral dedications and symbols: Lady's smock was dedicated to the Virgin Mary, the daisy to St. Margaret, while the evergreens, box, holly and ivy symbolize the resurrection, and palm stands for victory. Paintings reveal religious floral decoration—symmetrical pom-poms of flower heads topping shaped vases, as in Fra Angelico—'Madonna enthroned with child and four angels', and the ever-recurring lilies of the Annunciation. These were often held by the angel, but sometimes arranged in a balanced spray in a base typical of the period, as in 'Annunciation'—Simone Martini and a striking contrast—'The girlhood of Mary Virgin'—Dante Gabriel Rossetti.

Orange blossom, the symbol of virginity, bedecked brides in England during Victorian times, after its introduction from France, and the custom continues even in more recent times. Secular traditions and literature are steeped in floral symbolism. Ophelia in Hamlet prattled in her madness of 'rosemary, that's for remembrance' and 'pansies, that's for thoughts', and these traditional symbols remain with us. Rosemary, yew and cypress are still included in wreaths. According to the ancients, rosemary strengthens the memory, and was once used as a nerve tonic. As well as at funerals, rosemary was used at weddings, for in the language of flowers it meant 'fidelity in love'. Flower power was believed to exist from the earliest days: bunches of perfumed flowers and herbs were used to prevent plague, and the custom continues today in the presentation of nosegays to judges.

In the seventeenth century scientific studies were running side by side with the tradition and superstition, when it was discovered that pollen must reach the stigma before fertilization and seed formation could take place. The fact of sex in all plants (as opposed to the few with male and female plants) was not really recognised until the eighteenth century. The earliest recorded artificial cross of two closely related type of plants was that carried out in 1717 by Thomas Fairchild of London. He crossed a sweet william with a carnation and raised an offspring which was intermediate in appearance between the two.

While horticulturalists and scientists were taking a close look at sex in flowers, the ordinary British people were decorating their homes with picked nosegays and big masses of cut flowers and pot plants at windows and in summer fireplaces. The classic circular and triangular shaped masses of flowers, typical of the time in Europe were painted by Dutch and Flemish painters (a few are described on page 129), and much later by Cézanne ('Still life') and Van Gogh ('Sunflowers').

Industrialization gradually encroached on the landscape; for many people the beauties of flowers and trees were very distant and the Victorian age saw potted plants, domes of stuffed birds, and floral decoration and symbolism ad nauseam. The incredible conservatories and exotic glass houses of palms can be seen today

**42 'BLOSSOM BY BLOSSOM THE SPRING BEGINS'** *A. C. Swinburne*
Trees and water create peace and tranquillity. The two have been carefully matched by centuries of garden designers from the East (*Plate 41*) and the West. Not least was Claude Monet who created a beautiful water garden at Giverny which almost haunted him during his last twenty years, as he painted and repainted 'Water-lilies', 'The Japanese footbridge', 'The Water-lily pond' and many more (housed in Paris).

In the photograph, a quiet corner by a pond bursts into spring bloom, in the Cambridge Botanical Gardens, England. These gardens were founded in 1760 and the first tree was planted in 1831.

The distinctive branched form of blossom has been used as a basis for designs in *Fig D* and *Plate 15*.

in many localities in private and public gardens, such as Kew near London. The Victorian magnates created splendid gardens with European aspirations of symmetry and Baroque sculptures. Many gardens remained within the British style of a naturalistic landscape, such as the Cambridge Botanical Gardens, founded in 1760 and planted in the early nineteenth century (*Plate 42*).

Gardens that remained simple and functional throughout the centuries were the monastery gardens of Europe. In these, medicinal plants and herbs were grown, together with food plants. It was in one of these quiet unpretentious gardens that a discovery was made that has changed the course of modern civilisation, and could change the history of man. In the town of Brünn an unknown Augustinian monk, trained in mathematics and natural history, carried out some long and painstaking experiments on garden peas which he grew in a small garden plot at the monastery. Gregor Mendel published his proven laws of heredity in 1865, but his vital results were not recognised until 1900. It is tempting to surmise what the course of biology and history would have been if his discoveries had been recognised earlier and had come into the hands of Darwin. For there was one aspect of the evolutionary mechanism that Darwin could not satisfactorily explain, and it was this question that Mendel's work answered.

However, as it has always been through history, the significance of a great man's work was not realised until after the man was dead; at the end of the nineteenth century few biologists, even if they had known of the experiments, would admit that mathematics could explain a biological phenomenon. The application of Mendel's work on genetics had to wait for the future.

*The Present.* Against the background of centuries of selecting and breeding flowers for enjoyment in gardens and houses, as well as for biological investigation, flowers have been used as coy communication or a personal safeguard from disease. Where do flowers stand in the analysed and controlled world of the mid-twentieth century? Surprisingly, little has really changed. The Christian and heathen symbols are still with us, people still withdraw into gardens and parks which are now planned as part of the community, and, more than ever before, houses are beautified with floral arrangements.

But what of the flower arrangements of today? Yesterday's flower arrangements tended to be large masses of flowers and foliage arranged in beautiful vases, giving the impression left by the Flemish painters of still life, and the past.

The formal Mass is a traditional British style involving a classical shaped vase full of lots of beautiful flowers arranged in a conventional shape such as a triangle. The profusion of colours or tones of the same colour and the individual beauty of each flower used make the impact of this style.

As a style of arrangement the Mass Design flourishes, and modern treatment varies from carefree clusters to elegant symmetry—glamorous occasions are always decked with a beautiful mass of colour. This style demands large numbers of flowers, so can be an expensive style for the flat dweller dependant on the local florist. This fact, apart from natural progression and widespread communication and travel between East and West, may have influenced the still increasing growth of popularity of simpler arrangements.

During the years before World War II, Ikebana found a growing interest from people in the western half of the world. The growing preference in Britain for deceptively simple, elegant, yet inexpensive arrangements of flowers including the use of twigs, stones, and driftwood springs from an assimilation of the Japanese art. The modern trend has been towards the uncluttered clean lines of the Japanese style which uses only a few well-placed flowers. True Ikebana, mastered by some Europeans, demands a person who has, at least, time, dedication, and concentration to spend on the art. Eastern and western approaches have fused into the popular Line Design which retains the Japanese simplicity of line and shapes in space, paying scrupulous attention to the placing of a few perfect blooms, while dispensing with the discipline of religious rules and symbolism. With the scope of materials and style broadened, it was not surprising to find people taking a new look at containers that were not vases, and using anything from a casserole dish to a bottle for any type of design.

The free expressionistic style that has grown up has become widely adopted by Americans who have added rules of their own, such as the importance of the proportions of heights of plants to container, and the defined focal or interest point from which all stems spring. The modern interest in simplicity rather than profusion in floral decoration can perhaps also be attributed to the newly awakened consciousness of the basic elements which make up design, such as line, form and texture. The trend nowadays is for overall simplicity in order to accent these basics, whether it be architecture, sculpture, interior décor, furniture, glassware or childrens' toys.

A new chair nowadays is not always a mimic or extrapolation of past designs, but instead is an answer to the questions: what is the function of a chair? What is the simplest, most effective and pleasing arrangement which fulfils this function? In ever decreasing room space, the idea is to create more space by the use of plain colours, and smooth contours and shapes which fulfill their function without embellishment. Chintz and roses have given way to blocks of colour. As will be seen in Chapter 7, the latter lends itself far better as a setting for flower arrangements which, with artificial and growing plants, are becoming more a part of the interior. We are going the full circle and rediscovering the old Japanese ideas.

The ancient Japanese were one of many races whose attitude to life was reflected in their art. The Australian aborigines also showed a sensitive appreciation of natural forms in the shaping of wooden utensils, but the overall impression of the decoration contrasts sharply with that of the Japanese, in that it reflects an unsophisticated, almost fairy-tail, interpretation of man's place amongst living things. Their painting is a mirror of the Australian earth from which their materials derive: red, brown, ochre, yellow, white and charcoal. During the past thirty years the Australians have become increasingly aware of the unique stark beauty of much of the primitive aboriginal art, and it seems to have found expression in the hands of some Australian housewives in their approach to flower decorations. These are composed predominantly of the clay colours combined with white and grey driftwood, and black and white or chestnut red of the barks of different gum trees. Here, then, individuals' styles have been shaped by outside influences apparently unconnected with floral art, but which shares the same raw materials and the universal language of communication.

The evolution of the arts is now at a point at which there seem to be few boundaries of content and context. Environments are designed as a whole, architecture, gardens, and outdoor sculptures are carefully united. One sees examples of this reunion in some new towns, and universities where a whole living unit is planned at one time, rather than emerging piecemeal. For example in one of the new colleges at Cambridge—Churchill, sculptures of Hepworth and Moore fit beautifully with Sheppard's architecture and the surrounding gardens. Many sculptors set their work in gardens or rolling landscapes: location is part of the art.

Environmental planning incorporating the arts is not new; one has only to

**M** FREE STYLE IN IKEBANA
Modern materials in the form of bent sticks of black plastic and yellow plastic strips have been used in conjunction with two anthuriums, two trimmed palm fronds, and small leaves. The materials are held in place with the traditional kenzan or pinholder.

look at the Katsura Imperial Villa mentioned above to see the epitome of everything that modern architecture aims for. The interior of buildings and the exterior gardens are one. The design of buildings is functional, austere, yet anything but bound by conventions or sterile.

Content as well as context is changing. In 'painting', the incorporation of mass-produced food cartons, razor blades and dishcloths is almost old hat. In flower arrangment, equally astounding things are happening. Free Styles have emerged in the schools of Ikebana: anything can be incorporated into a design for a pleasing effect. 'Anything' covers cane curved like young fern fronds, copper wire contortions, hollow plastic tubing (*Fig M*) bent in graceful curves and sharp angles, carved chunks of polystyrene, stalked plastic balls and pieces of metal. The natural materials themselves are trimmed, tufted, and curved, often beyond recognition. Modern exhibitions of Ikebana include colossal tree trunks and landscapes twenty feet across, arrangements consisting of nothing but stones, and compositions of metal sheets and strips. So flower arrangements have reached the point where flowers are no longer necessary—new and shocking? Here one might recall the garden in Japan that consists of beautifully placed stones, set in a sea of carefully raked gravel. With the fine arts incorporating sculptures based on natural driftwood shapes and using the garbage of everyday life, and flower arrangement approaching metal sculpture and the disposition of stones in space, divisions between the extremes are sometimes difficult to see. The next phase and its surprises lie in the future.

*The Future.* For those who still do flower arrangements with flowers the future is promising: in America flowers are an industrial product which know no seasons. Flowering is artificially accelerated and controlled by treatment of seeds and control of artificial day length. These scientific techniques are spreading rapidly. There are now many more types of flower to choose from than there were before the war, and it is not just an idle boast of the young who do not believe in the good old days. Varieties of dahlias and roses have each increased by well over a thousand.

How is man creating new varieties? Mendel's discoveries of heredity started modern genetics, the study of inheritance and variation; of differences and resemblances between parents and offspring, whether they be ears of corn or man. Since Mendel's time, hypothetical things have materialised, such as genes, which carry hereditary messages from one generation to the next, and chromosomes which are strings of genes in each cell of living matter. Controlled coupling of male and female characters have produced most new varieties—man, rather then the insects, cross-pollinates varieties to make his own desired intermediate variety. Since the last war, mutations and radiation effects have come to the fore in their more sinister aspect. Mutations, however have made many modern flowers to man's design.

A mutation is a change in a gene or chromosome which casuses a change in the character of the animals or plant. Irradiation with X-rays and γ-rays, and treatment with some chemicals such as mustard gas, cause mutations which in flowers affect their colour, size of the flowers, leaf shape and so on, as well as invisible characteristics such as resistance to the cold.

Mutations produced by man have brought about new tulips (*Plate 43*), roses, chrysanthemums, petunias, snapdragons, geraniums and cyclamens by causing changes in the genes and chromosomes. Daffodils have also been changed to order: 'yellow cheerfulness' was produced from 'cheerfulness' which in turn was developed from 'Elvira'.

A frequent and fairly permanent mutation is one in which the number of chromosomes in the cell is changed—normally the number is fixed and constant for a certain species. Doubling, trebling or even greater mutiplication of chromo-somes can occur; the resulting plants are known as polyploids. In order to hold the extra chromosomes the size of the plant cells usually increases, which results in larger plants in which stems are taller and more rigid, leaves larger and thicker, and flowers and fruits bigger than in normal plants. The raspberry family contains polyploids, the loganberry and laxtonberry. Polyploid flower varieties include chrysanthemum, aster, iris, tulip, lupin, rose. Polyploids are now widespread, and many tetraploids have replaced their smaller ancestors.

Mutations are nearly always detrimental to the plant in some way. Some of the ornamental plants named above are flowers reduced to absurdity; their very raison d'être is lost, for the sexual organs, the stamens and pistils, are partly or wholly transformed into decorative petals. Such a progression is obviously detrimental to the normal reproduction of the species; however, as man has taken over the task of selection from the environment, sterility is no longer a disadvantage to the plant.

If such a mutation had occurred in nature, obviously the individuals carrying the new characteristic would have died leaving no progeny, so the variation would have died with it. Mutations do occur in nature, although infrequently. Many are thoroughly detrimental and disappear: it is the few that do not whose advantageous effects on plants and animals have provided much of the raw material for evolution. They are caused naturally by heat, cold, and natural radiations; man is simply accelerating them and making his own selection, rather than letting nature take its course.

Mutations could provide some of the answers to past over-exploitation of the environment; crops as well as flower petals are being doubled and trebled by their effects. The future, not only of flowers, but mankind, lies in mutations, good or evil.

**43** FLOWERS OF THE FUTURE
By means of mutations, the nature of a flower can be changed. Here, in an early flowering tulip, the familiar six smooth oval petals and six stamens (*Plate 27*) have been replaced with one leaf-cum-petal (at bottom of picture), twenty-five curled and jagged edged petals (many of which were streaked with leafy greenness, thickness and texture), two petal-cum-stamens (centre) and no conventional stamens at all.

Thus the male organs, the stamens, have been transformed into petals, but the transition is incomplete in this individual as two curled petals have purplish pollen bearing anthers along their edges (smallest petals at centre). The price of fertility and efficiency has also been paid by the female organ, the pistil at the centre; this has four crinkled lobes instead of the usual three straight ones, and the ovary wall, instead of enclosing and protecting the ovules, is parted, exposing its contorted contents.

# CHAPTER SIX

# Collecting and Preserving Plant Beauty

*Preservation In The Short Term*

Without water, plant tissue shrivels and dies. Water is the most vital constituent in living matter, and is necessary to transport food and raw materials around the plant. Also, by keeping the plant tissues turgid, water is sometimes responsible for supporting the plant. What, then, is responsible for the premature wilting and death of cut flowers and foliage when they are put in water?

'*Nor any drop to drink*'. The plant loses water all the time, mostly through its leaves, but also through the stem. The process is called transpiration: water evaporates from the surface of the plant and is lost into the air. This is not as catastrophic as it sounds. When the plant is growing in the soil the loss of water through the leaves assists the upward transport of water through the tiny tubes extending from the roots right the way up through the plant. The suction force of transpiration in fact pulls the water upwards. At the same time the roots absorb water from the soil and in some plants exert pressure pushing the water up to the leaves. Thus while the plant is growing in soil there is a continuous stream of water from the soil going up the plant and out in to the surrounding air. The water lifting mechanism is capable of lifting an unbroken column of water to a height of over 500 feet.

When a stem is cut and put in water, it is vital that the cut tubes at the base of the stem are clear so that water evaporated from the plant surface can be continuously replaced. There must be a free uptake of water comparable to the growing state if the plant is to survive.

One of the major factors responsible for the wilting of cut flowers is blockage of the cut end of the stem by bacteria growing in and around the minute water tubes. No matter how much water is available, or nutriment has been added to the water, if the passage of water up the stem is blocked the plant tissues can receive no benefit.

*Plant Hygiene.* One answer to the bacterial blockage is the use of a very mild disinfectant which will inhibit the growth of bacteria without having any detrimental effect on the blooms. Any old disinfectant will not do—the strength and mode of action is important.

Some people have found that a few drops of bleach or household ammonia in the water extends the life of flowers. There are several chemical preparations on the market which contain disinfectants of appropriate type and strength.

It is important that containers, knives, scissors and mechanical aids such as pinholders are kept scrupulously clean. Narrow-necked containers can be cleaned by shaking silver sand in with the washing-up water, or newspaper pieces and hot water (the vigorous shaking breaks the paper into tiny pieces which fall out easily afterwards). Oasis and Florapak both contain a chemical—formaldehyde —which restricts bacterial activity. These two, once thoroughly dry, can be stored hygienically in plastic bags without moulds appearing.

Leaves decay quickly, encouraging bacterial growth, if they are submerged in water. Some leaves deteriorate very much quicker than others: chrysanthemum leaves become slimy quickly, but evergreens last a long time without becoming foul smelling. Except for plants such as pine, box, cypress and their kind, it is wise to remove all foliage from the part of the stem which will be submerged. One of the traditional water additives is charcoal, which has been shown to help in keeping water odourless and clean. Metal containers also help in keeping water unpolluted.

Flowers and foliage are best cut with a knife (a very sharp one) which does not squeeze the tubes and stem tissue.

*Why Wilting Leaves?* Once an excess of water vapour has been lost from the plant without being replaced, the plant loses its rigidity, tissues become flaccid, the plant loses its inner support and wilts. To avoid wilting of cut plants one must aim at the least possible amount of transpiration. Under normal outside conditions the rate of transpiration is amazingly high; one maize plant transpires one pound of water per week.

Transpiration mostly occurs through the leaves, the upper and lower surfaces

**E marram grass** – in dry conditions tightly rolled

*The diagram shows a slice of leaf cut transversely

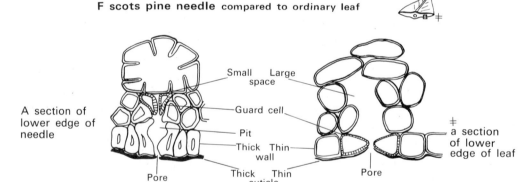

Leaf roll

= Hairs

= 'Hinge'

Position of pores

Thick cuticle on lower surface

Key:

▨ Leaf vein
▦ Sugar producing cells
☐ Strengthening cells

**F scots pine needle** compared to ordinary leaf

A section of lower edge of needle

Small   Large
space

Guard cell

Pit

Thick  Thin
wall

Pore

Thick  Thin
cuticle

Pore

‡ a section of lower edge of leaf

Both leaves have been cut through transversely and a small section including the edge magnified to show pore

## N DESIGN FOR WATER CONSERVATION

Although water loss through the leaves (transpiration) is a necessary process for a healthy plant, excessive transpiration is harmful, causing wilting or ultimately death. Plants that live in dry or arid places must therefore be on continual guard against losing more water to the atmosphere than they can replace from the soil.

E. Marram grass (*Plates 38, 46*) is one of the first plants to colonise sand dunes (described

of which nearly always have a different appearance. In the upper leaf surface there are usually no pores and there is often a thick protective layer lessening water loss. There are thousands of tiny pores in the lower surface of the leaf (for example one square centimetre may contain well over 18,000 pores). In some species there are pores on each side of the leaf, the proportion in the upper and lower surfaces varying from one species to another. It is through these tiny pores that the water evaporates, and gases, oxygen and carbon dioxide, pass in and out of the plant.

The pores are not simply holes in the leaf's surface (*Fig N*). The surface of the leaf is like a mosaic of cells—which are minute living building blocks. Intermingled among the mosaic are the pores—called stomata—which are usually bounded by two special kidney-shaped (when seen from above) cells. These guard and control the opening, hence their name, guard cells. These are special in that they change shape according to various conditions, one of them being the moisture conditions within the leaf: when there is plenty of water available they inflate with water and open the pore. When the leaf is less turgid the guard cells become deflated, change shape and close the pore. The leaf is thus partly in control of how much water it loses to the air.

The humidity immediately outside the leaf also controls the amount of water

on page 26); its environment seems comparatively waterless. The unquestionable success of the plant's survival in such a dry environment, and in the face of frequent drying salt-laden winds, depends on the neat protective mechanism which the grass has developed. In dry conditions the leaf rolls up as in the diagram, so that a microclimate is formed inside the roll. Moisture is held inside by virtue of there being very little air movement; the special ridges and hairs obstruct any free passage. The pores through which water is lost are positioned at the base of the ridges where any water vapour is most easily trapped. Since the pores allow a large loss of water from the leaf when the outside air is dry, very little valuable water is lost in this case as the mechanism has ensured that the air immediately outside the pore is as moist as possible. Transpiration is thus kept to a minimum. The hinges which are responsible for the amount of rolling are cells (living building blocks) sensitive to the amount of water vapour in the leaf. The pores only occur on the upper (inside) surface of the leaf, the lower (outer) surface being protected by a very thick waterproof skin, the cuticle.

F. The Scots pine (also page 94 and *Plate 51*) is adapted to an extremely dry environment (a cold climate is equivalent to dryness when the water is frozen in the soil and cannot be absorbed.) The narrowness of the pine needles, thick-walled cells and the thick cuticle covering them reduce transpiration. Also the pores are sunk low in pits to reduce the amount of air circulating and consequent drying round the pore—see diagram of part of lower leaf edge (an ordinary leaf has been drawn for comparison). Deciduous trees overcome the problem by losing their leaves and becoming dormant through winter. By virtue of their thick leathery cuticle the evergreens retain them—holly, laurel and the other shiny leafed plants. The effect of climatic changes on forests during the Ice Age is outlined in Table 1.

lost by transpiration. Dry air, wind, and rise in temperature cause a high transpiration rate by increasing the dryness of air around the leaf, and thus water passes from the moist leaf to the drier atmosphere outside. Whether the leaf loses water or not is not under a simple dual control: mechanical shock and severe water shortage close the stomata, and the pore size is less in the dark than the light. For free movement of water vapour and also carbon dioxide and oxygen in and out of the leaf the stomates must not be blocked by dust and small particles. A wipe with a moist cloth clears pores of large leaved plants, or a spray of water removes dust from smaller more delicate plants. This should be done fairly often to house plants growing inside.

*Water Conservation—Theory and Practice.* By keeping the air round the leaves moist one stops precious water being lost from them to the outside world. Japanese styled arrangements with few flowers in large troughs of water are not only peaceful to look at, but also are beneficial to the leaves: water continuously evaporates from the pool of water making a particularly humid atmosphere near them. Moss has a similar humidity effect, and stones placed on the earth of pot plants help in water retention. In centrally heated rooms it is best to keep to wide mouthed containers in order to keep up a good moisture level in the air around the plants, or alternatively a trough of water placed near the arrangement or source of heat will dampen the atmosphere. One can buy special humidifiers for this purpose which can be most attractive and are not too expensive. Alternatively one can beautify a plain trough of water with a layer

**44 INDOOR GARDEN**
Potted plants indoors can benefit each other when grouped together in a community. Humidity in a microclimate is held around the leaves so that less water is lost from the plant to the atmosphere.

Mother-in-law's tongue makes positive radiating perpendiculars at the back of the arrangement and other plants have been placed to give a circular outline, reflecting the circular brass pan and handle. Plants and pots have been tilted to give the impression of radiation from a central point.

Plants were selected for the similarities and contrasts in their foliage shape, pattern, colour and texture. Elongated tapering leaf shapes of spider plant, tradescantia, mother-in-law's tongue and ladder fern have been chosen for the edge of the arrangement, giving it a delicate outline. Although these four share a basic similarity of form they are also different from each other, lending interest. Spider plant has white stripes running along the leaf, mother-in-law's tongue has yellow edges to the leaves and horizontal dark green striations. The ladder fern leaves, divided and crenellated, give an interesting slatted impression and the larger leafed purple tradescantia picks up the purplish tinted veins in the green and grey

begonia leaves. The metallic silver sheen of these leaves, their large solid forms and red hairy stems and undersides, are a direct contrast to the other plants, and their growing pattern makes a focal point.

A sprig of ivy, cut for several months and still going strong, leads into the focus, and with the lower begonia leaf breaks the rim of the pan. The severe dark line of the handle has been interrupted by a few stray leaves. The arching overhangs of the spider plant are balanced by the flimsy fern on the opposite side, also adding an interesting variation of leaf form. The warm mellowed brass is a good foil for the cool greens and metallic purple grey.

of assorted shells (thoroughly washed) and stones, the appearance of which is greatly enhanced under water.

Draughts cause any valuable moist air near the leaves to move and be replaced by drier air which draws moisture out of the stomata. Plants, cut and potted, are best kept away from draughts, such as exist below an open window or an empty fireplace.

Increased temperature means increased evaporation from all moist surfaces: to keep transpiration down to a minimum the temperature should be kept as low as possible, and particularly for most pot plants, as constant as possible. Where a room is very hot and dry, it is often advantageous to remove an arrangement to a cool place overnight. Bright or direct sunlight should also be avoided as light increases stomatal pore size, and thus the amount of water lost from the leaf.

Treatments such as placing plastic bags over delicate blooms like hellebores, wrapping lily-of-the-valley stems in wet tissue, and rolling wet tulips in newspaper are merely making a miniature private atmosphere for the plants, full of moisture and sheltered. Grouping of pot plants together in one container has the same effect (*Plate 44*). Flowers, foliage and stems soon become full of water, turgid and stiff, as within the plastic or paper the leaves soon find themselves in a water packed atmosphere and cease transpiration, while still probably absorbing water. Spraying water over blooms and leaves has the same effect— it is most advantageous to pay attention to the under sides of leaves in particular. Flaccid pot plants are best treated in the same way; transpiration is slowed by putting the leaves in a wet atmosphere, not by watering the roots which very often kills the plant if done in excess. Some pot plants even require steam surrounding the leaves to get over a water loss; for example, azalea.

Even plants kept cool in still humid air will lose some water which must be replaced. The importance of keeping the stem tube apertures free of bacterial blockage has already been stressed. There is also another very important issue. For the transpiration force to pull the water upwards against gravity to the leaves and flowers, the column must be continuous. Any air lock in the stem destroys the upward passage of water and acts as a block in the same way as the bacterial growth. It is therefore important that as soon as they are cut, stems are placed in deep water. Best of all a bucket of clean water should be carried round the garden while gathering the flowers.

Warm water travels up the stem more readily than cold water. On this basis it is best that flowers are first placed in warm water; also, warm water does not give the sudden shock that cold water does. Once in their bucket of deep warm water, newly cut flowers lose least water if placed overnight in a cool dark place with a moist atmosphere and without draughts. Then all outside conditions are favourable to water being absorbed by the plant and remaining inside it. If flowers have been thus conditioned before being put in the arrangement they will be turgid and stiff and will last much longer. Wilting flowers in need of first aid, and floppy stems, can both be salvaged by placing in an inch or so of boiling water (with the flowers and leaves protected), left until it cools, and then rearranged in clean water.

Prior to arranging, many flowers are best recut under water so there are no air bubbles in the stem. For the same reason there should always be some water in the vase at the beginning of arranging so that those stems placed in position first are not without water for any time. Experiments have shown that recutting under water is definitely beneficial to carnations, pinks, marigolds, sweet peas, chrysanthemums, michaelmas daisies, snapdragons and water-lilies.

With bought flowers it is best to recut all stems as soon as possible and condition them directly as indicated above. Particularly in arrangements where stems abut on the floor of the container, it is advantageous if the stem is cut at an angle rather than straight across.

It is important that water in the design container is kept constantly topped up. The water in narrow necked containers falls very rapidly, and once the level has fallen below the stem ends, air blocks form in the stems. For the same reason it is essential that Oasis and Florapak are constantly waterlogged so that a continuous column of water can pass up the stem.

By removing foliage one is removing areas which are chiefly responsible for water loss and therefore benefitting the cut plant in one respect. However it must also be remembered that transpiration is not primarily detrimental; it is transpiration pull that largely accounts for water movement up the stem. In fact some flowers such as chrysanthemum and pansy keep best with foliage attached.

Woody stems take up water more easily if the stems are split a few inches with a sharp knife to increase the inner area in contact with the water. Smashing with a hammer tends to lacerate the tissues and may encourage decay, although many people recommend such treatment.

Stems containing milky or colourless fluid need to be treated to stop them from 'bleeding' so water can pass up the stem rather than the fluid come down. This is best done by placing stem ends in an inch or so of boiling water for a

**45** AUSTERITY AND OPULENCE—CACTUS AND GERANIUMS
Growing side by side, bulbous, water-packed stems of prickly pear and bright flowers of
geraniums make strange partners under a hot Mediterranean sky.
    Desert plants such as cacti have very few well protected pores from which water passes
to the atmosphere (transpiration) ; and to further reduce water loss, the pores are open at
night and closed in the day. Water therefore passes through the plant slowly. When the
rain falls, it is taken up quickly by the spreading roots and immediately stored inside the
plant whose special water storage tissues become swollen. During periods of drought, the
water is slowly used, very little being lost to the dry outside air. It is thought the thorns of
cacti are most probably protection against losing valuable foliage to browsing animals.

minute (meanwhile protecting upper stem and leaves from steam) or by holding the split stem ends in a flame for a few seconds. Hollyhock, poppy, poinsettia, hydrangea, fuchsia, daffodils and dahlias, dusty miller and lantana require this treatment prior to their long drink.

Evergreens and ferns are improved by careful immersion in cold water, also some flowers such as baby's breath.

*Natural Nutriments.* Water is not the only substance that the plant draws up. Dissolved in the life-giving water are small but vital amounts of mineral salts. These contain the main elements essential to a healthy plant; iron and magnesium are necessary for the formation of the green pigment, chlorophyll, without which the plant cannot trap the sun's energy. Sulphur and phosphorus are important components of proteins (which are basic building blocks of living matter); also potassium and calcium and many other elements are necessary to plants.

In cutting a flower one is cutting off the supply of mineral salts. It is therefore advantageous if these are introduced into water in which plants are to live. Chemical flower preservatives often contain small amounts of nitrates or phosphates of calcium or potassium, or magnesium sulphate. Once absorbed by the roots, mineral salts dissolved in water circulate round the plant; also there is sugar circulating. Sugar is the plant's food manufactured by the green chlorophyll-containing parts of the plant. It is made from the raw materials carbon dioxide (from the air) and water bound together into the compound sugar, using the sun's energy.

A low concentration of sugar added to the water acts as food for the tissues of cut plants—many of the traditional flower preservation recipes recommend the addition of sugar to water in the vase: for chrysanthemums, sweet peas, michaelmas daisy, maple and petunia.

Another factor is the acidity or alkalinity of the water. One can attempt to imitate the plant's outdoor environment: plants growing best in alkaline conditions keep fresher in alkaline water. Strength of the solution is important so home brews are at one's own risk—water can be made more acid by adding a small amount of vinegar and addition of household ammonia increases alkalinity, hence the presence of these two items in traditional recipes. Roses, carnations, hydrangeas, rhododendrons, pines and firs are 'acid plants', peony, iris and lilac are alkaline loving plants.

*True or False.* There are endless magic recipes quoted for making cut flowers last; some make sense, many contradict each other, and some make nonsense.

On the showing of one or two or dozens of flowers one cannot make accurate generalisations about plant preservation. If one wants to show the success of a new method it is not enough to remember how long the chrysanthemums lasted using one method last month and compare their state after using a new method this month.

There are many factors which would account for an observed 'prolonged life': temperature, humidity and draught conditions vary from one day to another, and from one place to another. There is the age of the flower at the time of picking to be considered, the number of flowers sharing the vase, the length of the stems, the number of leaves attached to the stems, and the size of the container to name but a few. Also wilting and withering do not always happen suddenly, they can be gradual, and are thus difficult to time exactly. It is easy to draw false conclusions unless one makes a carefully controlled study.

The traditional benefits of aspirins and pennies have apparently proved to be false hopes, probably based on inappropriate comparisons. Inventors of flower preservatives carry out scientific studies on cut flowers under controlled conditions. Rather than sort out the conflicting home brews, it seems more reliable, particularly for special occasions, to use the commercial preparations on the market. A further advantage of these are that plant hormones are often added which stimulate the opening of buds of some flowers or slow down the living processes to slow down maturation and aging (both hastened in a warm atmosphere).

Most of all, look at the situation from the plant's point of view. Water loss means wilting and ultimately premature death—essentials for plant health are clean containers and utensils to minimise bacterial interference, keeping the stems always under clean water and conditioning them prior to arranging, preserving a cool humid atmosphere around the plants, placing out of sunlight and draughts, with fresh air. Above all good quality flowers and foliage and the minimum of handling are essential for lasting beauty.

*When to Pick, When to Buy.* Transpiration is at its lowest during the evening and the night when the outside air is heavy with moisture and heat is at its lowest. It is therefore best to pick the flowers while in their most turgid condition in the early morning or in the evening. A convenient routine is to pick in the evening, leave conditioning overnight and arrange the next morning. Failing this, flowers can be stored in deep water while you look for a suitable container.

Some plants are more hardy then others because of their natural protection from water loss (*Fig N, Plate 45*). Ivy is particularly hardy foliage, and chrysanthemums are one of the longer lasting flowers (*Fig O*). Sweet peas deteriorate quickly if picked while the petals are still wet; others are less sensitive. Bulb flowers on the whole open from a bud in water, whereas roses need to be beyond the tight bud stage when picked. Poppies are best picked before the petals completely unfold.

Obviously it is best to choose young flowers when picking and buying—there is nothing more soul destroying than to see a lovely design which took valuable time and effort wilt beyond recognition within two days. There are no tricks in telling the age of flowers. One has simply to recall their raison d'être and check whether the stamens have released their pollen, or the stigma become receptive.

*How Old is a Flower?* One can find this out by looking at the state and positions of the stamens and the female parts of the flower. In some flowers such as the sweet pea the stamens and the stigma mature together and pollen is transferred by insect or wind on to the stigma of the same flower and fertilize the ovules. When this happens the flower has been self-pollinated.

Many flowers adopt cross-pollination, which means that pollen from one flower fertilizes ovules from another. The resulting seeds produce a more healthy and vigorous new plant which combines characteristics from both parents. Thus many plants have developed intriguing ways of guaranteeing cross-pollination rather than self-pollination, which conveniently tell the age of the flower.

In many flowers cross-pollination is favoured by the stamens maturing and shedding their pollen at a different time from the stigmas being receptive. In some, the positions of stamens and pistils change as the flower gets older—for example, a young flower of rose-bay willow-herb has the stamens, tinted bluish green, sticking straight out of the flower centre. As the stamens shed their pollen and the flower ages, the stamens bend back and splay out parallel to the petals, a long style emerges from the centre of the flower, the end of which opens out into a branched stigma when it is mature.

A similar change in position with age happens in sage (see also page 91). In the young flowers, the stamens hang down low inside the petal hood, shedding pollen downwards when mature, while the stigma is tightly closed in a single

## O DRIFTWOOD PAIR FOR WINTER

The driftwood pieces (*Plate 11*) formed the basis of this pair of arrangements; in both, the root wood framed a space. The similarity was accentuated by use of the same flowers with each—yellow and white spray chrysanthemums and ivy.

The most obvious reaction to the two framed spaces is to fill them with flowers; however, as the two windows were an important part of each shape, flowers were placed so as to emphasize rather than cover them.

The left hand design is essentially high lighting the diagonal line of the smooth silvery driftwood, the largest lemon chrysanthemum placed opposite the all-important space, the tiny white buds at the left suggesting a continuation of the straight diagonal pieces at the base of the wood. The ivy was placed along the same diagonal, linking the space with the largest and intermediate blooms. Peeping out from beneath the wood, small chrysanthemum flowers and leaves hide container mechanics and echo the diagonal. Flowers stems were wedged in a small cube of Oasis contained in foil, which was frequently watered.

In spite of its similar window, the right hand piece of driftwood was completely different to the other—shades of brown, rough textured with pieces of wrinkled bark still attached here and there. The line of this piece is very definitely vertical and horizontal. The main vertical was hollow, allowing insertion of a lipstick lid container of water for half open flower heads emerging out of the holes, keeping within the main vertical line. The base of the wood was weighted with a large lemon chrysanthemum and leaves held in a block of Oasis in foil, and meandering ivy leaves climbed up the vertical to break the severe line. The ivy also linked the upper flowers with the base and balanced the right hand branching of the wood. Flat stones made improvised bases for the pair.

Preservation note: the chrysanthemums were bought from a florist quite cheaply, and lasted for several weeks following pre-arrangement treatment with boiling water (described on page 201). Pieces of ivy, well protected from losing water by the thick glossy skin (cuticle) on the leaves, lasted happily without being in water.

strand, sticking out at the top of the hood. Later the style bows downwards and droops over the entrance of the floral tube, the stigma having opened out to expose a receptive bifid surface. In flowers such as the primrose there are two kinds of flower with the stigmas and stamens remaining at different levels throughout their lives. Some flowers have high standing stamens, others an elevated stigma. Others such as walnut have male and female flowers on separate plants.

If cross-fertilization does not occur, in many flowers the stigma bends back so that pollen from the same flower brings about fertilization. Self-fertilization is better than no fertilization.

When selecting flowers it is as well to bear in mind that young flowers bearing stamens should not have free pollen adhering to the anthers, and there should certainly not be pollen in profusion. Stigmas when young are often short styled and unbranched. If someone tries to sell you flowers with both burst anthers and opened out stigmas, the bunch is certainly not a good buy, as once pollen is freed and stigmas placed to receive it the job of the flower is drawing to its end.

**46** SEA-SHORE TREASURES mostly from shores of the North Sea, Irish Sea, English Channel and a few from the Pacific Ocean and the Mediterranean.
Wandering along the sea-shore one finds lots of design material—containers, accessories, focal and line material, not to mention items that make beautiful ornaments on their own. All are long lasting and each in its own way is unique.
Above the piece of fisherman's basket (used in *Plate 12*): green sponge; dried black seaweed, crinkle edged; to the right of the basket, flat stones for bases—smooth grey slates, one used in *Fig A*; tall straight spikes of marram grass, (*Plate 38*, here the drooping stamens of the flowers making up the spikes are just visible); wavy sedge stems; a sculptured pure white bone, on which bright pink seaweeds have been dried; driftwood. Curving round the bottom of the picture, underground stems of marram, used on page 239; and a curve of seaweed driftwood, same type used in *Plate 38*, *Figs G* and *L*. Below the basket: fisherman's floats, rough (used in *Fig 58*) and smooth; dried ribbon-like seaweeds, described on page 70, holdfast visible in one specimen; a reddish orange long-spined sea urchin; a horse tooth (*Fig C*); miniature tree shape of sea fern; coral; shells streaked and coloured like oil on water; rust stained wood. To the left of the basket: strangely imprinted rock; dried thrift; mermaid's purse (egg of the dogfish) brown and horny trailing curly 'tendrils'; pink and mauve patterned sea urchins, with and without spines; seed heads; part of a seaweed stem, dried and parted showing its fibrous construction—an interesting pattern. On the basket: the filigree complex form of part of the skull of a bony fish; an exotic spiked shell and cotton-grass from the cliff top.
The rest: periwinkles; limpets; mussel, razor and crab shells all shades of yellow, brown, white, green, red, orange and purplish-blue; glistening pebbles of white, pink, grey and orange; stripes, mottles and patterns, just a few of the thousands of treasures one can collect; driftwoods from the sea shore are pictured in *Plate 11*.

**P** METAMORPHOSIS OF A POT PLANT

Intricate pieces of driftwood are interesting natural sculptures when placed on their own, or, as one of a pair, linked with driftwood elements in a design. A Canary Island ivy and a contorted piece of root make an interesting tableau.

Climbing ivy leaves straddle an elongated, curving length of silver-grey. The shine of the wood accents the shine of the leaves (ivy leaves shine beautifully, and are cleaned and protected with a wipe of milk) and pottery. Grey-blue leaf colours and limey-green and green and grey striped pebbles unite with merging bands of green, turquoise and Prussian blue pottery glaze. The theme of blue-green is relieved by cream edges and slashes in the leaves and white, lemon and orange stones scattered over the compost.

Composition note: a space between pot rim and first leaves looks ugly with straggling stems, and brings any pot plant composition to an abrupt end. An undulating stem of driftwood, striated and wrinkled hints at an old gnarled trunk to the ivy plant. Close to the 'trunk' and reaching upwards from its roots, twisted seaweed-like strands of grey-green lichen bristling with disc and finger-like projections add weight and interest to the base of the design. Their texture and dull surface give them the appearance of tiny fossilized shrubs rising from between miniature boulders.

*Collecting and Hoarding*

The hoarding of oddments has already been justified—as a cheap and interesting means of making a small bunch of fresh flowers or foliage go further, and as a stimulating source of variety and quantity from which one can make the 'right' choice when selecting material.

Where does one start to look for useful objects? Many of them one finds on walks in the country, or sorties round waste land and derelict buildings, or by the wayside when walking the dog—oddly shaped twigs, angular branches and lumps of wood, fir cones, larch twigs, bracken, lichens on their own or still attached to twigs and stones, sprigs of pine needles, seedheads of sorrel, cow parsley and its many relatives, rose-bay willow-herb, old man's beard, bunches of sycamore keys, thistle heads, grasses, stray heads of crop plants—wheat, barley, oats, birch bracket fungi, old twisted ivy stems, stones of all colours, shapes and sizes as camouflage, bases or part of a design, snail shells—bright yellow, olive green and brown striped ones as well as the brown mottled garden variety. All of these are ready to be used immediately, without further ado; and in addition countless types of leaves can be preserved with minimal time and effort by standing in glycerin.

On the sea shore (*Plate 46*) there is marram grass: flower spikes, leaves and roots, many different types of driftwood, fisherman's cork floats and bits of wicker baskets, shells both subtle and brilliant patterned and coloured, pebbles and pieces of rounded ground glass, at the same time shiny and opaque, mermaid's purses (dogfish egg cases), fossils, sea urchins and starfish, dried seaweeds and their skeletons, feathers, sponges, and occasionally beautifully weathered bones transformed into weird sculptured shapes. Properly washed and dried, there is no stale seaweed smell.

Storage space for such items can be a problem—a corner of the airing cupboard or attic is best of all, but even a few boxes of grasses, twigs, driftwood and shells can make life awkward in a one-roomed flat. A reasonable compromise is to live with one's trophies—a bunch of grasses and long stalked seedheads look very graceful in most sorts of container, be it an old make-up bottle, an alabaster urn or a jam jar. The most beautiful and unusual driftwoods make impromptu sculptured ornaments when not in use (held on a temporary base of a table mat with plasticine or Bostik). Many junk shop accessories and containers also make attractive ornaments when not in use. Shells and pebbles look pretty in a colourful heap in a glass container, or any shallow bowl and make a pleasing ornament in a bathroom which has the space available (and above the stretch level of toddlers at the inquisitive-eating stage). Having started collecting, your 'stock box' will appear never ending, for you will continue to automatically pick up odd twigs or driftwood whenever the opportunity occurs; ideas will form in your mind as to how you will use a certain item.

Many hardwearing foliages last so long that they could be included in the hoarding category. For those in cities and flats, these foliages are a valuable acquisition. One can have them attractively stored in water for weeks before they are actually used in a design—evergreens such as pine, box, ivy and holly. From the vegetable basket, carrot, parsnip, swede and beetroot tops sprout interesting foliage after a matter of days in a saucer of shallow water, continuing growing and sprouting for weeks.

Another saucer garden of 'storage' material is different types of moss, so useful for camouflaging the mechanics of flower arrangements and many of them are beautiful enough to make miniature arrangements on their own with lichens and tiny shoots and flowers. These saucer storage items are an absorbing interest for children, and look very pretty in a kitchen with a few stones filling the spaces between the brilliant green of the moss and the frosted bluish-white of lichen heads.

*Everlasting Beauty.* Dried arrangements are a good compromise when flowers are scarce or expensive, when a warm dry atmosphere indoors is inevitable, or when time for planning and arranging is short. Preserved plant material can provide bright (*Colour Plate 10*) or subtle shades to compare favourably with any flower, lasts indefinitely in a dry atmosphere, and will stay arranged and pleasing for as long as required. Apart from these advantages, a dried store packed away on shelves is invaluable for that missing something that will make the design perfect, and an asset if the house is flowerless, garden bare, shops closed, and dinner guests imminent! Above all the dry store can make a tiny bunch into a big bunch.

The same combination of flowers, seedheads, leaves, or grasses can be arranged in lots of different ways. Dried plants are perfect for the uninitiated—most take endless handling, can be altered over a long period until 'just right', and prove the flexibility of an apparently limited supply of raw material.

Semi-permanent material can be selected as part of the room's colour scheme: golden Chinese lanterns look tailor made for a room with golden cushions. It is best not to keep dried arrangements too long, or they can become boring, and even the best arrangements need to have the dust blown off! The boundary between a dried arrangement and an ornament is slender, particularly if one makes permanent showpieces such as hanging balls, garlands or pictures of dried pressed flowers.

The human urge to preserve floral beauty is not new: rose buds from a tomb dating 500 B.C. are said to have opened when placed in warm water, and ancient lotus seeds have germinated and flowered—a miracle of life from the past in the present. For those who wish to mimic the ancients it is apparently possible to preserve roses for long periods by selecting long-stalked buds just before they open, dipping the stem in melted wax as a sealer, and wrapping individually in tissue paper before sealing into an airtight tin. These keep well in a cool place and will slowly spring forth into full blown roses once the waxed stem is cut away and the clear stem immersed in warm water.

*Drying Methods*

First and foremost the specimens to be dried should be as near perfect as possible; it is a waste of time and space to dry and preserve carefully a nibbled, tired or damaged flower or leaf. It is therefore best to pick flowers for preservation while they are still in bud or when approaching full bloom; on no account should they be past their best, otherwise one ends up with an unattractive dead conglomeration of petals. Accidents will happen, so it is sensible to dry at least twice as much material as is needed. Material is best picked on a dry day to avoid any mould developing one it has been brought inside. To keep their colours, flowers are best dried quickly and in the dark. Many exotic seed heads, already dried, are available at a florist's: lotus, okra, and others.

*Natural Drying.* This is the lazy way of preserving plant material, and is just as successful as the more fiddly procedures, its disadvantage being that one's raw material is limited. Foliage, moss and flowers are simply left in an arrangement or some sort of receptacle and allowed to dry by not replacing water in the container. Quicker still, stems which are to remain straight can be laid in boxes once they are thoroughly dry. The airing cupboard or a similar dry place is an ideal venue for this method.

## Poppy

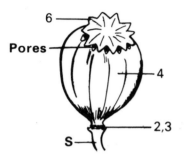

6

**Pores**

4

2,3

S

## Sycamore

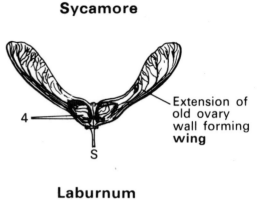

4

Extension of
old ovary
wall forming
**wing**

S

## Traveller's joy
lots of fruits

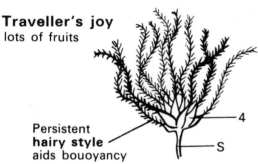

4

S

Persistent
**hairy style**
aids bouoyancy

## Laburnum

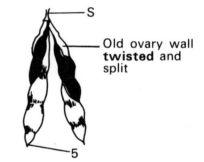

S

Old ovary wall
**twisted** and
split

5

## Dog rose hip -cut open

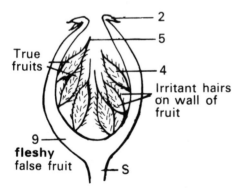

2

5

4

True
fruits

Irritant hairs
on wall of
fruit

9
**fleshy**
false fruit

S

## Plum -cut open

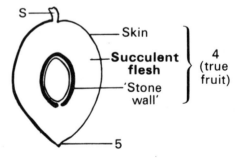

S

Skin

**Succulent
flesh**

'Stone
wall'

4
(true
fruit)

5

This effortless method of preservation is good for broom, seed pods, berries on branches, box (remains green), holly, ivy, viburnum, grevillea, sorrel, heather, baby's breath, and grasses including cereals—corn, barley, etc., which bow gracefully if stood upright in a jar. Leaves should be removed as these shrivel and look untidy. Drying takes two to three weeks.

## Q FRUITS FOR ALL SEASONS

Popularly called seed heads or seed boxes, these winter standbys are true fruits. A true fruit is the ovary (female part of the flower) and it contains seeds.

The purpose of the fruit is dispersal of the seeds far from the parent plant. Many intricate structures and mechanisms have developed to take full advantage of the dispersal agents available: wind, and to a lesser extent, animals (also water).

The attractive poppy fruit relies on the wind shaking the dry fruit held on its elastic stalk. The movement shakes a few seeds at a time out of the pores.

The sycamore also relies on wind—here the entire fruit is carried away, not just the seeds as in the poppy. To aid its wind travel, the wall of the ovary has extended to form a long wing structure.

Whirling and gyrating in the wind is one method of movement; floating is another. Traveller's joy and dandelion produce fruit parachutes for this purpose. In the former the thin prolongation of the ovary, the hairy style, remains.

Some fruits are independent of wind, water and animals, having explosive mechanisms which fling the seeds away from the parent. The ovary wall of laburnum tightens as it dries and the tensions set up cause the wall to suddenly burst open, twisting and scattering the seeds.

Fruits are rendered attractive to animals by brightly coloured edible ovary walls. The succulent part of the fruit is eaten and the seeds discarded, or they are passed straight through the animal's body, well protected from digestive juices. The ovary wall is fleshy in the plum, the receptacle in false fruits such as wild rose. In the latter the swollen tip of the stem (the receptacle), which bore the flower has enlarged around the old ovaries, or fruits, and become succulent. The dog rose effects dispersal of the true fruits inside the hip before they are irretrievably digested, by providing them with irritant hairs (responsible for the 'itching powder' manufactured from hips by school boys). These cause the animal which has plucked and eaten the hip to vomit, regurgitating the fruits unharmed by digestion and ready to release their precious cargo, the seeds.

Dried fruits have been used in *Colour Plates 7* and *10*.

*Flower/Fruit Parts* (as in *Figs E, H, I, J*)

2,3—remains of sepals and petals
4—wall of old ovary (now fruit) enclosing seeds
5—remains of style
6—old stigma
9—receptacle
S—old flower stem

*Hanging*. This method is generally used for most flowers as it retains their shape, and if hung in a dark place colours can be preserved. As with the previous method leaves should be stripped and the material kept in a dry place to avoid moulds. Examples of raw material are: delphiniums, lamb's ear, love-lies-bleeding, larkspur, acanthus, everlastings (heads can be dried individually in sieves) and the more complicated flowers, such as rose, hydrangea and peony—these larger flower heads should be hung on their own; others can be successfully preserved without damage hung in small bunches. The true flower of the hydrangea is a tiny central swelling, the outer 'petals' being bracts (modified leaves, see *Fig 19*). The true flower should have finished and the bracts should no longer be fleshy when the flower is picked for drying. While drying, hydrangeas turn the most beautiful shades of pink, deep reds, purple and bronze. Hooks in the ceiling, strings, coat hangers make good points from which to hang things. The fewer the petals the easier is the good preservation of the flower.

*Sand, Silica Gel or Borax*. Sand from beach should be sifted, and the other two commodities can be bought from a chemist. This method keeps the original shape and colour of the flower, and should take place in a dry cool atmosphere, in the dark. The bottom of a box or carton should be covered with the solid to a depth of two inches and the flowers placed face down in it and gently covered with more powder. Stems are best propped up against the side of the box, the lid should remain off the box to allow free passage of air. When the petals feel crisp the powder should be carefully poured off; borax can be used repeatedly.

This method is best used for open-faced flowers; awkward shapes like daffodils have to be very carefully handled and the trumpet carefully filled with powder in order to retain the shape. Flowers to be treated by this method are: chrysanthemums, roses, sunflowers, geraniums, bleeding heart, delphiniums, pansy, zinnia, dahlia, marigold and anemone. Coleus leaves which are highly coloured are best preserved by drying under powder. The time taken for drying depends on the texture of the flower; delicate petals dry quickest—in a few days.

*Pressing*. As well as dryness this requires warmth. Leaves and flowers should be carefully placed on several layers of newspapers so that there is little wrinkling of petals and no overlapping which would result in material sticking together. More newspaper is placed on top of the specimens which must be weighted down with books; an alternative position is under the carpet. This method is ideal for leaves which grow in a single plane, such as beech or ferns. Other leaves and silver foliages are also good for pressing. A quicker method is to gently iron foliage in between newspapers with a cool iron—ideal for ferns.

*Skeletonizing.* Many seed heads, such as poppy and bluebell become skeletonized while growing and somehow the delicate filigrees survive the wind and weather. Sometimes on the floor of woods one can find a partly skeletonised leaf, but very rarely a full skeleton.

It is a fairly easy job to skeletonize leaves at home, and these, once dried, make a delicate rather ethereal edge to any fresh or dried decoration. Pure white vein patterns silhouetted against a glossy fresh leaf look stunning. The Victorians used to skeletonize leaves by boiling them for thirty minutes in a quart of water containing one teaspoon of soda, leaving them to cool in the soda solution afterwards. The softened leaves were then spread carefully on paper and the fleshy parts on either side of the skeleton removed with a blunt edge such as a knife back. The cleaned skeleton was then bleached for an hour then rinsed and pressed in the usual way under newspapers. Tough leathery leaves are ideal—holly, magnolia, laurel, oak. A more natural method of skeletonizing involves immersing leaves or seed heads in stagnant rain water until the outer skin will slide off the vein skeleton. Afterwards the leaves should be washed in running water.

Sometimes glycerine-preserved leaves of magnolia or iris lose their fleshy parts slowly by disintegration. Careful flicking with a paint brush will remove the rest of the flesh, and the skeleton is clear. These skeletons can be stored between wax paper to retain some moisture.

*Glycerine Preservation.* This method gives best result in summer heat. Green leaves frequently turn brown, such as magnolia, beech and bronze-reddish leaves retain their colour, hawthorn and crab-apple leaves have reddish colours when preserved, others change colour as they absorb the glycerine, and should be removed as soon as they reach an appropriate colour. Eucalyptus, ferns, and beech picked young; ivy, hydrangea, and barberry stay green when dried. This method is another one which requires little time and effort and is used for most types of foliage.

Branches and leaves should be cleaned, bark removed from the bottom few inches of stem and the stem split to increase the area for absorption. Stems must be under six inches of a solution of one part glycerine to two parts water (made by boiling the two together for several minutes) which can be used repeatedly if stored in a covered jar.

Autumn colours can be preserved by spraying leaves with plastic lacquer, or painting it on carefully. The forms of thistle seed heads and bulrushes are kept in check if sprayed with plastic or hair spray.

*Dry Storage*. Most of the drying methods take two to three weeks unless particularly large blooms or fleshy stems are being preserved. Things must be thoroughly dried before being put away to avoid any growth of mould.

Specimens should be stored in a dry dark place, preferably packed away in upright boxes. Delicate items should be kept separately from the more sturdy heavier ones to avoid breakage. Although it is initially time-consuming to label the boxes before putting them away, it is a good investment of time in the long run and saves frantic rummaging through box after box. Boxes can be kept upright by weighting them down at the bottom with sand or stones. Very delicate flower heads or those with lots of petals are best stood in jars or a vase so that nothing touches them.

Dried seaweed, fungi, and lichened twigs and stones are best stored in the same conditions, also bark and driftwood. Before storing, bark and wood must be cleaned and should be carefully checked for any livestock which might have been sheltering in it. It is also a good idea to check for tell-tale wood worm holes before bringing into the house.

*Subtle Shades*. The colours of dried flowers are generally softer and more subtle than their fresh counterparts. On the whole, splashes of vivid brightness must come from preserved autumn leaves, dried fruits such as peppers and Chinese lanterns, and the everlasting flowers—strawflower (helichrysum) in bright reds, orange, yellow, white and pink, and the softer colours of pink, lavender, blue and white of sea lavender.

The foliage of many vegetables improves with keeping; broccoli dries tan with a mauve tint, cabbage turns pinkish-mauve, and cauliflower become tinged with pinkish-purple. All of these should be dried flat. A dramatic contrast is provided by pear leaves which dry almost black.

It is as well to experiment; one makes lots of exciting discoveries—things dry differently according to their age when picked—young bulrush heads dry drooping and curvy, a complete contrast to the stiff older forms. The veins of some leaves are intensified with preserving—ivy leaves just left to dry naturally retain their shine for some time and the bulk of the leaf becomes darker until it is almost black and the veins stand out in a clear green.

The hoarding instinct pays dividends, as sometimes things dry out through forgetfulness and exceed one's wildest hopes. Having peeled a beautiful spike of sweet corn, never destroy the leaves and tassels—these dry well to a delicate greenish yellow, a beautiful shade set against brown glycerined leaves.

*Arrangements—A Little Unusual*

As regards the placing and selection of materials, preserved designs are much the same as fresh ones. The same mechanical aids can be used, with the proviso that the dried items do not get wet. If perchance they become damp accidentally, then they should be thoroughly dried before re-storing. Dried stems can be easily supported by plasticine, dry Oasis is also very useful.

If one is tired of orthodox dried arrangements, there are lots more possibilities open. A ball of bright strawflowers hanging from the ceiling or a shelf brightens a corner. Suspending ribbon could match or contrast, and colours can be selected for the room's colour scheme. Strawflower heads stick easily with glue, and any ball-shape can be used, as long as it is light and can have ribbon easily attached.

An equally permanent ornamental arrangement can be made with light dried flowers, foliage and grasses, dried in their natural form or pressed. A strip of heavy material textured or plain makes an attractive backing for a design of flowers, casual or formally placed. A light blob of glue will secure the plants, or they can be stapled into position. This hanging decoration looks almost like a Chinese silk embroidered banner coming to life. The colour of the material is best contrasted with the flowers and must fit into the overall scheme of the room. A more traditional treatment would be to frame the flower picture in an old world picture frame (a few pence each at auctions); the subtle dried flower colours add to the antique appearance.

A similar breath of the past can be conjured up by wiring seed heads and leaves into a close packed garland by winding wires and stems round each other.

This makes an attractive wall ornament looped in a Hogarth curve, or makes an ornate edging to a straight edge such as a pelmet or a circular frame for a mirror. The rich browns can be brought out with a plastic varnish to look like old wood, carved and mellow. Such an arrangement can be successfully mounted on wood if desired, and ideally pods, seeds and leaves merge into the wood and they all look as one. Inspiration and ideas for these more fussy and permanent ornaments can be suggested by decorative stone and wood carving on antique furniture and architecture.

CHAPTER SEVEN

# Suiting Locations and Occasions

It is as well not to adhere too rigorously to a particular style of arranging, as a floral design is not going to be seen in the glorious isolation of a book illustration. It is going to be seen in the context of its immediate background and its supporting furniture, in its relation to the overall décor of the room, and in conjuction with other highlights in the room such as ornaments and mirrors.

A sleek modern asymmetrical Line Design is as out of place in front of a fussy wallpaper as a large classical urnful of formal arrangement is in a cosy cottage nook! Flowers, together with the colour scheme, style of furnishings, the furniture, and objets d'arts make up one unit, harmonious or otherwise; plant materials can highlight and harmonise with the surroundings to make a pleasing overall effect, or look disturbingly inappropriate.

The recent boom in flamboyant paper flowers, both bought and do-it-yourself, reflects the growing awareness of planning a colour scheme down to the smallest detail.

*Back To The Fore*. In Japan, a special large recess about six foot wide and containing a long hanging picture is used solely for plant arrangements, plain and uncluttered; there is an almost altar-like focus of complete calm and peace, as the typical room is very plain, containing no permanent furniture. Seating cushions are brought out of cupboards as and when required, so that far from being a subsidiary decoration the flower arrangement and its related picture

**R CLASSICAL CORNER**
The mellowed colours of antique mahogany and a quiet Victorian painting and a Sèvres piece demand a traditionally styled arrangement in an antique container. Delicate dried grasses and muted tones of preserved berries and seed-heads in a 'silver lustre' jug make an arrangement which fits the old world setting and embellishes the overall effect without stealing too much attention.

dominate the interior. In dreamy moments one imagines some future and incredibly spacious dream house, full of plain uninterrupted wall space and tidy and individual recesses for flowers and ornaments . . . but in the meantime one must make do with the present—albeit often cluttered and overcrowded with all the bits and pieces that make a house lived in rather than an ideal home exhibit.

All designs, traditional, modern, or crazy, look best against a plain background. Stripy wallpaper and curtains can be overpowering, if not disturbing; curvy patterns, particularly floral ones, tend to absorb the arrangement, the two merging into one round the edges! One cannot decorate one's own, or anyone else's house at the whim of a flower arrangement, and it's only occasionally that one can match flowers to the walls and curtains. One gains the best from both worlds by importing a background for the occasion—a piece of painted hardboard or covered picture backing propped or hung against the wall, a length of material (with the advantage of texture) or plain wallpaper pinned to the picture rail or suspended from a horizontal strut. Even if one is continually moving house these are easily transportable items and, for those living in miniature, storage of a short roll of material or paper is an easy proposition.

Less lasting, sugar paper has a pleasant rough texture and can be obtained in several colours from art shops very cheaply; coloured card is a slightly stiffer and more expensive alternative. Predominantly light coloured designs show themselves to greatest advantage against a dark background, and vice versa.

Moveable backgrounds give one great scope with colour schemes. Several different backings can pick up different colours in a room, giving it different accents, and also use left over paint and curtain material to advantage. Intensity variation can be achieved by adding white or black to a colour; thus a background could be a light echo of dark coloured chair covers, for instance.

Another background idea is a piece of covered cardboard tailor made to fit in between shelves—thus part of a shelf can become a micro-setting for a design. Several coloured backings highlighting a room scheme used in a set of shelves or a shelf unit bring new life and interest to that furniture as well as making an attractive setting for flowers, ornaments, driftwood 'sculptures', and knick knacks. For extra focus and illumination a concealed battery light is a luxury, but awakens new contours and textures in objects. For a change, backings are easier to move around than the furniture.

Backgrounds can focus attention on a design, highlight a flower or cushion colour, but above all isolate a small space for peaceful contemplation. Stands have the same effect, whether they be converted Victorian pedestals, modern wrought iron scrolls, a tea pot stand, or a leftover polystyrene tile from the bathroom ceiling. Stands also define the limits of the design and can thus act as a frame for a picture. Where a pair of components make up one design, a single base can be the important unifying factor. Low squat stands on legs look very dainty and oriental. Tiles and pieces of smooth painted or natural wood have a modern aura and look neat. A definite Japanese effect can be given to a Line Design by standing it on two elongated rectangles of wood set side by side, one jutting out beyond the other, making a slatted base. Designs needing extra texture can be improved by standing on well grained wood or a rush mat base, improvised from table mats or a square of floor matting, both neutral coloured. Bases need to be carefully chosen for a design—preferably there should be a contrast of base and container.

Any ornaments or bric-a-brac to be incorporated with the design must also be chosen with care. Light delicate designs need delicate accessories. There must be a unifying something between artificial accessories and natural materials— colour, form (*Fig S*), or an idea, for instance.

*Locating Practical Points*

Window sills make an attractive nook for flowers, out of the way and framed by curtains. When using the window sill certain aesthetic and practical points must be remembered. The silhouette will be most accentuated by light shining into the room, and also incoming light will show up any spaces between stems at the focus of the display—obviously undesirable. A further point to be remembered: most flowers and leaves once cut are deteriorated by direct sunlight. At the other end of the scale an evening drop in temperature (including frost) can penetrate glass and touch flowers on a window sill unless curtains have been carefully pulled round the back of the vase for insulation.

Mantel-pieces are ideal for flower arrangements. Classic mantel-pieces demand classically shaped arrangements—symmetrical if placed centrally, or if placed to one side, a diagonal design 'leading along' the mantel-piece. Where a flower arrangement must be placed near a low hanging picture, it is most advantageous to both if the two are related, with the arrangement leading the eye to the picture, complementing rather than competing. Echoing a colour or form in the picture is one unifying factor, or reflecting its atmosphere and style (*Fig S*).

Unless a small low table is to be completely transformed into a vase plinth, a small design is appropriate. On a low surface an arrangement must look its best when viewed from above, rather than from the sides. Drooping flowers such as snowdrops give the best of both views when placed on a mirror. Since shape is thus limited particular attention can be focussed on placing colour in the arrangement; posy rings are useful in this context.

Fireplace arrangements are also seen from above and in contrast to the small table setting they need to look larger than life in order not to be dwarfed, particularly in the case of old walk-in fireplaces. Tall stems in these designs should be much larger than usual. Another point not to be forgotten is that a fireplace means a draught which will harm more sensitive varieties and certainly pot plants (see page 200).

Wall vases or vases on high shelves are ideal for those to whom lack of space is a major problem. Designs look most pleasing trailing over the rim and obviously tall perpendicular stems are best dwarfed and lateral and drooping stems accentuated as the arrangement will be viewed probably at eye level, or from below when sitting down.

### S  A DESIGN FROM THE WILD

The inspiration of this design was the sweeping curve of an old larch twig from a felled tree, encrusted with a thin coat of velvety bright green lichen—no dark brown showed through at all. Two slim curves of living larch were picked to embellish the old one, and a rosette shaped shoot of limey-green oak leaves, just bronzing at the edges and the veins.

The dominant upright element of the design is the dead twig, the two living twigs almost echoing it as they fan outwards. The old twig is further emphasized by tilting the focal oak leaves so that they are linked more closely with it than the other twigs. The radiating pattern of twigs is rounded off and the line of the dominant curve completed with a tiny tip placed at the base of the container, which was improvised from two stainless steel dishes, one shallow and one deep.

The delicacy of larch and the light greenish yellow of autumn needles and leaves seemed in keeping with the delicate Chinese silk painting above it, 'The old man of the mountain', in whimsy pastel shades with draped and curving forms. The African carved head was used as an accessory as it shared form and emphasis with the twigs—the gentle slope of ridged antlers linking with the curved notched twig forms.

Preservation note: over a few weeks, the needles and oak dried out naturally, ending up completely bronze but retaining their shapes. When thoroughly dried they were useful additions to the dry storage box.

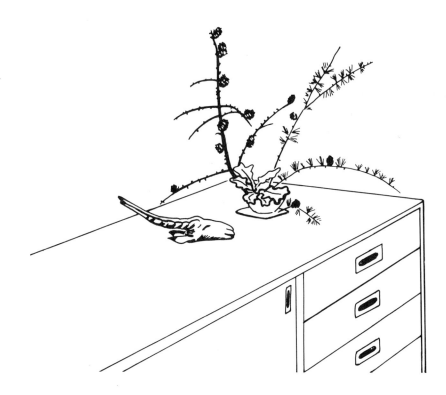

*An Individual Table.* Arrangements on dining tables should be appropriate to the purpose of the table and the occasion. The main requirement is an attractive centrepiece as a focus of the table which will look beautiful from every position at the table and at the same time not dwarf the table and make conversation awkward. A very important point in favour of keeping the design low is avoiding the embarrassment of a guest knocking it over while passing the salt!

Flowers can set the atmosphere of a meal or an occasion; they can formalise, or give a carefree casual appearance to the table. A formal triangular arrangement of a mass of flowers in an urn vase is as inappropriate at a teenage barbecue as an offbeat avant-garde 'flower' arrangement of stones at a formal banquet. On the other hand, a child's miniature plastic umbrella filled with bright flowers and an accompanying doll makes a good start for a little girl's birthday party. The occasion rather than inspiration must take first place.

In choosing flowers for occasions, colour schemes, or lack of them, can be the key of success or dismal failure.

Table designs look very pleasing if table cloth or mats are of the same or related colours to both fresh flowers and candles if the latter are to be incorporated into the design. If matching is not possible, candles look best either toning or brightly contrasting to the table colour scheme, or at least to the fresh flowers. For example, with an olive green cloth, golden candles and chrysanthemums are mutually enriching; other possibilities could be green candles and white flowers, turquoise candles and lemon flowers, or simply plain pure white decoration. These sort of planning details are what makes the difference between a pleasant and a stunningly beautiful arrangement. Even cheap crockery and glasses on gingham look something special if tastefully mixed and teamed with flowers to make an overall scheme. Careful use of colours can lift the humblest starting materials to unexpected heights.

*An Individual Room.* Often a particular feature of décor can be highlighted by judicious choice of materials. A copper fireplace hood is accentuated and featured by a copper container and autumn hues; the warmth of light natural wood is brought out by copper or yellow brass and warm flower colours, or echoed in a wooden slice design base. Dark wood has even more depth when contrasted with light fragile flowers such as white camellias.

Floral designs also make good a room's shortcomings—dark corners can be lightened by bright lemon, white, pink, and cream flowers—it works in nature

## 47 CENTRE PIECE

Centre piece for an informal luncheon, a first prize design by Mrs. Rehana Savul (Pakistan Horticulture Society).

This apparently casual arrangement of red roses, fern and leaves in a wicker basket fits the requirement imposed by a dining table perfectly: the arrangement is designed to be looked at from all angles, it is low and, above all, not too large and cumbersome. An all-round design like this with only a few flowers demands great skill in making the arrangement attractive from every viewpoint, and hide the mechanics. The trick is to keep turning the arrangement all the time while making it, never to leave it in one position.

The arrangement looks casual but in fact the placing of its elements has been done with great skill—it would have been so easy (and uninteresting) to mimic the wheel shape of the basket, making a static, almost geometric arrangement with 'spokes' of living material. In fact the design is just the opposite to a static wheel. The meandering line of the roses moves from one side of the circle to the other, at the same time making an all-round design with a focal point. The radiation of the arrangement from a central focus is very much assisted, but not dominated, by the spokes of the basket—thus container and design are perfectly suited and have been combined to make one beautiful unit. Round-faced flowers and round leaves are a perfect choice for a round container.

Colours have also been carefully chosen; the warm colour of the golden brown basket is in sympathy with the red roses, the glossy green leaves making a direct contrast. The edge of the design is less dense than the central focal point—leaves and flowers are placed closer together towards the centre than at the edge of the design. The plain leaves, acting as a foil for sculptured roses, also cover the pin holder.

Fern, as well as contributing a filmy light edge to the design, makes a useful light green filler, and breaks the severe circular rim of the basket. The roses overhanging the rim also serve to relieve its regular line.

for attracting night flying moths (see page 84) so why not mimic a well tried trick of light indoors?

*Ideas for Christmas*

It is in the winter, when days are grey and the garden and countryside drab, that one feels most need to brighten the house. The dried materials stored in the attic come into their own as fresh flowers and foliage rocket in price.

Many people decorate their homes by simply going out and buying ready-made Christmas arrangements. For those who want something a little more personal and original, or those who are loath to buy what they could economically and enjoyably make, here are a few arrange-it-yourself ideas.

*Five Ways With a White Tree.* A tree shaped branch can be made into an attractive non-needle-dropping Christmas tree cum arrangement that is eye-catching and unusual. Traditionalists need not wring their hands in horror at the thought of leaving fir and pine trees growing, for these were only absorbed into British custom at the time of Queen Victoria's marriage to Albert which gave rise to a craze for German things. Decorating with holly is the more truly ancient custom; it is thought that the Roman custom of decorating with holly in December on account of the feast of Saturn was adopted by early Christians, and duly transferred to the feast of Christmas. Tradition satisfied, a white skeleton branch has much more design potential than a small conifer.

The final tree shape will probably be asymmetric when the branch is stood upright, so the upright shape should be carefully considered before actually cutting. Cluttering or superfluous twigs spoiling the line of the branch removed, paint with gloss white paint. Small evenly spread branches can be mounted upright in a mound of putty or plasticine. Larger and asymmetric ones likely to topple can be held in position once in a heavy base of cement or sand. Depending on its size and form, the tree may be best placed on a well protected small table or covered box.

The basic white tree shape can be decorated in the traditional manner with lots of different colours and shapes: balls, icicles, bells, candles, tiny presents and so on. Streamers, ribbons, and lengths of tinsel draped horizontally among the branches tend to detract from the delicate tree shape, the coloured draping competing with linear branch shapes. These types of decoration are best hung in short lengths like icicles.

Home-made Baubles: For greater economy and originality, bright tree baubles can be easily made (particularly by children on a rainy day) instead of bought— match boxes covered in offcuts of Christmas paper and ribbon, tinsel or coloured string, bright miniature crackers and candles made from the same materials, snowflakes cut from kitchen foil or bright tissue, hoops of tinsel and miniature bells from milk bottle tops pressed on lemon squeezers. Improvised candles can materialise from white and glitter spangled plantain heads and beech nuts forming the cradle bases.

Very tiny painted cones can be stuck onto branches with glue, but the bigger cones need to be wired on. This is done by looping wire round the base of the cone, pushing it right in between open scales so that it encircles the central cone stem, and the loose ends entwine the branch. A loop of tinsel hides any wire from sight. Any bare twigs can be brightened and made interesting by a dab of glue followed by a sprinkling of glitter.

Off-beat Sophistication: A more austere decoration can be created by keeping to a few colours, possibly blending with the room colour scheme—say, in a green and gold scheme, lemon and gold icicles and balls, peacock blue, emerald green and gold paradise birds (metallic or fluffy), glittering skeletons of chinese lanterns and fir cones, and green evergreen sprays round the tree base.

If a colour scheme is difficult to match, the strictly traditional theme of red, green and white is a good stand-by. Such a planned and fitting design looks deceptively expensive although it is cheap to make.

Oriental Make-Believe: Still on a white tree theme, an unusual and natural-looking oriental design can be made from a very simple branch shape, set in a relaxing quiet scene with branches overhanging a shimmering pool of a mirror or silver foil. Silver water can be shimmered with a dust of sifted icing sugar, opaque or silver glitter. Cleverly placed stone slabs (arrangement bases from the storage box) and chunky rocks and stones, in as many contrasting colours and textures as possible, overhang and cover the mirror edge and make a natural

**48** WINTER ARRANGEMENT

A lichen covered branch makes the basic triangular outline of this simple arrangement. A piece of heavy sculptured driftwood makes a solid base to the focal point of two large chrysanthemums, and completes the triangular outline. Orange crusty lichens intermingled amongst the branched blue-grey clusters are echoed in the mustard coloured underside of the chrysanthemum petals, and a triangular piece of lichen covered slate at the base.

An oval meat dish made a plain flat base—its grey-blue upper side echoing the lichens. Behind the driftwood, a small container with pinholder was hidden.

Lichens are unusual plants in that they are really dual plants—consisting of a fungus and an alga (tiny simple plant) associated together. Usually the fungus makes up most of the lichen, and the form varies from a flat crust (seen here), to a flattened lobed form like a liverwort, or erect or pendant branches( as on the twig). The fungal growth protects the tiny alga, and in return consumes a substance produced by that plant.

Found on tree trunks, twigs, old walls, exposed rock, and amongst moss, lichens are very important in the formation of soil from rock. They adhere very closely to a rock's surface (and are painfully difficult to remove without breaking the rock) and cause its gradual disintegration. The broken rock fragments and decayed dead lichens produce minute quantities of soil on which other small plants can grow, such as mosses. Their humble size and appearance is deceptive.

As well as their natural importance in soil formation, lichens are useful in the making of dyes, tanning materials and soaps and perfumes, and lichen extract is the familiar litmus of chemistry school days.

slope up to the tree. Mica naturally glints silver catching the light, so makes an ideal stone to include. Small potted plants, succulents, or evergreen sprays can be grouped around the tree base and, overhanging the water, pots buried in stones.

Natural type decorations are best for such a 'growing' tree—possibilities are bright paradise birds in exotic colours, the longer the tails the better for an oriental effect. Stuffed Victorian birds would also look attractive perched in the branches, reflected in the water. Exotic foil or tinsel blossoms give the impression of magical winter blossom bursting from the branches; failing these, dried flamboyant flowers from summer, or everlasting strawflowers, white and wintry or brightly coloured with petals tipped with glittering silver. For interest at the trunk of the tree and to link the spreading branches to the 'growing' focus of the design, silver edged ivy can be easily attached to the trunk to creep up the tree. Appropriately styled and sized ornaments of browsing animals and oriental figures look well in such a tranquil scene.

Miniature Magic: Small very simple trees with few side branches and twigs are transformed once the main trunk is encased with silver foil, and branches wound with tinsel. Such a tree demands little further embellishment except for a scene round the base to give it weight and interest. For grown-ups, a focal spray of foliage, berries, a few flower heads or cones. For the children, cotton wool snow touched with glitter, reindeers, a tiny Father Christmas, ornaments and models such as deer, birds, squirrels, rabbits, and miniature dolls—anything that fits into a child's fairy-land. The scale of the decoration and such accessories must be appropriate to each other, or else the magical effect is lost. With this type of decoration in mind, it is as well never to throw away ornamental chocolate containers, Christmas cracker trimmings and so on. For adults and children alike the little scene is thoroughly enchanting if lit by a concealed torch, perhaps coloured with a sheet of cellophane across the glass; tinsel shimmers beautifully in coloured light.

*Driftwood Mobiles.* So far, tree shapes have been used. Another possibility is a single shapely branch or contorted driftwood piece attached to the wall or suspended as a mobile. Since so much emphasis lies on the single piece its shape is of prime importance; it should have a definite line and look reasonably

balanced on its own. Twigs crossing the main line of the branch should be removed so one has a basic uncluttered and fairly bold starting shape.

Keeping simplicity well to the forefront, variations on a single embellishment
theme are attractive, and are difficult to overdo. For instance several different
sized metallic balls hung singly or hugging the branch in close clusters like
multicoloured berris look both festive and interesting. No other shapes are
necessary. For a pleasing overall design the shape and space around the branch
should be 'consulted' before hanging the baubles so that the two elements of
the design are complementary. Droplets and clusters hung here and there
regardless of the form of the branch would look unbalanced and disturbing.

*Plate 49* shows an unusual Christmas mobile. The inspiration was a driftwood
tree base with wide spreading roots reminiscent of a chandelier shape. The root
ends and tree trunk had fortunately been tapered off naturally by weathering
thus avoiding any clumsy pruning. Instead of candles mounted on the chandelier
arms, fir cones of different types and at different stages of opening were used.
These were mounted on wire which was subsequently covered with tinsel (see
page 229). The whole decoration was white and silver, naturally silver-grey
driftwood, white daubed cones and plaintain heads touched with silver glitter,
and silver spangled white strawflower heads.

The sprawling octopus-like tree roots could look quite different mounted
flush against the wall, supporting metallic baubles.


*Driftwood, Bark and Ivy.* Driftwood with a silver-grey patina makes an attractive
setting for festive designs—shining and subtle with dark ivy or holly, light and
bright with two or three gold chrysanthemums or sprayed fir cones and seed
heads.

For wood in which a sheen is lacking, a quick dip or brush in white paint
makes a good second best. Another whitening treatment is to submerge the
wood for a few days in fairly strong bleach solution, but the whiteness so produced does not really compare with the natural bleaching processes of wind and
rain; artificially bleached wood looks a very matt dead white.

Pieces of well cleaned bark and logs (beware of inner livestock) make ideal
improvised containers or bases at Christmas time; silver birch makes a light,
not too heavy base—darker barks can be lightened by a touch of artificial ice and
snow.

Ivy, traditionally yuletide foliage, combines beautifully with bark. As a

### 49 CHRISTMAS CHANDELIER

An unusual aerial arrangement was inspired by a silver grey piece of driftwood : the spreading roots and base of a tree from an ancient forest. Emerging from the dark brown peat and spreading over the sandy shores of lakes, these old skeletons are strange relics from the past; for a tree trunk *in situ* see *Colour Plate 2*.

The tapering roots extending in all directions and in three dimensions made an ideal sturdy base for heavy cones. Large cones were placed towards the centre for aesthetic and physical balance, and smaller more delicate ones at the ends of the arms. Slender and textured 'candles' were made from plantain seed heads (rolled in glue and silver glitter), and cones touched with white paint (powder paint) and then glittered. To focus the interest to the centre of the design, white strawflowers, with outer petals dipped in silver, were pinned to the wood, and a chain of silver bells suspended for the central column. Supporting wires were covered in tinsel giving the appearance of cones almost growing out of a cluster of silver sepals. The whole design was as close to the drift colour as possible—a mixture of silver grey and white. Except for strawflowers raw plant materials were found in the wild.

**50** FROSTED LEAVES
'. . . hoary-headed frosts
Fall in the fresh lap of the crimson rose.'   *Shakespeare*.

A pretty wintry touch can be added to Christmas arrangements by edging fresh or preserved
leaves with white and silver, mimicking the frost in nature. A light touch is far more effective
than an overall white wash.

continually glossy evergreen (the property which symbolised everlasting life to
early Christians) it is invaluable raw material, fresh or dried. A spray of dark

green leaves make a pretty contrast to textured silver birch bark, the silvery tree whiteness echoed in a few leaves, touched at the edges with frosty white paint and silver (*Plate 50*). If desired, a brightening touch can be added with brilliant red anemones, with bright white centres and blue black pollen. Gold sprayed leaf skeletons or seedheads brighten the green and white theme, or just one sprig of holly, crowded with glossy sparkling berries.

Twigs, left dark and textured, or daubed white and glossy, make good linear material for off-beat Line Designs and traditional Mass shapes. In *Fig U* an angular twig, left natural, has been pruned and upended to make the basic design shape. Whitened alder twigs are similarly vital to the triangular shape in *Fig T* and provide positive solid lines compared to the drooping grass and diffuse sorrel shapes.

In *Fig T* completely white twigs would have looked very monotonous; thus parts of the alder stems and catkins were left dark for interest value. Similarly the sorrel stem skeleton forming the highest point in the design was blotched white, and also the red-brown sorrel heads.

*Summer and Autumn Revisited.* Preserved foliage, flowers and seed heads are Christmas lifesavers. White, gold and silver paint transform ordinary looking seed heads into bright and fascinating forms. The filigréed skeletons of poppy and Chinese lantern, and the exotic large pitted lotus seed head, look particularly beautiful when gilded. Treated seedheads and preserved berries make a festive focal point in orthodox Line and Mass Arrangements as well as adding interest to a hanging festive swag.

Also for the centre of designs, fir cones of all shapes and sizes (the more different ones the better) unite happily with the other materials. Uniformity gets monotonous so a mixture with differences in size, background, colour and shape, such as pine, larch, cedar and fir, makes for variety and interest. Intermingled spiky globes of plane, conkers, and beech nuts also look natural and interesting. The cone's own pattern is best accentuated by daubing the tips of the scales with paint, making it thicker and more completely covering the scales nearer the base than the top. The merest touch of glitter gives a sparkly effect without making the cone look excessively 'made-up'; touches here and there are more economical on the glitter, too.

A quick and economical way of daubing paint that also saves time, brushes, floor, and paint-covered hands is to pour a small amount of paint into an enamel

bowl of water. The paint droplets float and are caught up in anything swished in the water.

Last year's preserved anemones, snowdrops and daffodils add to any December design. Muted, dried tones can be enlivened with a line of glue and glitter along the outer edges of the petals. For really bright floral colour from the storage box, everlastings never disappoint, particularly bright orange, and crimson straw-flowers.

Edged or streaked with silver or gold like touches of frost (*Plate 50*), bronzy leaves of autumn can also be transformed. As with the other dried materials, these look best edged and veined with paint rather than all overcoated which tends towards a heavy appearance.

Dried grasses turn into silver glittering cascades, once touched into a pool of glue and dipped in glitter (*Fig T*). These add something of Christmas to the outline of an otherwise unseasonal arrangement. Dried bracken and skeletonized leaves can be similarly treated and make delicate tapering edge material.

These dried plant materials, wild and cultivated, are a cheap and quick solution to the problem of Christmas arrangements when fresh material is so

**T MAKING BOUGHT FLOWERS GO FURTHER**

Fresh material for this design was very limited—a few sprigs of variegated holly and three amber coloured chrysanthemums. The storage box furnished most of the arrangement; starting materials were: unpressed dried bracken, selected for creamy colour echoing flowers and holly, and for patterned form; a solid curve of dark brown driftwood, as camouflage and echoing sorrel colour, also to give a solid base; two winter alder twigs, for overall shapes and interest of catkins; two heads of sorrel, as solid perpendiculars and colour related to flowers; a skeleton stem of sorrel, a shadow shape of stems bearing seeds, and to taper edge of design; grasses as delicate fillers to complete outline; white paint to break up 'heavy' colours and forms, and add lightness; silver glitter for interest and to add Christmas sparkle. The container was an oval meat dish (that used in *Plate 48*), dark greyish-blue and white, blue a direct contrast to other warm colours and white linking with white daubed sorrel, twigs, and bracken.

The angular branching stem of bare sorrel makes the highest point of the design, anchored with Plasticine; in front of it, a full rich reddish brown head of sorrel. A less dense and more spreading head of sorrel was used as a transition between the tall slender perpendicular stems and the lower part of the arrangement. Grasses of varying droopiness were silvered for a seasonal effect and placed to make a triangular shape. Flimsy grass outlines were linked to the centre of the design with white-blotched twigs held in position with a pinholder.

The trio of gold chrysanthemums are framed by their own leaves and variegated holly, held in position with Oasis in a small hidden container. The strong horizontal line of driftwood is broken by a flower head and leaf, and the dark brown lightened with creamy holly leaves and whitened bracken curving out from under the flowers.

limited. Better still, they can be completed without fear of deterioration before the rush starts.

A few traditional bought materials such as coloured candles for height and outlines, metallic balls and spangled bells for focus and interest, and strands of tinsel, are stretched a long way with transformed leaves, ferns, cones, flowers, seeds and fruits from dry storage. Different textures and forms can be introduced with off-cuts of Christmas string, and tinselled ribbon to dangle or cluster in loops for extra depth in the centre of an arrangement. Odd bits of braid, sequins, sparkly ear-rings and beads are also worth remembering for that little bit of extra something to complete a pretty picture. Most of all there is the personal pleasure of creating something original from next to nothing, and forgiveable pride at the compliments.

*Fresh and Festive.* For those who dislike streamers and paper chains, yet want a whole room bedecked with the colour of Christmas, garlands of holly and ivy make a good compromise. Pelmets, mantel-pieces, door frames, and picture rails are ideal bases for a garland effect in a hurry. A few panel pins hold sprays in place, or a length of string stretched between two nails. Italian paintings of the Renaissance show luxurious garlands, laden with heavy fruits, complete with knots of string!

If holly is being kept for any time before being used, it keeps fresh if left outside or in a cool place, covered by a damp sack or paper. Ivy and fir can be kept fresh in the same way, or put in a bucket of water. When gathering greenery, inclusion of just a few variegated twigs of holly will make all the difference to arrangements—the hints of cream and gold break up a mass of dark glossy green, and make a light contrast for berries. Trimmings of variegated pot plants also help to break up a mass of dark evergreen.

Crab apples (improved and preserved with a coat of varnish), nuts, green and black grapes, mandarins, satsumas and blushing apples savour of rich harvest, quantities of good food and traditional Victorian Christmases, as well as making large and bright focal areas. Bright fruit colours are perfectly foiled by dark holly and ivy and whitened ferns which also lend a little pattern and detail to a design. Fir cones and coloured balls also look well amongst heaps of fruit.

Christmas time is a splendid excuse, table or sideboard space permitting, to make a sumptuous central fruit and fir cone arrangement in the old master's style, twice as good as any other, set on a large mirror. Fresh green foliage and white Christmas chrysanthemums can be cunningly introduced in tiny bottles. Rosy apples can be prompted with lipstick and edible frost and snow improvised with white of egg and icing sugar.

Less demanding on space are classic all-round table arrangements of candles, sprays of horizontally spreading evergreens, 'growing' gilded cones, and a few fresh flowers, berries or coloured balls for colour. Fir sprays can look very awkward, almost too geometric to be real if stood upright as a design backing, but once placed horizontally in their natural growing position look perfectly at home. A hole cut in Oasis supports small candles; larger ones need a pin-holder, wire netting, or stones and plasticine. Stalked sundae dishes and soup bowls are also ideal containers for individual arrangements or table places as they have plenty of depth for anchorage and water. Trails of ivy, tradescantia, cellophane strips (as used in festive packaging), or small ribbon-suspended balls soften the outside and rims of stalked containers and make attractive overhangs.

*Hogarth Curve.* Embellishment of a curving branch of holly can make a graceful Hogarth curve. Sweeping curves of marram grass stems bound together make the basic leaning S-shape, with a few slim larch twigs carrying cones. Then, two curved holly sprays, one bending up the curve, the other tapering away from the centre so that the tips of the two sprays point in opposite directions. If possible it is best to choose really lush branches crammed with berries for this diagonal part of the curve. With the outline shape and distal ends of the curve complete there is a central space and two overlapping holly stems to cover.

To use more holly would be uninteresting—oddments from present wrapping and last week's left overs come to the rescue. Two small tips of blue tinted fir set opposite each other and crossing the main diagonal at a slant provide textural and colour interest, and also break a too ordered outline. In the absence of any large leaves and seed heads, a long length of white satin ribbon is folded into three clusters of loops and pinned into position near the centre, floppy loops propped up with offcuts of three or four variegated holly leaves. A leftover of green and gold tinselled ribbon breaks up the white adding extra depth and focus, and a cluster of small silver balls peeps out from the centre, 'growing' with the berries from a central gleaming sprig of holly, and pin-pointing the centre from which all stems and clusters radiate. A touch of white on the marram stems, larch, barely a dusting of white and silver glitter on fir and holly, and a beautiful wall decoration is complete. Hogarth curves unite beautifully with

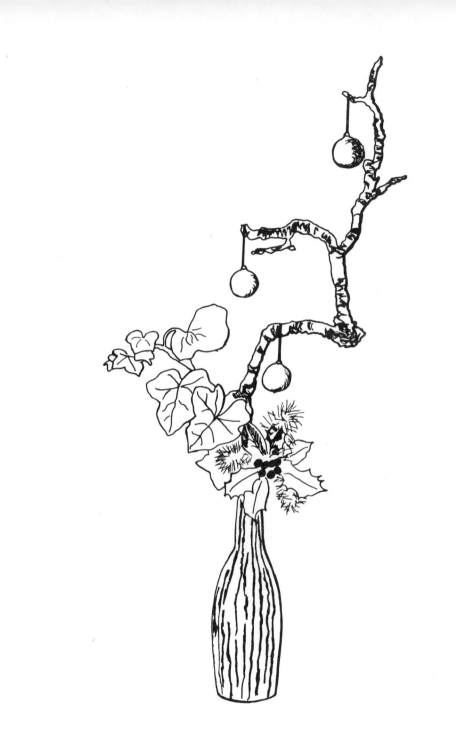

bottle shapes, and heavy decorations can be wired into the neck or around it without fear of mechanical support being visible.

*Bright Entrances.* Most children love Little Grey Rabbit books, and little grey rabbit's kissing bunch hanging in the porch or the hall is a definite hit. Wire netting squeezed to football size makes an ideal base on which holly, ivy, and any greenery can intertwine. Cones, mistletoe, coloured balls and seed heads look attractive peeping out of the greenery, and the whole entrance assumes enchantment if coloured lights are strung among the leaves, with occasional wisps of tinsel catching the light and brightening dark stems. First and foremost the efficiency of the string of coloured bulbs must be tested, and the bulbs fixed to the ball before any of the foliage. The hanging ball of strawflowers suggested in Chapter 6 could easily be adapted for Christmas festivities by the judicious inclusion of small light cones such as larch and tinselled ribbon loops.

A glass window can be converted to vivid stained glass in an hour, given a few scraps of different coloured cellophanes. Children can be absorbed for much longer than an hour drawing the proposed picture on paper, cutting the cellophane shapes and sticking them carefully together. For the genuine touch, thin strips of black masking tape can be used to mimic the lead strips of the real thing.

A variation on the wreath of the front door is to select a well balanced spray of holly, tie a perfect red bow near the base and embellish with coloured balls,

## U BOTTLE OF CHRISTMAS CHEER

An old wine bottle was previously used as a lamp base and painted mat dark olive green to match a room wall. To add interest and pattern, a razor blade was scraped over the paint, making irregular perpendicular stripes of shiny glossy green. This bottle seemed an ideal container for the horizontally notched twig. The upended twig, bedecked with metallic balls, continues the perpendicular line of the bottle. A diagonal spray of wild ivy acts as the third and biggest offshoot of the twig. This type of ivy leads in beautifully to the focal point, as the leaves are regularly arranged—tiny leaves at the tip gradually increasing to large ones at the focus.

A single sprig of holly with berries acts as a focal point, and also completes the overall triangular outline (drawn from the tip of the twig to the tip of the ivy shoot, to the holly leaves, and so to the highest point of the twig). The dark green ivy and holly have little colour contrast, and so a strand of silver tinsel was made into three loops and tucked behind the leaves to lighten the focus, add an interesting texture, and above all help to draw attention to the base of the design. The neck of the bottle was narrow enough to hold the twigs and shoots in place with only the aid of a small wedge of stick to keep the stems apart.

tinsel and ivy. Even more unusual, fix a cheap wall vase or covered improvised container on to the door, and have coloured balls on foil and tinsel covered wires frothing over the rim, cascading downwards, and radiating upwards. Trails of ivy overhanging also look pretty and add a traditional flavour.

*A Fir Cone—a Flower?* A fir cone is more than an attractive symbol of winter and cosy Christmases—it represents the first simple flower. Not easily recognisable to the uninitiated as petals are absent, but more vital than these, it bears the important female parts of the flower which after fertilisation grow and enclose developing seeds, nourishing and protecting them as they grow. Male cones are smaller and most often pass unnoticed.

The conifers—pine, yew, larch, spruce, juniper, cypress, cedar and monkey puzzle were amongst the first plants to truly dominate the rigorous conditions of the land. Until their arrival in the late Palaeozoic (Table 1) all plants such as ferns and horsetails were dependent on the reproductive parts of their structure being in the presence of water so that the male cell could swim to and fertilise the female cell. Water was the vital link between generations.

Reproduction in the conifers is dependent only on the wind: with this giant step forward land plants were freed at last from the swamps and damp places.

Conifers produce male and female cones (or 'flowers'): large numbers of pollen grains containing male cells are blown from the male cone, some reaching the female cone. In the Scots-fir, really a pine, the pollen grain has become specially adapted for this journey and bears two balloon-like air-sacs which make it more buoyant. The female cone (*Plate 51*) consists of a central axis or column bearing a cluster of scales (equivalent to flat open pistils, the outer edges of the scales are visible in the picture). Within these are the female cells or ovules. The ovules are fertilized when pollen grains are blown into the waiting cone and penetrate inside.

The brightly coloured flowers seen and described in the previous pages are thus equivalent to a cluster of scales borne on a cone axis (floral counterpart— receptacle *Fig E*). The difference between the flower and the cone is that in the former the lower scales have been modified and sterilized to form sepals and petals, becoming bright where appropriate to their job of advertisement. Stamens and pistils are equivalent to the upper scales of the primitive cone, still retaining their function of reproduction.

The conifers lack a true ovary enclosing the ovules (seeds, once fertilized).

The ovules lie naked on top of the scale, unprotected and exposed, the primitive feature dividing the gymnosperms (or conifers) from the angiosperms (or flowering plants).

In conifers, after fertilization, the seed develops within the protecting cone and ultimately is ready for dispersal, provided with a food store, a tough outer covering and a wing for assisting its wind travel once it has been shed from the cone. In the Scots-fir it takes three years for the female cone to reach maturity and release its seeds.

The cone has a particularly cunning method of guaranteeing that the seeds are freed only in the most advantageous dry and windy conditions—on a humid day the scales of the cone absorb any water in the surrounding air, thus altering their shape and relative positions and locking the seeds inside the tightly closed cone (*Plate 51*). When the air around the cone is dry, the scales lose the water and contract and twist, gaping apart and allowing the seeds to escape: hence the stories of cone weather forecasting.

In conifers having 'berries' rather than cones, such as the yew, the 'berry' or 'fruit' does not really merit this name. After wind pollination and fertilization a cup-shaped structure (an extra seed covering) grows up round the embryo, developing at the tip of the female cone (or flower). This envelope becomes fleshy and red, attracting birds to eat the seeds. Birds are used for seed dispersal rather than wind and the seed has been adapted accordingly. Here one sees a beautiful example of the forces of evolution achieving the same thing, using different materials. In flowering plants, the ovary wall or the receptacle (*Fig Q*) becomes fleshy and brightly coloured for the attraction of birds. In conifers there is no true ovary as such, and so another structure is called in to play; thus the two different structures have the stamp of similarity as their purpose is the same. (This phenomenon has been mentioned before, in connection with bracts acting as petals, see page 47).

The conifers have only one foot on the rung of the ladder of higher plants—their pollination is an uncertain process. Most important of all, the seeds of the conifers are naked, lying on the scales of the cones rather than being enclosed in the safety of an ovary. There is still a wide gap up to the next rung of the ladder—the flowers of small plants and deciduous trees.

In trees one sees some of the lower and higher levels of plant evolution (Table 1). They are the quintessence of man's relationship with the plant world: their products are valuable—they have been plundered and nurtured, their variety of form and seasonal change are awe-inspiring and often the city-dweller's only touch of nature. The great age and endurance of our trees, and their place in the vast environmental jigsaw epitomise the continuity of life processes against which we as individuals, and our times, may be measured.

**51**
'If Winter comes, can Spring be far behind?'   *Percy Bysshe Shelley.*

# Index

Many common and colloquial names (erroneous and otherwise) are given in the index for ease of identification for those who know a plant only by a local or general name.

References to all Plates and Figures include the caption as well as the illustration and are printed in italics. Colour Plates appear between pages 112 and 113.